1,001 Things You Always Wanted to Know About Cats

1,001 Things You Always Wanted to Know About Cats

J. Stephen Lang

Howell Book House™
An Imprint of WILEY

Howell Book House
Published by Wiley Publishing, Inc., Hoboken, New Jersey
Published simultaneously in Canada

Design and production by Navta Associates, Inc.

For general information about our other products and services, please contact our Customer Care Department within the United States at (800) 762-2974, outside the United States at (317) 572-3993 or fax (317) 572-4002.

Wiley also publishes its books in a variety of electronic formats. Some content that appears in print may not be available in electronic books. For more information about Wiley products, visit our web site at www.wiley.com.

Library of Congress Cataloging-in-Publication Data:

Lang, J. Stephen.
1,001 things you always wanted to know about cats / by J. Stephen Lang.
p. cm.
Includes index.
ISBN 0-7645-6926-0 (paper)
1. Cats—Miscellanea. I. Title: One thousand one things you always wanted to know about cats. II. Title.

SF445.5.L35 2004

636.8—dc22

200400947

Printed in the United States of America

10 9 8 7 6 5 4 3 2 1

To my family,
for having homes where
cats were always adored

Yes, it *is* strange that anyone
should dislike cats.

—C. S. Lewis

CONTENTS

INTRODUCTION

Nine Lives, and Thousands of Books

Your reaction to seeing this book might have been the same as that of my agent, Ed Knappman, when I proposed the book: *another* book on cats? My reply to him, and to you: yes, and why not? Cats are a great subject, they now outnumber dogs as pets in the United States (see entry 347 for more details) and lots of cat owners love to read about cats. Add to this the fact that a book about cats is, for me, a labor of love—I've been a cat fancier since infancy. Finally, the "1,001 Things You Always Wanted to Know About" formula has proved profitable for me in the past, demonstrating to me that readers love these "tidbit" books, which are perfect for browsing. So here you have it: yet another book about cats, yes, but one that I've tried to make fun, user-friendly and browse-worthy—made to be enjoyed, just as cats are.

Cats are intriguing in form, so I've included an entire chapter on the amazing feline body, truly a marvel of beauty and design. Naturally there is a chapter on feline behaviors—behaviors that fascinate and puzzle us (purring, grooming, mad dashes through the house) and frustrate us (clawing furniture, spraying). There is a quick tour of the various breeds of cats (all beautiful, of course), from the placid longhaired Persians to the nearly hairless Sphynxes. You'll also get an education in pedigrees and cat shows. And despite cats' reputation for having "nine lives," they do get sick, so there's lots of information on cat health, and on mating and motherhood as well.

Since I am a history-minded person, you'll get a nonboring history lesson in cats, including details about their prehistoric ancestors, their wild cousins of today and their early associations with the Egyptians, Greeks and Romans.

This is a book about cats (obviously), but, just as important, a book about human responses to cats. Thus there is an entire chapter on famous people who have doted on their cats—writers, artists, musicians, politicians and other notables. The human affection for cats has resulted in thousands of books, movies, artworks, cartoons and songs with cats as the subject as well as the use of cats as advertising gimmicks, and you'll find these items covered in this book. Both fondness for cats and detestation of cats have resulted in innumerable lies and legends about them, and there is a chapter about these stories. My favorite chapter deals with the many "catty" words and phrases that add color to our language—phrases sometimes rooted in reality, sometimes in misconceptions.

This book is not an encyclopedia, but it can serve as one if you make use of the index. If you are curious about how cats purr, for example, look up "purring" in the index to find the numbers for the entries that deal with purring. If you recall that the author Ernest Hemingway was fond of cats and you want to know more about his relationship with cats, you'll find Hemingway in the index, too. If you've heard the rumor that the cat-loving ancient Egyptians made mummies of their deceased cats, you can confirm that rumor (it's true) and find out more by looking under "mummies" in the index. In short, the index is a neat alphabetical list of nearly every cat-related subject you can think of (and plenty that you never thought of).

A black-and-white shorthair named Lucy was usually just inches from the keyboard while this was being written and served as both inspiration and (at times) sedative. Given her role in the creation of this book, this purring refugee from the county animal shelter probably merits being listed as coauthor.

1

How They Behave, and Why

The Habits We Like

1 The purr-fect sound of contentment

To a cat lover, it is one of the most pleasant sensations in the world: the contented vibration that we know as purring. Why do they do it? Scientists think it is a kind of "homing device" used by a mother cat to help her newborn kittens (whose sight, hearing and sense of smell are all underdeveloped) locate her when it's time to nurse. Purring is a kind of "dinner bell" to young kittens. A mother cat purrs, the kittens fasten on, and the purring stops. We can't be sure, but it appears that from kittenhood on they associate purring with pleasure.

2 Share the purr

Your contented cat may purr in your lap or lying near you, but you won't hear (or feel) him purr as he lies contented in the sun. Purring is never a solitary act; cats only purr in the close proximity of a human—or another cat. Cat experts think purring indicates not only contentment but also submission. That is, purring is the kitten's signal to his mother and the adult cat's signal to his owner that "I'm yours." No wonder owners take such pleasure in it.

3 They knead you

Kneading refers to a cat's habit of using its front paws to massage a person's chest or stomach. It goes back to kittenhood, when a nursing kitten uses its tiny paws to massage its mother's udder while sucking. Kneading is inevitably accompanied by purring, and both adults and kittens are clearly in cat heaven while kneading. Some cat owners love this evidence that cats can pet their owners as well as *be* petted. On the other hand, kneading can be downright painful to people, because a cat's claws are definitely *out* while kneading. Owners of declawed cats (including the author) find kneading to be a perfectly painless and delightful aspect of cat ownership.

4 There's a name for it: "bunting"

There's a fabric called "bunting," and you can "bunt" a baseball. Likewise, your cat will "bunt" you and your furniture as part of a familiar habit: rubbing the side of his head against a person or an object. This isn't just affection; the cat is actually leaving behind some glandular secretions from his face as a kind of "I was here" signal to himself and other cats. We can be thankful that this form of scent marking is practiced on us instead of the much more obnoxious spraying of urine.

5 Mad dashes

It amuses us as much as it mystifies us: for no apparent reason a cat suddenly makes a mad dash through the house. Many cat owners claim cats do so after using the litter box, perhaps to express a sense of relief and release. Conversely, some do it right after eating. But often the cat's mad dash is connected to no other event. Experts in animal behavior suggest that running fits might relieve tension, but tension doesn't seem to be much of a problem for many cats. Perhaps the best and most satisfying explanation is that it just feels really good to run and frolic, even if it's just for a few seconds.

6 The "I see you" call

Cats vary greatly in their "talkativeness," but most of them will give an "acknowledgment" call to people with whom they are familiar. This is a very short, soft "meow" uttered when, for example, you walk through a room where the cat is sitting. The acknowledgment call isn't urgent or pleading, and you won't hear it if you've just walked into the house after being gone for two weeks. Cat owners find it to be a pleasant part of owning a cat, for it seems to be the cat's way of communicating, "Yes, I see you," rather than ignoring the person.

7 Allogrooming and autogrooming

Yes, we all know that cats are fanatical groomers (that is, lickers) of themselves, but every cat owner also knows that a cat will also groom his owner, and other cats as well. Naturally there are technical terms to employ here: *autogrooming* refers (of course) to the cat's grooming of himself, while *allogrooming* refers to licking other cats or humans. The cat spends less time and attention on you than on himself for the obvious reason: he assumes (correctly or not) that you are responsible for keeping yourself clean.

8 So much primp time

If a human spent one-third of his waking hours on grooming, you would call that person vain and self-obsessed (unless the person was you, of course). But it is estimated that cats do indeed spend about one-third of their waking hours in grooming, and no cat owner would argue with that.

9 Covering their traces

The fact that cats use their litter boxes (usually) is one of their finer traits. Owners assume that covering up their wastes is another sign of cats' fabled cleanliness. It is, in part, but it's also part of their wild genes: by covering up their traces they are acting in the role of wild animals who do not want to leave anything behind that will lead to their being trailed.

10 High as a cat

If you've ever given your cat the herb known as catnip, you know how much pleasure it gives. The cat rubs his face in it, licks it, then stretches, rolls around on the floor and in general gives the impression of being in extreme ecstasy. If you've ever seen a female cat in heat, you know that a "catnip high" appears very similar to a "heat high." However, these two highs aren't quite the same; plus, male cats respond to catnip exactly as females do. Catnip is available in stores everywhere, and lots of people grow their own. As with drugs and alcohol for humans, catnip can lose its zip if given too often to your cat.

11 The urine-catnip common bond

To the human nose, catnip has only a faint smell, but obviously cats respond to it in a flamboyant way. Curiously, cats can also get a high by sniffing a concentrated extract of tomcat urine, which humans respond to in quite a different way. It appears that the chemical compound nepetalactone, which is the pleasure-inducing ingredient in catnip, is similar to something found in tomcat urine. (Here's a hint: If you want to please your cat—and yourself—stick with catnip and avoid the urine extract.)

12 Privacy, please

Dogs are notoriously "public" animals, perfectly willing to urinate and defecate in a busy area with lots of people observing. Cats are more reserved, and while they don't object to being watched, they do object to having their litter box placed in a high-traffic area. One way they show their displeasure with this situation is that they cease to use the box and find their own spot somewhere else in the home. A litter box, to satisfy both the cat and the owner, ought to be in a quiet, low-traffic zone in the home.

13 Love your smell

Whether cats can truly love in the human sense has been endlessly debated. Those of us who truly love cats look at it this way: they probably love as much as they are capable, which is all we can expect of any being. At any rate, they do seem fond of the smell of those they know well, which explains why a cat can be found sleeping on something that has your smell on it—not only the bed, but a sock, shirt, sweater, etc. Some, in fact, like sleeping on a pile of the owner's dirty laundry. You might not be aware of your distinctive scent on the object, but your pet certainly is.

14 The "leave no traces" phenomenon

Dogs are lovable but klutzy, and a dog doesn't give a thought to what he might be knocking over with a wagging tail. Not so the cat. Your cat may occasionally knock over a vase or other household item, but such events are rare because cats are fastidious about not disturbing their environments. (This doesn't apply to prey or potential prey, obviously.) A cat walking across a desk, for example, plants his feet carefully, so as to leave things much the way he found them. This is unnecessary behavior for house pets, of course, but it's the instinct of their wild ancestors, always trying to keep themselves hidden from both potential prey and potential aggressors.

15 Mice aren't stupid

It has been estimated that a young healthy cat could easily kill a thousand mice in a year. Most homeowners will be happy to know that their own houses are unlikely to have a thousand mice in a year, or in ten years. So in short, if you do own a cat, you probably won't have mice around, or not for long. Rodents are not stupid, and they will tend to avoid a house where a cat lives. Unlike the cartoons, where the wily mice always get the better of the cat, in real life rodents either get eaten or move on to a catless home.

16 All-natural extermination

Here in the sanitized twenty-first century we like to think that the household woes of bygone days—including rodents—no longer bother us. But it isn't so, as proved by the thriving business of pest control companies, plus the huge sales of traps and poisons. Rodents were around before humans were, and though we live in a high-tech world, low-tech rodents are still a serious problem. Homes and businesses too might be wise to "go natural" and fall back on the original pest-control system, cats. In fact, factories and other businesses find that traps and poisons aren't always the best solutions, since rodents can learn to avoid them.

17 The sound of the sack

Almost all cats are fascinated by the sound of a paper bag, and every cat owner has probably witnessed the familiar scene of bringing home something from the store and watching the cat turn the bag into a toy. The featherweight plastic sacks that have now largely replaced paper bags don't seem to be quite as much fun for cats, but, whether paper or plastic, bags that make some kind of rustling or crackling noise do hold some fascination. (Aside from the sound, bags are fun places to hide in.) For owners who want to keep their pet supplied with a noisy sack at all times, there is the Krinkle Sack, a machine-washable item that provides the right sound and lasts much longer than the usual throwaway store sack.

18 Snow as prey

Kittens do it, and so do some adult cats: swat or bite at falling snowflakes. To a cat, each falling snowflake is a potential toy—or to be more accurate, a potential prey to play with before "killing." Most cats seem to like snow (or at least a few minutes of it), and as long as it isn't too terribly cold an outdoor cat will go about its normal business with snow on the ground. Some find their usual outdoor "latrines" covered with snow, forcing them to go elsewhere temporarily, but some cats will forge right on through snow, insisting on using the same old spot even if it does have an inch of snow over it.

The Habits We Don't Like

19 Ah, the taste of urine

Like many animals, cats use their urine to mark their territory, and this is especially so of unneutered tomcats. The flip side of this habit is that cats habitually sniff about to determine if another cat has urinated in the vicinity. When another cat's urine has been detected by smell, the cat will then lick up the urine, then move the tip of the tongue against the upper palate. Yes, it does sound disgusting, but the reason he does this is that above the hard palate is the vomeronasal organ, a sense organ that (probably) can tell the cat the sex of the cat who produced the urine. Some scientists consider this organ to be the source of a cat's sixth sense.

20 Yes, cats do it too

Dogs are notorious for sniffing each other's rear ends (and, embarrassingly, the rear ends or crotches of human beings also). We'd like to be able to report that cats aren't so crude, but in fact they are, though less showy about it than dogs are. Two cats new to each other will, assuming they don't fight, at some point get around to sniffing each other around the anal region, probably cautiously circling a few times before the actual sniffing takes place. (We can be thankful that some of these behaviors are not practiced by their human owners.)

21 Drinking from the toilet

We associate this habit with dogs, but cats love to do it, too. Why, especially if the cat has a perfectly good water dish available? No one knows for sure, except that we can assume these very independent creatures like to seek out their own watering places, just as they would in the wild. A cat will drink not only from your toilet but from a birdbath, a fish bowl, a gutter or anything else with water in it, and cats aren't fussy about whether the water is fresh or stagnant. The toilet-drinking habit seems disgusting, but remind yourself that your cat would *not* drink from the toilet if it contained anything besides water.

22 Do they know their names?

Dogs certainly do, but do cats? The answer is yes—but whether they choose to come to you when called is another matter. Even the most loving cat still retains his streak of independence. A tip for teaching the cat his name: call out the name just before you feed him, so that he comes to associate the sound with coming to a full dish. In time he will connect his name not only with the food but also with the act of coming to you.

23 Shedding, molting, whatever

Technically, it's called molting, but owners usually just speak of shedding, and it's one of the less pleasant aspects of cat ownership. Cats living in the wild molt hair in the spring, leaving them with a shorter (and cooler) coat for the summer. But most house cats live in an environment that is artificially lit, heated, and cooled, so your cat is most likely to shed to some extent year round. (An analogy: a cat in the wild is like a deciduous tree, dropping old leaves at one time in the fall, but your house pet is like an evergreen, dropping leaves or needles a few at a time no matter the season.)

24 Love that wool

This isn't as common as other cat problems, but you'll see it occasionally among Burmese and Siamese cats: the cat will chew on cloth, sometimes creating large holes. They seem to prefer wool, which is why vets refer to "wool chewing" and "wool sucking," but some cats will chew on other fabrics as well. No one knows exactly why they do it, though it might be related to a craving for fiber in the diet. It isn't easily solved, though some people work around it by giving the cat an old wool sock or glove to chew on.

25 Wetting the tires

You may have seen dogs urinating on car tires, but did you know that tomcats do it too? As with dogs, unneutered tomcats who do this are marking their territory (and, like dogs, don't understand that the "marked car" isn't going to stay in one place).

26 The three marking methods

In marking their territories, cats use three methods, one related to sight, the others related to smell. To provide visual evidence of "This is mine!" cats scratch. (And you thought they were just sharpening their claws.) To provide olfactory evidence, they rub objects with their muzzles, leaving glandular secretions that humans can't smell but that are picked up by other cats. And even more noticeable olfactory evidence results from spraying urine—unneutered toms are the worst (and most malodorous) perpetrators.

27 Sampling the vegetation

Cats are carnivores, with no interest in vegetable food, and yet they will occasionally chew on plants. The author has watched his cat roam in the yard, which contains several poisonous plants, including dieffenbachia and allamanda. Happily, his cat has sniffed at these but never bitten into them. In fact, outdoor cats very rarely chew on poisonous plants, but sometimes bored indoor cats do bite into houseplants, and some of the common ones—dieffenbachia and philodendron, for example—are poisonous. While few cats are ever poisoned this way, it might give you peace of mind to ask your vet for a list of poisonous shrubs and houseplants, plus information on emergency treatment.

Discipline, More or Less

28 "Shut up!" just doesn't work

If a cat's meowing is getting on your nerves, here's one thing that won't work: telling him to stop. Cats respond to sound with more sound. By telling a meowing cat, "Stop!" or "Shut up!" you are making sure that the "conversation" continues. The only way to silence him is give him what he wants—food, water, attention or an open door. (On the other hand, if it's a female cat caterwauling because she is in heat, you won't be able to give her what she wants.)

29 Blow equals hiss

Cats really don't like having air blown at them, particularly in their faces. In fact, if your cat is getting too rough while playing with you, blowing in his face is a good way to get him to back off. Why, since a puff of air is harmless? Apparently cats associate blowing with hissing—their own sign to the world that a serious threat is near. If you are close to a hissing cat, you will experience not only the distinctive sound, but also a jet of air being expelled from the cat. So, when you blow air at your cat, you are (so the cat believes) hissing at him, and he will respond accordingly.

30 The squirt gun technique

Many cat owners swear by the use of water pistols in training cats. Here's how it works: Keep a water pistol filled with water in a convenient place in your home, and when you catch the cat doing something he shouldn't be doing, give him a squirt of water. It seems more effective than physically hitting the cat with your hand, since the cat doesn't seem to associate the squirt of water with you. He only knows that when he does a certain thing—urinate on the rug, bite your heels, claw the drapes—he gets spritzed with water, which he doesn't like. It doesn't work with all cats in every situation, but it is worth a try.

31 The ketone "No"

The Hartz Mountain Corporation is a major marketer of pet products, and one of their products has the catchy brand name No. It is essentially an aerosol spray containing chemical compounds known as ketones. The human nose can barely smell ketones, and we find the smell to be slightly sweet. But to the extremely sensitive snoots of both cats and dogs, ketones are highly offensive. No can be sprayed on furniture, rugs or anything else that an owner wants the pet to avoid. Incidentally, ketones are present in the breath of people who are in the advanced stages of diabetes, which explains why it was observed long ago that cats seem to avoid people who are seriously sick from diabetes.

The Claw Problem

32 The itch to scratch

Why do they scratch furniture and drapes? The main reason seems to be to loosen the dead layers of cells on the claws, but scratching is also a way of marking territory. Cats also learn that it gets their owner's attention (definitely!), and scratching may just be a way of releasing built-up energy. Whatever the reason for it, scratching is one of the least attractive cat habits, and the best solution (other than declawing) is to make a scratching post available to the cat. Some cats use them, others never do, but the best way to ensure that the post gets used is to introduce it while a cat is still a kitten. Also, a kitten that has seen his mother use a scratching post is likely to use one, too. It's worth noting that a scratching post needs to be in the center of things, not tucked away in a corner, since cats definitely prefer that their "graffiti" be easily seen.

33 To de-, or not to de-?

Many cat owners have strong opinions about the subject of declawing. For people who love their cats but who want to preserve their upholstery, drapes, and the like, declawing seems like the ideal solution to the age-old problem of clawing. You take your cat to the vet, and when you bring him home in a couple of days, no more shredded furniture. The cat never understands that he is missing his claws, and owners get a kick out of seeing the pet go through the motions of clawing a chair or drape when in fact no damage is being done.

34 . . . and the other side of de-

Opponents of declawing state an obvious fact: if a declawed cat gets loose and is confronted with a dog (or a cat who *has* claws), he is practically defenseless. Vets who declaw cats strongly recommend to owners that the cats never be allowed to roam outside, since the outside world is an especially dangerous place for a declawed animal. Owning a declawed cat does require some extra care and caution, but most people who choose declawing claim it is more than compensated for by the absence of shredded furniture.

Incidentally, many vets refuse to perform declawing on the *back* paws. Cats use their back claws to scratch themselves, and those back claws can help the cat climb a tree if he is being pursued by another animal.

35 Surefooted as a goat—or cat

"Surefooted as a goat" is an old cliché, but "surefooted as a cat" would be just as accurate, for cats have an extraordinary sense of balance, enabling them to walk on narrow ledges, tree branches, and so on. (They have an obvious advantage over goats: claws to help steady themselves.) As it is in humans, balance is connected to the inner ear. The cat's inner ear has an organ called the vestibular apparatus, which, working in conjunction with the eyes, gives the cat a perfect sense of his location in space. With the smallest movement, he will act reflexively to balance himself once again.

36 The belly problem

Almost every cat owner has experienced this: your cat is lying in your lap or beside you, you try to rub his belly, and he begins clawing you vigorously with his back feet. (And yes, sometimes it hurts—and bleeds.) Don't blame the cat. Nature (meaning instinct) has taken hold, and the cat is protecting his most vulnerable spot, his belly. A cat has to *learn* to relax enough to let his belly be rubbed, and even in the most trusting of lap cats, the old instinct still tends to kick in (literally). Consider yourself lucky if your pet is so secure with you that you can stroke his belly with impunity.

37 Bite, scratch—then lick

Here's another familiar situation of instinct kicking in: you are stroking your cat with your hand, he seems to be enjoying it thoroughly, then suddenly he bites or scratches that hand—then stops and licks the same hand he just bit. Is your cat confused? In a way, yes. A cat has to *learn* to let a human being stroke him, for the natural instinct would be to regard stroking as threatening. Nature programs the cat to bite or scratch the hand, then run. So instinct goes head to head with the learned behavior of relaxing under a human touch. When a cat bites or scratches and then licks your hand, he is very suddenly doing a switch from instinct-led wildcat to taught-to-be-relaxed-while-touched house cat.

38 Call the fire department!

It's an old cliché, but like most clichés, it's based on truth: cats easily climb *up* a tree but often can't climb *down*. Hence we have all the old jokes about calling the fire department to get the pitifully meowing cat down from the tree. Why can't they climb down by themselves? After all, squirrels do it with ease. The problem with climbing down is that cats, like squirrels, want to do it headfirst, in order to see what's ahead of it. But while a squirrel's claws are perfect for moving headfirst down a tree trunk, a cat's aren't. The cat wants to go down headfirst, senses he can't, so stays where he is, and makes a lot of noise until rescued.

The Gold Standard of Independence

39 Lone wolf cats

"Lone wolf" is actually a misnomer, because wolves are social animals that live in packs. Ditto for dogs, which are descended from wolves. But cats, of course, are basically solitary animals, and this is true not only of house cats but of all wild cats as well. The one notable exception: lions, which live in groups known as prides. For all other cats, single is the name of the game, and male and female come together strictly for mating.

40 Harness, not collars

Cats and collars go together, but not cats, collars, *and leashes*. Unlike dogs, cats simply can't accept the notion of being *led* on a leash, and tugging on a leash attached to a collar is (in the cat's view) like hanging him in a noose. If you have any hope of ever getting a cat to walk on a leash (and many cats never will), the only hope is the use of a harness, not a collar. A good flexible harness fits around the cat's front legs and torso and, when snapped to a leash, is much less threatening than a leash fastened to a collar.

41 Too dumb, or just indifferent?

"Cats never learn their own name." Ah, but they do, especially if it is short (only one or two syllables) and you repeat it often. What frustrates many people is that a cat will not come to you just because you call his name. He might, or he might remain totally indifferent to you, coming out only when he chooses. Unpredictability and stupidity are not the same thing. The fact is, if you want an animal that will come to you every time you call, you would do better with a dog than a cat.

42 The W. C. Fields syndrome

"Cats hate kids." That's about as true as the statement "W. C. Fields hated kids." He didn't—but he despised *obnoxious* ones. Cats don't like noise or unpredictability, and both seem to accompany children. But cats will happily allow themselves to be stroked and handled by quieter kids, and will gladly play with a person dangling a string, whatever the person's age. If you have children in the home and there is a lot of noise and confusion, owning a cat isn't impossible, but the poor cat may wish he were somewhere else.

43 "Enough play already"

A dog, especially a young one, will romp and play with an owner as long as the owner's energy holds out. Not so the cat. The cat's energy seems to come in short bursts, and after a few minutes of tearing around the house, chasing a toy or whatever, something inside the cat whispers, "Playtime's over, let's nap!" The cat who has reached his "play limit" may start moving his tail in agitation, signaling to his owner, "Give me some space, OK?" A cat simply is not a "party animal," for his inner batteries have a short life and need to be recharged often with withdrawal and sleep.

Some Truly Mysterious Senses

44 ESP looks suspicious

Cats are mysterious, which fascinates cat lovers but puzzles (and sometimes angers) everyone else. Cats may stare intently at nothing, make mad dashes through the house for no apparent reason or otherwise appear to be responding to some unseen phenomenon. The fact is, a cat is not responding to "nothing," but to something he can see, hear or smell, something that our human senses are not attuned to. No extrasensory perception (ESP) is involved, merely more-sensitive-than-human perception, which also figures into cats' mysterious sensing of earthquakes coming (see 46). In a prescientific age, a lot of people tended to assume that an animal with such mysterious behavior and powers was in cahoots with Satan and the powers of evil.

45 Psi-trailing

You may have seen one of the movie versions of *The Incredible Journey*, about the cat and two dogs who somehow manage to track down their owners hundreds of miles away. Truth is as amazing as fiction, and there are numerous stories of cats locating their owners far away—or, conversely, finding their way back home after being displaced. The stories are legion: a man who moved from New York to California gave his cat to friends in New York before moving—and, five months later, the cat showed up at his home in California. Scientists refer to the ability as psi-trailing, and they are as amazed as we laymen are at cats' ability to find their way around, since apparently they do not rely on sights and sounds as humans would. (Let's also admit that many humans seem to possess an uncanny sense of direction.)

46 Cat seismologists

Seismologists are scientists who use many sophisticated instruments to study and try to predict earthquakes. It appears that their instruments are not quite as sophisticated as cats, for there are numerous stories of cats acting frantically and agitatedly shortly before an earthquake occurred. As the story goes, in China in 1975 seismologists ordered the evacuation of the city of Haicheng based on their observations of cats. The city was evacuated, and the quake hit within a day. The damage was enormous, of course, but because of the evacuation, many lives were saved. How did the cats "know" a quake was coming? We can only assume they are more sensitive to earth vibrations than are humans—or human technology.

47 Napoleon the weathercat

Let's face it: in spite of all the technological advances in weather forecasting, your local weather person isn't always right. That was even more true a generation ago, pre-Doppler. In the 1930s, a woman in Baltimore found that her cat, Napoleon, was a better predictor than the local forecasters. The woman noted that the cat would lie on the floor with his head tucked between his extended front legs as a sign that rain was coming. He did so in 1930 at a time when the local forecasters were sure of an extended drought. Napoleon proved to be correct, and he so dazzled the locals that his "forecasts" were made public until his death in 1936.

48 Tornado predictors?

Those of us who have lived through tornadoes know that they are the most unpredictable weather phenomenon, and professional meteorologists would agree. Unlike hurricanes, tornadoes are "sneak attacks," appearing suddenly, lifting and touching down with no rhyme or reason. So how is it possible that cats sometimes seem to know a tornado is coming? There are several stories about mother cats moving their kittens out of a house or barn hours or even days before a tornado destroyed the site. Sheer coincidence, or do cats have a "storm sensor" that we humans do not possess?

49 Air raid predictors

England, and London in particular, had to endure a lot of German bombs during World War II, so Londoners grew accustomed to the sirens that warned of an imminent bombing. Some Londoners still recall that their cats would become frantic and seek out a hiding place—before the sirens even sounded. How did they know? Vibrations in the air that humans—and human radar—could not sense?

Such Sleepy Creatures

50 City vs. country

Scientifically, all house cats are grouped into a single species, *Felis catus*, but aside from the many differences among the breeds, there are also behavioral differences based on location. Curiously, some of these location-based differences correspond to differences among humans. For example, it's an old stereotype (and a true one) that country folk are more likely to "live by the sun," being active during the day and sleeping at night, while urban dwellers are more likely to stay up late and, at times, "party till dawn." This seems also to be true of cats. Farm cats do most of their sleeping at night and most of their hunting, feeding and grooming during the day, whereas city cats are most active from dusk until dawn.

51 Say "crepuscular"

Most people assume that cats are night creatures, and certainly their amazing eyes (see 99) make them suited for night activity. But the fact is, although your cat might be active at night, he is not active *all* night, and in the *middle* of the night he is as likely to be asleep as you are. No matter how domesticated your cat is, he retains hunter genes, which tell the cat that the best hunting time is around dusk and dawn. Cats are crepuscular—most active at twilight—and least active in the middle of either day or night.

52 To sleep, perchance to dream

Dog owners know that dogs dream, as evidenced by their occasional twitching and whimpering while asleep. Do cats dream? Most definitely. During deep sleep, a cat's eyes move rapidly at times, even though the eyelids are shut. The scientists refer to this as "rapid eye movement," or REM, and deep sleep is often called REM sleep. While in REM sleep, cats may move their paws and claws, twitch their whiskers, change their posture and make sounds—in short, show that they are responding to something going on inside their heads, not outside.

53 Cat EEGs

Scientists use a sophisticated device called an electroencephalograph (EEG) to monitor the activity of the human brain and the brains of some animals as well. By using the EEG, we've learned a lot about cats' sleep habits, as shown by the wavy line displayed on the EEG. We have learned that a cat typically sleeps lightly for about thirty minutes, and then goes into a deeper sleep, called REM sleep (see 52). Most often, though, cats aren't sleeping deeply. Of their daily dose of about sixteen hours of sleep, probably 70 percent of it is light sleep—the "catnap" that is their trademark.

54 Dead to the world—not!

No matter how deep the sleep, cats are never totally "out of it." Every cat owner knows that even a cat who appears "dead to the world" is very easily awakened, as evidenced by the cat's response to touch, a loud noise or even a smell (such as the odor that wafts from the opening of a can of sardines). No matter how domesticated the cat may seem, he still retains this aspect of the wild animal, ever alert to the presence of a threat.

55 Are you listening to me?

If a person appeared to doze off in your presence, you could feel fairly certainly he wasn't too interested in what you were saying. What would be rude in a human being isn't at all rude in a cat, however. A cat settling in your lap or nearby who half-closes his eyes isn't showing a lack of interest; rather, closed eyes imply total trust and relaxation. (And whether you're saying something fascinating or boring doesn't much matter to the cat anyway.)

56 Stretching or curling?

Cats are notorious for being able to sleep practically anywhere. Regardless of the location, however, the sleeping position is definitely related to whatever the temperature happens to be. The basic rule: they stretch out when it is warm, curl up when it is cool. So you'll see a cat stretched out in the sun, but never curled up in the sun. If the room is cool, the cat will curl up into a ball, keeping his body heat turned in on himself. Even better, he will curl up into a human lap—or sidle up to an unaggressive dog, or even another cat.

57 The hiding instinct

Throughout this book you will run into this fact over and over: cats are only partially domestic, and some of their wild instincts will always remain. You see this in their choice of sleeping places: make a box, bag, open drawer, closet, even a suitcase available, and they will probably sleep in it. Why so, especially if you've seen them week after week sleeping openly on the floor or the bed with no fear of attack? The old instinct is still there: find a safe and enclosed place to sleep. A variation on this is an elevated spot, such as a windowsill or the branch of a tree—high up and, above all, *safe.*

58 The need (?) for a bed

You don't have to be an experienced cat watcher to know that cats can sleep darn near anywhere—your bed, carpet, tile, linoleum, concrete, gravel, grass, a tree branch, even on top of radiators. Unlike humans, cats do not require a soft (or flat) surface for sleep. In fact, part of the joy in owning a cat is observing all the varied places he chooses to sleep. Given that obvious fact, why do owners buy special beds for their pets? Go with the obvious answer: cat beds, like numerous other pet products, are made to appeal to the owner, not to any real need of the cat. If you buy your cat a bed, he will probably sleep in it—there, and everywhere else in your home.

59 The fan blade syndrome

If you've just come home from a drive and your cat is outside, there's a good chance he will seek out the hood of the car, taking advantage of the warmth, especially in cold weather. Cat owners have come to expect kitty footprints on their cars as an inevitable part of having a pet. Unfortunately, there is a downside to cats seeking out the warmth of a car: on occasion they will crawl up inside the hood (warmer there than on top of it, obviously) and, sadly, some cats have met their death by falling asleep on the engine and being cut by the fan blades when the vehicle is started again. On a happier note, though, some cats have survived after traveling several miles under the hood of a car.

60 The radiator bed

Not many homes have radiators now, but in those that do, the radiator is a prime sleeping spot for cats, since it's a nice source of moist heat. Cats willingly sleep on top of any heat source that won't actually burn them. This does not harm them, but it does tend to dry out their fur, especially on the belly, making them shed more. If the cat is a radiator sleeper, a thick towel or small blanket atop the radiator is a good idea to prevent belly dryness.

Predators Will Hunt

61 Playing with their Food

It's been observed for centuries: cats play with their prey before finally killing it. A cat pounces on a mouse but instead of chowing down at once, he swats at it, tosses it into the air and otherwise prolongs the death for several minutes. Many humans find this rather sadistic, but words like *sadistic* hardly apply to an animal that, by nature, catches and kills other animals. One thing that surprises some people is that the cat may continue to play with the prey *after it is dead*. Here's something that won't surprise you: if the cat is *really* hungry, he will eat his prey without playing with it.

62 Attack!

Some owners are disturbed by watching their pet stalk and kill something, but in fact cats are natural predators, and their technique is poetry in motion. A hunting cat keeps low to the ground and uses a natural cover (such as plants) for concealment. The closer to the prey, the slower the cat advances. When lying in wait, only the tip of the tail moves. Cats are good judges of distance, leaping to attack when they know they can reach the prey in two or three bounds. They rarely miss their target, of course.

63 Hunting: nature or nurture?

You don't have to teach your cat to chase birds, rodents or fish, for the predator instinct is very much in his genes. However, it is true that the hunting instinct is affected by what kittens see their mother do. A mother cat living in the wild or on a farm will catch rodents or birds and, of course, bring them home to the kittens. But they won't eat right away, for the mom cat will release the prey and allow the kittens to capture it again, and even compete with them for it. The killer instinct is already there, but mom is nurturing it with this training. Needless to say, kittens who observe their mothers killing prey become more effective predators than kittens raised in a cat-food-only home.

64 Eating what you kill

It's a standard line among human hunters: a good hunter eats what he kills—which means that you don't kill for the sheer pleasure of killing, leaving a dead beast to lie and rot. Well, a cat in the wild definitely follows that rule, devoting its predator skills to finding food, not engaging in sport. But well-fed house pets don't follow that rule at all. They gladly kill when they aren't particularly hungry, and they will even kill nasty-tasting things like shrews, which they have no intention of eating (and which, if the cat was hungry, he wouldn't bother pursuing).

65 Will they eat bugs?

Indeed they will. The human eye (and mind) draws a distinction between "higher animals" (mammals, birds, reptiles) and "just bugs," but cats' eyes don't. Cats have no conception of biological classes, whether an animal is a vertebrate, invertebrate, warm-blooded, cold-blooded and so on. Domestic cats retain their predaceous instincts, and their prey can be a mouse or a bird or a lizard . . . or a grasshopper. Probably the first prey of kittens is something small and easily caught, such as the nearest bug. All these creatures fall under the very broad category of food. While a well-fed adult house cat is unlikely to go after an insect, feral cats are not so finicky.

66 Don't play with your food!

Human parents tell their kids not to play with their food. Cat parents don't do so, and kittens do indeed play with the food served to them—or more precisely, try to kill it before eating it. The predaceous instincts are so strong that even a very young kitten will sometimes pounce on a bowl of food, even though that food is about as "dead" as can be. The kitten seems to think that, since this is food, it has to be "killed" first. As they mature, kittens seem to learn that the food given by humans is not "prey" and doesn't need to be attacked before being eaten.

67 Chattering teeth

Humans associate teeth chattering with cold temperatures, but you won't ever see your cat's teeth chattering for that reason. Rather, chattering is the "frustrated hunter reflex": the cat, a natural predator, is in a place where he spots a potential prey, but he can't get to it, so his teeth chatter. You may have observed this when your cat was sitting on a windowsill, looking out at a bird, lizard, mouse or other outside creature. The cat's teeth would not chatter if the cat was *outside* the window, with the prey within reach.

68 The bird predator myth

It's no myth that cats are natural predators, and, yes, they do eat birds. But nature lovers have unfairly exaggerated the role that cats play in decimating bird populations. While cats do indeed eat birds, they also eat mice and rats, which themselves are notorious for preying on young birds and eggs. Cats actually aid birds by keeping down the population of egg predators. (Cats do not eat eggs.) Cats also prey on several other egg eaters—blue jays (the most notorious nest robbers in the world), young raccoons, young opossums, and the like.

69 Will a cat fish?

Of course it will, as any owner of an aquarium or goldfish pond knows. Yes, cats hate water, but cats just love fish for dinner, so many a cat can forget (for a few seconds) his fear of water and dip his paws and claws into a fishbowl. At times the willingness to fish is more urgent: a house cat in the wild who is seriously hungry and hasn't managed to find enough birds or rodents will seek out a stream or pond, hoping for a fish dinner, and will even (if things are truly desperate) wade into the water to do so.

70 The no-lizard rule (seldom obeyed)

Any small creature is a potential prey (and meal) for the house cat, and in Florida the most common small creatures around the house are the many species of lizards available—anoles, geckos and several others, none very large, all harmless to humans, and all tasty to cats. The author's cat is a typical Florida cat, making a meal of whatever lizard is foolish enough to enter the house or the garage. The received wisdom is that the skin of these lizards is toxic, so cats should not be allowed to eat them. In this situation, the author is more willing to trust the cat than the supposed human experts.

71 Why hunt when you're full?

The wives of hunters ask this question, and so do cat owners. In olden days, men had to hunt to survive, ditto for cats. It's a "guy thing," and a "cat thing," too. Your cat may be sleek and well fed, but let a bird or rodent come within sight and the predaceous genes take over. Sometimes the hunt can be more involved than that, with a cat waiting by a small hole for hours for the desired prey to come out. A lot of waiting, a lot of stalking, then a few seconds of pursuing and killing. Perhaps men who truly enjoy hunting have a better understanding of the cat as predator than others do.

72 The cat-chicken truce

Since ancient times, every farm had its chickens and its cats, and somehow they lived together in peace—usually. In my own experience, our family's aggressive and hyperactive Siamese tomcat had no qualms about killing and eating baby chicks. And why not, since cats like to prey on birds, and what easier prey than birds that can't fly? But the usual rule is that cats have a certain grudging respect for barnyard chickens, partly because mother hens are very protective of chicks and partly because roosters are a force to be reckoned with too.

73 A semi-dead token of affection

The author has had half-dead lizards dropped in his lap or at his feet, and countless cat owners get presented with similar "gifts"—dead or half-dead birds, mice, toads and so on. It horrifies some people but delights others. Give a cat credit for good intentions: an animal who is mostly selfish is sharing the spoils of the hunt with you. There may be some pride involved, too, which you can see on the face of a cat marching home with the prey held high in his mouth. A combination of "Look what I did!" and "Here, master, I brought you something!" Isn't it kind of silly to get angry when this happens?

74 Scavenger buffet

If you've ever lived in a situation where your household garbage had to be put in a Dumpster trash receptacle, you may have had the funny (but frightening) experience of opening the door and having a cat (or several) jump out wildly. The cat was probably scavenging for food inside, and while he might have been someone's pet, he was most likely a feral cat dining at one of his favorite feeding sites. Humans throw away a lot of high-protein garbage, and feral cats (especially in urban areas) find any open garbage container to be a great source of food. Feral cats still *hunt* for a lot of their food, of course, but much of it is supplied by wasteful humans' table scraps.

Defense and Offense

75 Go for the gut

Cats use their hind claws to scratch themselves, but those long hind claws serve a defensive purpose as well. A cat under serious attack by another animal will roll onto its back and use its large thigh muscles and its hind claws, aiming at the attacker's belly. The aim is, of course, to literally go for the guts, perhaps even to disembowel the enemy. (Owners, if they behave themselves, are never on the receiving end of this.)

76 Not glad to meet

The author C. S. Lewis noted that cats seldom seemed to like each other, and he had a point, especially in regard to first encounters. Most cats feel threatened when meeting a cat they've never seen before, and two unneutered toms can be hostile in a very noisy way. Normally the two approach each other with tails moving slowly from side to side, all the while making direct eye contact. The smaller of the two cats may size up the situation and slink away, but if two cats feel they are evenly matched, they will walk past each other; then, one will spring onto the other, who will roll onto his back. The one on top will try to bury his teeth into the other's nape. While lying belly to belly this way, they will claw, bite, urinate on each other and create the noisiest ruckus cats are capable of. At some point the attacker will jump free, giving the other a chance to slink away or engage in a counterattack.

77 Paws together = I'm scared

A truly frightened cat will not only hiss and arch his back, he will literally gather all four feet together under his body, as if his back feet were moving forward and his front feet were moving backward. The cat seems to be preparing for any eventuality—springing forward, leaping straight up, jumping backward or otherwise responding to what the perceived enemy does.

78 Urban manners

Sociologists have long noticed a basic fact about human beings: the farther apart they live, the more pleasant their relations are. The flip side: the closer together, the more fights and murders. Stating the obvious, there are more assaults and murders in cities than in rural areas. This seems to apply to cats as well. Jam a lot of cats together in a city, and you can count on some loud nocturnal battles among toms attempting to stake out their territories. And no wonder: a farm cat might have ten acres to himself, while city cats have to share a relatively tiny amount of space. "Good fences make good neighbors" doesn't apply if you are small, agile and can easily climb on the tops of the fences!

79 Hiss vs. growl

Neither is exactly a sign of pleasure, but hisses and growls don't communicate quite the same thing. Basically, a hiss is a sign of fear. Something in the vicinity has really rattled the cat, who hisses at it and, if pressed, will attack but, more likely, will try to flee. A growl is more of a sign of anger and aggression than of fear. If you've ever witnessed a serious cat fight (see 76), you'll hear both cats loudly growling throughout the whole ordeal.

80 Read the eyes

Is the cat frightened, or fighting mad? The eyes are a good signal. When a cat is frightened, the pupils of his eyes dilate. (And if you're familiar with cats, you know those pupils can become *really* large.) You may literally see red in the eyes of a frightened cat, because the retinal blood vessels may be visible through the dilated pupils. The pupils of an aggressive, angry cat will constrict rather than dilate.

81 The significance of "belly up"

A cat basking in the sun may lie on his back at times, but in interactions with humans or other animals, "belly up" is bad news. It means the cat is the loser in a two-cat brawl. It frustrates many cat owners that cats, quite unlike dogs, don't usually like to be held on their backs while their bellies are rubbed. But, obviously, the cat associates "on my back" with "I'm in the middle of a fight!" It is not a position with pleasant associations. If you're fortunate enough to have a cat who willingly exposes his belly for you to rub, you can assume the cat trusts you totally.

82 Blessed are the peacemakers

How do you make two cats get along? That is a logical question if you have a cat and are bringing in a new one, but it also happens that, for whatever reason, two cats who have gotten along suddenly start fighting. Here is one peacemaking technique: keep the cats separated for a time, then put each in a separate cage or carrier. Next, put them in the same room several feet apart and then feed them at the same time. Gradually, over a period of a few days, move the cages closer together at each mealtime. Eventually the two should feel more relaxed near each other, so that in time they can eat in the same room together with no aggression.

Cat vs. Dog

83 Must cats and dogs fight?

There is plenty of truth in the old phrase “fight like cats and dogs.” In nature, the two would avoid each other and fight only if they happened to meet. However, humans have brought them together under the same roof, and they can in fact get along just fine, particularly a kitten and a puppy who are raised together. An adult dog and an adult cat may require a period of adjustment, but they will learn to be friends or at least to tolerate the other. The sight of a cat and dog curled up beside each other in blissful sleep is not all that rare.

84 The occasional kitten eater

Having just said that cats and dogs can get along, a word of warning: some dogs have a strange—and dangerous—reaction to very young kittens. In a word, they eat them. Sadly, this can occur even if the dog had been friendly with the mother cat. Dogs and cats are both creatures of instinct, and even a dog comfortable with adult cats may look upon tiny kittens with their high-pitched mewing as (alas!) something to eat. Naturally the mother cat, if present, will fight the dog tooth and claw, but the dog is more likely to do its dirty work while the mother is absent. A word to the wise: if your cat just had kittens, try to keep them out of the way of dogs.

85 First blood

If cats and dogs fight, you can rest assured that the dog started it, even if unintentionally. A dog might be attacking—or might be licking a sleeping cat in a perfectly friendly way. Either way, the cat's space has been invaded and he won't tolerate it. In the case of a clearly aggressive dog, the cat will assume his classic "inflated" posture—back arched, hair bristling out, looking larger and more menacing than before. It's a bluff, since the cat can't kill a large dog, while a large dog can kill a cat (see 86). But many dogs will be taken in by the "inflated cat" and be content to bark and nothing more. The cat whose bluff fails will run when he can or fight if cornered. But the cat is never the aggressor in a cat-dog battle.

86 The neck snap

Both dogs and cats seem to understand a secret of killing: break or sever the spine and your work is done. A cat delivers the deathblow as a sharp bite to the neck, trying to sever the spinal cord. Alas, predator sometimes becomes the prey, and a cat who finds himself in the grip of a large and aggressive dog may die quickly if the dog grabs the cat by the neck and gives him a quick and life-ending snap. If you've ever seen this happen (and I have) it seems terribly cold-blooded. Suffice it to say, if you and your cat live near a large dog, do what you can to keep your cat out of harm's way. The dog is just doing what comes naturally, but that isn't much consolation if a beloved pet dies.

And a Few Choice Behavioral Tidbits

87 Water—yuck!

Like all animals, cats require water for drinking, but house cats are notoriously averse to getting *in* water. In spite of that, they can swim, though they make for shore as quickly as possible. In fact, all species of cats can swim. Lions and leopards do it reluctantly, but, curiously, tigers and jaguars enter the water with no hesitation and actually seem to take pleasure in swimming.

88 The dreaded B word

Bathing, that is. In general, it should never be necessary, given that cats are cleanliness fanatics. But accidents happen: they get splashed with mud or motor oil, fall into a puddle—in short, they need cleaning that their tongues just can't handle. Needless to say, bathing a cat (especially one that is not declawed) is a daunting task, but some owners do it often, and apparently cats can learn to tolerate being bathed. Suggestion: arm yourself with gloves and an apron, and pray for patience. (Note: A few breeds, including the Turkish Van, actually seem to *like* bathing.)

89 The dry-cleaning alternative

If you survived giving your cat his first water bath, you might be thinking of possible alternatives. In cases where the cat isn't terribly soiled, you can "dry clean" him by sprinkling him with talcum powder and then brushing it out. Pet stores also have dry shampoos that function the same way. Some owners give bran baths, using bran sold for either humans or horses. The bran is heated in an oven, then massaged into the fur, then brushed out, taking dirt and oil with it. In the case of tar or oil on the hair, you can daub the spot with mineral oil, let it set for several hours, and then try to swab it off with soap and water.

90 Making the squirrels chatter

Squirrels are rodents. They hate and fear cats, and with good reason, because cats can climb trees. If you have squirrels on your property, you are probably aware that when they see a cat, they immediately head to the highest part of the nearest tree and raise quite a ruckus, chattering noisily to one another. This distinctive chatter (which some people mistake for birds) is both a cry of fear and a warning to any squirrels in the vicinity that—horrors!—a cat is nearby.

91 Cats in cars?

If you've ever emerged from your car with several nasty scratch wounds, you probably learned (the hard way) that cats don't like to travel in automobiles. Everything about the experience disturbs them: the engine noise, the stop-and-go movement of the vehicle and, probably the worst aspect, other vehicles passing by. They meow noisily, and some will scratch anything available, including you. Most cat owners choose (after losing blood) to put their cat in a cage or carrier when he has to be transported. However, some cats can learn to ride peacefully in a car, but only if you train them as young kittens. Kittens who remain placid on a trial run may turn out to be among the few happy car cats around.

92 No heaving in the car

Most dogs *love* to ride in cars and are fascinated to pass by things they haven't seen before. The bad news is that many dogs get carsick and throw up in the car. Not so for cats. Assuming your cat rides well in a car (see 91), you need never fear him getting motion sickness, for a cat's legendary equilibrium will keep him steady. The average cat detests riding in a car, but not because of balance problems.

93 Feline *melomanes*

Do cats love music? Some owners claim their pets seem happy curled up next to a speaker—assuming the speaker is emitting something pleasant and harmonious, that is. At least one writer has referred to cats as *melomanes*, "music lovers." The author's own opinion is that a cat's preferred environment would have no sound at all, but that cats definitely prefer pleasant music over any kind of noise, whatever the source.

94 The bag drag

If your cat really trusts you, you can do things with him no stranger would be allowed to do. One pastime that a few coddled cats will endure (and even enjoy) is the bag drag, which needs to be done on either wood or linoleum: have the cat lie in a bag (either paper or cloth) while you spin the bag in a circle, the cat's belly touching the floor. The majority of cats probably wouldn't tolerate it, but a few seem to like the gentle friction generated by the spinning.

95 Kitty Falsetto

We do it without thinking: call out "Here, kitty" in a high-pitched voice. Both men and women will, for reasons we never analyze, pitch our voices an octave or so higher than normal when calling a cat. The habit actually makes perfect sense, for the simple reason that cats' ears are sensitive to higher-pitched sounds. Those hypersensitive ears are much more likely to respond to a soprano than a bass. (Then again, even after hearing you, they can still choose to ignore you.)

96 Cat alarms?

We cat lovers joke about our slumbering pets, assuming they would probably sleep through a fire or would exit the burning house with no thought for us. We tend to assume that the only threat to a burglar would be that he might trip over the cat in the dark. Dogs, so people assume, are the "hero pets," warning their owners of fire or other dangers. But in fact there are true stories of cats waking up their owners when the house was on fire or raising a ruckus when someone was breaking into the house. There are even cases of cats saving the lives of people (or other cats) who were being attacked by vicious dogs. Yes, cats do seem to be selfish creatures, but they do have their noble moments.

97 Making eye contact, George Burns style

It's a basic rule of good communication: look people in the eye when speaking to them. It seems also to apply when humans communicate with cats, for cat experts observe that a timid or frightened cat responds to direct eye contact with a human—not an intense stare (which intimidates cats) but unbroken eye contact involving a slow blink (think of comedian George Burns). The experts think that the slow blink is the cat equivalent of a warm, welcoming smile.

98 The vacuum—friend or foe?

Most cats despise and fear vacuum cleaners (so do most dogs) because of the noise they make. To the cat, the vacuum is like some noisy, threatening animal. But a few cat owners manage to get their cat comfortable with a vacuum cleaner, enough so that they can use a hose attachment and groom the cat. This is amazing to watch, but if your cat will tolerate it, wonderful, for it is a tidy way to groom loose and dead hair off cats, especially longhaired ones. But don't be surprised if your cat won't cooperate.

The Amazing Feline Body

99 Light in the eyes

Yes, cats' eyes really do reflect light, and there are a couple of reasons why. One is that they have a reflective layer, the *tapetum*, within the eye that intensifies any light coming in. Couple that with the fact that in a low-light situation the cat's pupils are dilated enormously, and you are, in effect, looking into two small mirrors when you look at your cat's eyes. Some humans seem to have eyes that are more reflective than normal, and we often say that such a person has "cat eyes."

100 Can they see in color?

Most people assume that cats, like dogs, have only a monochrome view of the world. You might remember from science class that eyes have two types of sensory cells: rods sense shape and cones sense color. (The old memory trick for sorting out which is which is to remember that *cones* and *color* begin with the same letter.) Cats do have cones in their eyes, two different types, in fact, one for blue and one for green. That doesn't exactly give them a full-color view of the world, but it does mean that they do have *some* sense of color.

101 Focusing on details

Cats amaze people with their ability to focus in on some tiny object—say, a gnat or a tiny lizard crawling on the fence. The retina of a cat's eye contains the *area centralis*, a heavy concentration of cone cells, and thus the most sensitive area within the entire eye. When your cat "locks in" on something small that had escaped your attention, you can be sure that that object is right in the center of the cat's area centralis.

102 A soft-focus world

In many ways, cats' vision is superior to ours. Their amazing ability to sense motion (obviously something that would be highly useful to a predator seeking prey) is one example. Apart from their poor sense of color (see 100), however, cats also are not very good at distinguishing sharp details. You might say they see the whole world in "soft focus." The large lens in the cat eye is useful for gathering lots of light but is not so useful for seeing detail. Cats could not "read the fine print" even if they had the mental capacity to read.

103 Nictitate = wink

Your cat possesses one more eyelid (per eye) than you do. This is the haw eyelid, or nictitating membrane. (The verb *nictitate* means "to wink.") The haw eyelid shuts horizontally (like a drapery being closed sideways across a window) instead of vertically (like a window shade drawn up and down), and is an extra layer of protection for the cat's eye. Many other animals have them; humans don't.

104 Bi-eyes

It happens occasionally: a cat has eyes of different colors. The most common combination is one blue and one amber, and you'll usually find it among white cats. It's a genetic oddity that is little understood. Some people find it unpleasant to look at on first glance, but owners of these "bi-eyed" cats claim that the distinctive look does grow on you after a while. (And considering that these cats are usually white, it does add an extra dash of color.)

105 Bright-eyed to the end

Some cats develop vision problems as they age, but most don't. In fact, old age is much kinder to cats' eyes than to dogs' eyes, since dogs are prone to cataracts. Most cat owners are pleased to find that their pets remain bright-eyed to the very end, even if those eyes seem to close more often for sleep.

106 Ear range

Recall that an octave is the range of sounds, higher or lower, from one musical note to the next corresponding note—say, from C to the next higher or lower C. The normal human ear can detect sounds over a range of about 8.5 octaves. Cats, as you might expect, have a wider range, about 10 octaves. Specifically, they are good at sensing higher pitched sounds than humans—such as the faint and high-pitched calls of kittens or rodents. In scientific terms, cats have an upper hearing range of 65 kilohertz.

107 Do the external ears really help?

Some breeds have fairly small ears, some have fairly large ones, but all cats, as already noted, have excellent hearing. Do the external ears really help that much, or is their sensitive hearing all a matter of internal sensors? As with human ears, cats' external ears play a large role in hearing—in fact, a larger role than human ears, since cats are able to turn their ears more than humans can. Humans who have had their external ears removed do not go deaf, but their hearing does suffer, and this is true for cats as well. The external ears are extremely useful "funnels" for sound.

108 Grate tongue

If you've been licked by a cat, the odds are that you endured it but did not enjoy it. It is remarkable that anything as supple and innocent looking as a cat's pink tongue could feel so abrasive, like a pliant file on the skin. Under a microscope, the tongue's surface is far from flat, but has "barbs," called *papillae*, which are slanted toward the back of the cat's throat. These barbs are multi-functional: they help lap up water and food, "polish" the coat, clean off helpless kittens. The rough tongue even has a function in defense and hunting, for those barbs cause the wounds of the prey to bleed more profusely.

109 No sweet tooth here

The cat tongue, like the human tongue, can taste four general categories: saltiness, sweetness, sourness and bitterness. Cats' favorite tastes are salty and/or sour, and they definitely do not share humans' (or dogs') love of sweet things. But there are curious exceptions to every rule. In spite of being carnivorous, and in spite of what was just said about sweet foods, some cats like sweet tastes, especially floury sweet objects like cookies. (Note that cookies and other sweet treats like pastries do have fat in them, and it's likely that the fat is the draw, not the sugar.)

110 First the baby teeth . . .

Like humans, cats have two sets of teeth in their lifetimes (not counting dentures, that is). The cat's deciduous teeth (baby teeth) appear between her fourth and sixth weeks. These are shed around the sixteenth week and replaced by the adult teeth, which are all in place by seven months.

111 Alas, they're called "canines"

We're referring to the most noticeable teeth in the cat's mouth—the "fangs," two on the top, two on the bottom. Biologists referred to these sharp, prominent teeth as "canines," regardless of what animal has them (including humans). They are the "rippers" in the cat's mouth that not only do the serious business of tearing large bits of food, but also do the equally serious work of biting an attacker. As in most animals, the cat's canines are pointed slightly inward, so whatever they fasten to—food or enemy—finds it difficult to escape.

112 Whiskers First

A bit of fetus trivia: the kitten in the womb acquires whiskers before acquiring body hair. This is appropriate, for when the kitten is born, her eyes are shut and her ears are practically deaf at first, so the fully functional whiskers are one of the chief sources of information about the world around her.

113 Flexible whiskers

Compared to a cat's whiskers, a human male's beard and mustache are stiff and unexpressive. The cat's whiskers—technically, the vibrissae—are controlled by various facial muscles, which can point the whiskers out or, when feeding or fighting, pull them backward toward the head. The long upper-lip whiskers are called mystacials, and the muscles under them can move the bottom and top rows of hairs independently. The short whiskers on the lower jaw are called mandibulars. The whiskers on the cheeks are called genals, and the antennalike whiskers above the eyes are known as superciliaries. Quite apart from the face, each front leg has backward-pointing hairs that serve the same function as the head whiskers. All of them are, of course, supersensitive touch receptors.

114 No clipping here!

Whiskers are part of the total look of the cat, and most cat owners like them. But occasionally an owner will notice a wild hair (pun intended) and decide to trim the cat's whiskers, the same way we trim our own whiskers and eyebrows. No permanent harm is done since they do grow back. However, trimming whiskers should be avoided because they are the cat's "antennas"—her sensitive feelers of the world around her—and are especially needed in the dark. There is even a kind of "whisker reflex": in the dark, if something brushes against the cat's eyebrow whiskers, she will shut her eyes immediately to protect them.

115 Pad vibes

The pads on a cat's paws make excellent grippers, which your cat proves through her agile climbing.

But the pads are also sensitive as all get-out, sensing vibrations and other movements on whatever surface the cat touches. The cat's pads feel slight movements that would not be perceptible to the human palm or sole, and they alert the cat to be aware of where she's walking—or, better, turn around and flee.

116 The no-slip grip

Cats, like humans, have sebaceous glands in their skin that secrete sebum, a fatty substance that gives hair its sheen and also provides a water-repellant covering to the skin. The one area totally lacking in sebum are the pads of the paws, which explains why a cat's paw pads always feel dry. It also explains why the pads are such excellent grippers—they're oil-free!

117 Toe-walking

Let's learn some fancy scientific terms: *digitigrade* describes animals that walk on their toes, while *plantigrade* refers to those that walk on the whole foot. Bears are plantigrade animals (so are humans, usually) whereas cats are digitigrade. Generally, digitigrade animals can run faster than animals that put their whole paw, foot or hoof on the ground.

118 It means "many fingered"

Occasionally, through the Russian roulette of genetics, a cat is born with more than the normal number of toes on her feet. Some of these, like the descendants of the many cats at the Ernest Hemingway home in Key West, Florida, are literally collectors' items, fetching high prices. The scientific term for the condition of having extra toes or fingers is *polydactylism*.

119 Global position systems

Automobile makers tout their sophisticated global positioning systems (GPS) in vehicles, but GPS is nothing new in nature. For centuries birds have migrated huge distances, and cats, dogs, horses and other animals somehow find their way home, without depending on computer technology. Chalk some of it up to sensitive vision, hearing and smell, but also to some mysterious natural forces we barely understand, such as their perception of magnetic fields, reactions to the slant of the sun's rays and other phenomena. These senses have delighted pet owners who had given up their pets as hopelessly lost, but whose pets somehow managed to come home again. The flip side: a cruel owner who carries his pet off and abandons it is often dismayed to find the pet back on his doorstep in a few days. (Serves him right!)

120 True and false vocalists

Both you and your cat possess a larynx, also known as the voice box, at the opening to the windpipe.

Vocal chords, made up of cartilage, produce the "voice" of the cat. Veterinarians distinguish between the "true" vocal chords—those that produce meowing, crying and growling—and the "false" vocal chords—those that produce (you guessed it!) purring.

121 Nose leather

Cats are almost entirely covered with hair. One of the few bare areas is the end of the nose, which is known as the leather. Kept damp by secretions from the nostrils, the leather is highly sensitive to touch. The cat version of "kissing" a human, or another cat, is to touch her nose leather to the other's nose. Interestingly, the nose is the only part of a cat's skin that has no sweat glands.

122 The cold nose test

It is true for cats as well as for dogs: a healthy animal will have a slightly cool nose. In both animals the nose is a kind of external thermometer. If your cat's nose feels warm or hot, she may have a fever, a sign that something is wrong internally that needs a vet's attention.

123 Three types of hair

Whether short or long, a cat's coat, or fur, is of great appeal to humans, especially those of us who like to touch. Nature made cats touchable but also provided them with three different types of hair to protect them against the elements. The longest are the guard hairs, which form the topcoat, along with the shorter, bristly awn hairs. Underneath these is the undercoat, which insulates and is composed of short, soft down hairs. (Some hot-climate breeds, such as the Siamese, lack down hair, while cold-climate breeds, like the Maine Coons, have thicker down.) A cat's skin, like human skin, has erector muscles that raise or lower the hairs in response to emotions or temperature.

124 Fat acceptance vs. averages

Cats, like humans, are unique individuals and each cat differs in size and weight. However, it's possible to generalize about the "average" weight of different breeds. The Ragdolls are "biggies": adult cats average from ten to twenty pounds and most of them closer to twenty than to ten. The Maine Coons can be even larger, averaging nine to twenty-two pounds—again, many of them lean toward the heavier end. The "generic" American cat, the American Shorthair, averages from eight to fifteen. On the lighter side (literally), the short-legged Munchkins average five to nine pounds, but lightest of all is probably the quiet little Singapura, averaging from four to nine pounds. Not even the Ragdolls are anywhere near the record set by Himmy, an Australian tabby who died in 1986. Hefty Himmy weighed almost forty-seven pounds.

125 Chest appendices

"Useless as teats on a boar hog" is an old country expression. Well, most male mammals (including humans) have teats, and they are all useless. A male cat has five or six pairs and their purpose is as mysterious as the human appendix—or as a man's nipples.

126 Do cats freckle?

They do indeed. Cats whose coats are red (orange, that is), cream or calico develop freckles as they age, with the spots appearing on their eyelids, mouth, nose and paw pads—in short, on all the exposed areas of skin. Note the cat-human connection: red-haired humans are prone to freckling, and so are red-haired cats.

127 "Hair up!" in Latin

Let's learn some hair-related Latin terms: *piloerection* ("hair standing up") and *arrector pili* ("raiser of hair"). Piloerection occurs in humans, cats and many other animals. The *arrector pili* are muscles under the skin of all areas of the body where hair is present. When the muscles contract (due to fear, excitement and so on), the hairs stand on end. It probably won't surprise you to learn that the most developed of a cat's arrector pili muscles are on the back and tail.

128 Gut juices

A cat's digestive juices are similar to those of humans but different in some key ways. As in humans, the cat's mouth is phase one, with saliva as the first digestive fluid to start working on the food, but cat saliva contains hardly any ptyalin, the enzyme that breaks down starches. (Cats do not naturally seek out starchy foods, and there is little point in their owners giving them starchy snacks.) But what they lack in saliva power, cats make up for in phase two, the stomach, where their stomach acids are much more powerful than those of humans. The cat stomach has no difficulty digesting bits of hard bone and other things that send the human stomach into a tizzy.

129 Sprinters, not long-distance runners

You probably know that the fastest land animal is a species of cat, the cheetah (see 430). Talk of the cheetah's amazing speed has to be accompanied by a disclaimer: very fast, *but only for short distances.* Every cat, including your pet, is the same as the cheetah: made for fast sprints, not endurance over long distances. Some house cats can run thirty miles per hour—faster than you, probably, but you could outlast the cat, and so could a dog. A cat will literally overheat after a minute of running and will have to stop. Such is the nature of the cat's muscle cells.

130 Jumping, pouncing, etc.

Humans have to envy the cat's jumping ability, for the cat can jump six times her own length. (And that's from a still position, not a running leap.) This comes from the same powerful but fast-tiring muscle cells that enable the cat to sprint swiftly. The same muscles are involved in the classic pounce: using the hind legs to spring forward, arching her back, then landing with her front paws on the prey.

131 Tails talk

A cat's tail is a great communicator, as every cat owner knows. When excited, the cat's tail flicks quickly from side to side. If it is still, and raised, the cat is friendly. If it is raised but twitching, the cat is on the alert. When stalking, the tail is carried low, either still or with a slight twitching at the end. In the classic "fright" pose made famous in Halloween decorations, the tail is straight up with the hair standing on end, in accompaniment to the arched back and loud hiss.

All About Breeds and Shows

132 The root of "breed"

Since there is much discussion about breeds of cats and other animals, let's pause here for a quick history of the word *breed*. It comes from the Old English *bredan*, meaning "to nourish, to keep warm." (The word *brood* is rooted in the same word, by the way.) In times past an individual offspring in a litter could be called a breed. As farmers and animal experts became more aware of animal heredity and how to control it, the term *breed* took on its current meaning, that is, "a specific type within a species, having distinctive traits that are passed on through genetics." In addition to cats, there are breeds of dogs, horses, cattle, hogs and so on.

133 Sizing up cats

Dogs range in size from tiny Chihuahuas to bulky Great Danes, even though they are technically the same species. There is no such size difference among the many breeds of *Felis catus*, the common house cat. Humans have been breeding and crossbreeding dogs for centuries, which is why we have tiny breeds, huge breeds and every size and shape in between, all so different that the proverbial visitor from Mars might conclude that these dogs are different species. Not so for cats, which have never lent themselves to the same kind of genetic manipulation. So the largest breed of cats (the Maine Coon) isn't that much bigger than the smaller breeds, and frankly there isn't much variation of the basic body shape of cats. The differences are mostly matters of hair color, hair length and texture, eye color and head shape.

134 Tabby, the "default" setting

If domestic cats were left to breed on their own, with zero interference from humans, there would be very few longhaired cats and very few solid-colored ones. Genetically, the "normal" cat would be a tabby, with a mostly grayish-brown coat and the familiar striping. That is also the typical coat of many of the world's smaller wildcats (see 405 for more about wildcats). Most of the larger cats, such as leopards and tigers, have spots or stripes to help conceal them when they stalk prey. Even solid-colored cats—lions and cougars—have coats of muted colors that serve as camouflage. For a predator in the wild, a gray-brown coat with irregular stripes is the perfect camouflage, so the gray-brown tabby is, because of the coat, the perfect stalking machine.

135 Melanism, the original mutation

While the tabby's camouflaging coat is the "default" pattern for *Felis catus*, the most common mutation is melanism, or blackness. You might say that a solid black cat is nature's first variation on the tabby pattern, occurring without any human involvement in the breeding. Melanism occurs not only among domestic cats but also among thirteen species of wild cats. Genetically, tabby is dominant over black, and as a result there are far more tabby cats than black ones in the world.

136 Don't say "mongrel"

Many dog owners are perfectly content with their "mutt" or "mongrel" dogs, and that is certainly true for cat owners as well. It is safe to say there are a lot more "mutt" cats around than purebred ones. However, you seldom hear a cat owner speak about owning a "mutt" or "mongrel," and there is no generally accepted slang term for such cats. Some owners refer to their pets as "alley cats," and some say the pet is "just cat." The proper term is "mixed-breed." There are signs that the British term *mog* may slowly be catching on in America.

137 The back-crossing phenomenon

In human terms, this would be considered incest and would be frowned upon universally, but it's a regular occurrence among cats, particularly when there is a desire to reproduce a trait in a particular breed. The idea is: a kitten is born with a physical trait that a cat breeder likes and then tries to reproduce in kittens. This is done by crossing the kitten who has the desirable trait (when he or she matures, obviously) with the parent.

138 "Natural" breeds

The various cat associations divide cat breeds into three broad categories: natural, man-made and spontaneous mutation. Among the natural breeds are Persians, Turkish Angoras and Russian Blues. They are natural because the breeds' distinctive traits (color, body shape and the like) occurred without any deliberate interference from humans. But take "natural" with a grain of salt: the basic Persian look may have occurred naturally, but the various natural breeds have, over the years, been refined by selective breeding.

139 "Man-made" breeds

Strictly speaking, man can't make a cat. (Only God—or nature—can do that.) But by mating one type of cat with another, humans can create an entirely new type of cat. A female cat of breed X mates with a male cat of breed Y, and their kittens are the new breed, Z. A "man-made" breed results from this deliberate hybridizing. Once the new breed is established, of course, new litters can be produced by mating the hybrids with other hybrids, instead of reproducing the original mating of breed X with breed Y. As you will see in later entries, many of the newer breeds are man-made.

140 "Spontaneous mutation" breeds

A mutation is any unexpected deviation from the norm. A certain cat is born with an odd trait. By mating that cat with a cat with the same odd trait, an entirely new breed results, all the offspring of which have the same odd trait. The most famous example of this is the Manx, the tailless cat (see 193). A more recent example is the Scottish Fold, with the famous flattened-down ears (see 178). No one knows what causes genetic oddities, and not all of them are attractive enough that humans would want more of them.

141 "Foreign" vs. "cobby"

Serious cat fanciers describe cats' body types as either "foreign" or "cobby"—essentially, slim or stocky. The quintessential foreign breed is the Siamese: slim and lithe, the cat equivalent of what would be called a swimmer's build in a human. The cobby body is heavier, shorter in the legs and sits closer to the ground. Persians are the classic example of the cobby body. Naturally some breeds fall somewhere in between, and they are called "moderate" or "modified." The average mixed-breed house cat is a moderate.

142 The pedigree

A pedigreed cat is a cat with "the papers"—specifically, registration papers listing the cat's purebred parents, grandparents and great-grandparents (and even further, if that information is available). In other words, it is a family tree that ensures that the cat is not a mixed breed (not that the cat himself gives a hoot). The papers will also list the cat's ancestors' titles—awards won in cat shows, that is.

143 Their countries of origin (not!)

What's in a name—specifically, the name of a cat breed that links that breed with a spot on the map? Not much at all. Siamese cats probably did come from Siam (Thailand), and Burmese came (probably) from Burma, but otherwise the geographical names of various cat breeds have little or no connection to where the breed actually originated, as you will see in some of the breeds' descriptions later in this chapter. Chalk it up to bad guesses, the choice of names that sound exotic or other factors.

Hair, Fur, Coat

144 No hairless cats

The Mexican hairless dog breed isn't *totally* hairless (no dog breed is), and no cat is totally hairless, either. The closest thing to hairless is the stubby-haired Sphynx (see 179), which has received a lot of publicity thanks to the cat Mr. Bigglesworth in the Austin Powers movies. A lot of viewers left theatres talking about "that hairless cat," but Sphynxes do have a coat of suedelike fur.

145 Double or single coat

In discussing cats' hair, the proper term to use is *coat*, not *fur*. Shorthaired cats have a double coat or a single coat. A single coat means the hair is very fine and lies close to the body, resulting in a smooth, satiny look, which is especially attractive in black cats. A double coat has long guard hairs and a thicker undercoat (see 123). Naturally the double coat looks thicker and more plush than the single coat.

146 Don't call it "mane"

The mane, the thick hair around the head that gives the male lion its distinctive look, has its counterpart in several longhaired breeds of cats. In house cats, however, this thick growth of hair around the face is not a mane but a ruff. (Remember that in the 1500s, a ruff was a very fancy type of lacy starched collar worn by people of the upper classes.) Fans of Persians consider the ruff to be one of this breed's most attractive features.

147 "Brush," not "bush"

We often speak of a cat or dog as having a "bushy" tail, but among cat fanciers, it is proper to speak of the "brush" of a tail, as in "The Turkish Angora's tail has a full brush." Obviously every type of brush has its admirers, from the extremely full brush of Persians and Maine Coons to the practically brushless Siamese. Fans of longhaired cats cite the long, thick fur on the tails as one of the most appealing features.

148 The true meaning of "tabby"

In times past, "tabby" could refer to any house cat, though this name was more often used to refer to a female (as in "toms and tabbies"). Later it came to mean a cat whose coat showed bands, or stripes, of a darker color than the base color. Strictly speaking, there is no cat breed named "tabby," but, as you will see in the following entries, the word *tabby* is used among cat fanciers to refer to several types of coat patterns.

149 "Classic tabby"

As you might guess from the name, the tabby cat is so named because of the coat pattern that people associate with the word *tabby*. The cat's coat has clearly defined bands on the body. There are also bars of this darker color on the face, and there is a defined M-shape of the darker color on the cat's forehead.

150 "Mackerel tabby"

This is similar to the classic tabby, except that the stripes are narrower. There is the familiar M on the forehead, just as the classic tabby has. In case you're curious, *mackerel* comes from the mackerel fish, which is striped. (We can safely assume that a mackerel tabby cat would eagerly *eat* mackerel, also—as would any other cat.)

151 The unicolor

Some cats are consistently the same color all over—that is, each hair is the same color from tip to root, and hairs all over the body are the same color. Among cat fanciers, this is referred to as the "self coat" pattern. It is very attractive, but so are the various patterns listed next.

152 Tipping

When a cat has a "tipped" coat, the individual hairs are not the same color from root to tip. Rather, the tips are of a contrasting color compared to the rest of the hair. If the tipping is light, the cat is a Chinchilla. If the tipping is medium, the cat is Shaded. And if the tipping is heavy, the cats are Smokes.

153 Tortoiseshell

True tortoiseshell (the shell of an actual turtle, that is) is black with attractive highlights of orange or cream.

It has been used for centuries in making furniture inlays and ornamental articles, such as hairbrushes. The name has long been applied to cats whose coats resemble tortoiseshells—that is, black cats with highlight patches of orange or cream. These beautiful cats are often referred to as "torties." People often confuse the terms *tortoiseshell* and *calico*, but the two are not the same (see 156).

154 "Blue" (but not really) and "ginger"

You might describe your own cat as gray, but in the world of breeding and cat shows, there are no gray cats, only *blue* ones. (As far as that goes, no human or cat is naturally "red," yet when we refer to a cat or person having "red" hair, people know exactly what we mean.) Likewise *ginger* is applied to orangey-coated cats, even though real ginger (the spice, that is) is brown, not orange.

155 "Lilac" and "apricot"

Here are two other coat color names that, like blue, aren't meant to be taken quite literally. Lilac, which has also been called "lavender," is basically a beige-gray or a light brown-gray but is distinctive in having (barely) a hint of pinkish purple. (The colors purple and brown are not that different, as any artist would tell you.) "Apricot" is a cream color that (again, barely) has a hint of orange-red. Neither lilac nor apricot seems to occur in nature; they are the result of selective breeding.

156 Calico

As noted above, people often call tortoiseshell cats "calico" and calico cats "tortoiseshell," and some people assume these words mean the same. The confusion probably arises because both tortoiseshells and calicos have a mix of black and orange. Calico cats, however, also have a lot of white—in fact, a mix of white, black and orange (or cream) in clearly defined patches—whereas tortoiseshells are black all over with the orange appearing as highlights all over. Put another way, calicos' coats give the impression of being stitched together from various large scraps of white, black and orange.

157 "Van" cats

The breed known as the Turkish Van, which is described elsewhere (see 171), was named for an area around Lake Van in southeastern Turkey. In recent years, the name Van has been used to describe a cat (of any breed) that has the coloring of the Turkish Van: mostly white, but with a few patches of another color, usually the entire tail and part of the face.

The Breeds

158 Longhairs, in general

Genetically, short hair is dominant in cats, meaning that the default setting for the hair of domestic cats is short, just as it was for their wild ancestors. But there is a recessive gene that results in long hair, and the breeding of longhaired cats was a fairly simple matter of getting together males and females who shared the recessive gene. Where exactly this first occurred isn't known for certain, though it was probably in central Asia (which would include Persia, the country we now call Iran). We have it on good authority that some of these longhairs reached France and Italy sometime in the 1500s, and from there they reached other countries in Europe. No one tried very hard to be "scientific" about naming cats, so longhaired cats might be called Russian, French, even Chinese. (Obviously "Persian" was one name that caught people's fancy and stuck.) Europeans, especially aristocrats who could afford to buy exotic beasts, were enchanted by longhaired cats, as are millions of people today. In the descriptions of the longhaired breeds that follow, note that many of them began as longhaired mutations of an existing shorthair breed; for example, the Balinese are descended from longhaired kittens that showed up in litters of normally shorthaired Siamese.

159 Persian

Say "Persian cat" and most people think of something longhaired, elegant and quiet. And so they are, although they probably aren't from Persia. Their longhaired ancestors were brought to Europe from Turkey around 1520, and Europeans (and later Americans) were taken with these lovely creatures. (One proof of their popularity in the United States: there are more Persians registered with the Cat Fanciers' Association than any other breed.) The Persian (or Longhair, as the British call this breed) is fairly stout-bodied and has the trademark "pushed-in" nose, round face, round eyes and soft voice. The Persian is the quintessential lap cat, even though Persians surprise their owners with their mousing ability. Their long hair is beautiful but needs regular grooming with a fine-toothed comb, particularly if the cat is allowed to wander outside. British (but not American) breeders consider the various Persian color types to be separate breeds.

160 Himalayan

Imagine what would happen if you crossed the two most popular breeds of cat—Persian and Siamese. That's exactly what breeders did back in the 1930s, and the result is the longhaired Himalayan, which some call the Himalayan Persian. This cat inherited the stocky body and round face of the Persians, but the distinctive "pointed" coloration and the blue eyes of the Siamese, giving an appearance (obviously) of a longhaired Siamese. (Its blue is more subdued than the blue of the Siamese.) Personality-wise, this cat seems more Persian than Siamese—fairly quiet, soft-voiced and less demanding than the typical Siamese. Thanks to a thick coat, a Himalayan also requires a lot more grooming than a Siamese does.

161 Birman

Supposedly, this breed originated in the Asian country of Burma, so why is it Birman instead of Burman? To distinguish this breed from the Burmese, obviously. (The two breeds are not related at all.) The Birman, like the Himalayan, gives the appearance of being a longhaired Siamese, but the Birman occurs naturally, while the Himalayan is the result of deliberate crossbreeding. The Birman has an off-white coat and the Siamese-like "points" of black or dark brown on the face, ears, legs and tail, plus attractive blue eyes. Though not as rambunctious as Siamese, Birmans are not as laidback as Persians are.

162 Balinese

The third breed that looks like a longhaired Siamese, the Balinese started out as a real Siamese—specifically, as a genetic mutation in a litter of Siamese kittens in the 1950s. Having too long a coat to be exhibited as Siamese, the mutant kittens were given a new breed name, even though they had no connection at all with the island of Bali, except perhaps that their graceful movements reminded people of Balinese dancers. The Balinese has long hair, though not as fluffy as the Himalayan or Birman. Personality-wise and body-wise, this cat is all Siamese—playful and slender.

163 Javanese

This breed derived from the Balinese (meaning that, going further back, this breed was derived from the Siamese), and like the Balinese, was named for an Indonesian island (even though both breeds originated in the United States). The Javanese are longhaired, white or cream in color, with "points" like their Siamese ancestors and the blue eyes of the Siamese. Like all the longhaired breeds descended from the Siamese, the Javeneses' points are much less distinctive than those of their shorthaired ancestors.

164 Turkish Angora

This lovely breed was named after Angora, the old name for Ankara, now the capital city of Turkey. Like Persians, Angoras are prized for their rich coat of long hair, and even though many people confuse the two breeds, they are different in many ways. The Angora has a more slender build than the Persian, with a more triangular face that is more "catty" than the round, snub-nosed Persian face. The Angora's long coat does not mat and tangle as easily as the Persian's does and comes in as many colors as a Persian's. They also share the Persian's genetic flukes: blue-eyed white cats that are often deaf and "odd-eyed" cats that have one blue eye, and one copper or green eye. Though we can't be certain, it's highly possible that the Angoras were a naturally occurring breed, and that Persians were developed from them.

165 Selkirk Rex

This new breed has a curly coat like that of the other two Rex breeds (see 180 and 181), but is longhaired, making this Rex even more of a "poodle cat" than the Devon Rex or the Cornish Rex. Like their shorthaired cousins, the Selkirks have a playful personality. The kittens go through a rather unattractive phase before taking on the distinctive longhaired curly look of the adult cat. It is the "ugly duckling" syndrome at work, for the adult Selkirk Rex is truly a beautiful animal.

166 Maine Coon

Not all longhaired cats are foreign. The large Maine Coon cat is all-American—in fact, this cat is the offspring of American farm cats and wild raccoons—or so the legend goes. (Cats and raccoons do not mate.) Probably the Maine Coon resulted from the breeding of shorthaired farm cats with Angora cats brought back to New England by sailors. (A more "all-American" explanation is also possible: the Maine Coons resulted from a genetic mutation in Maine farm cats, with no help at all from foreign longhairs.) These lovable, longhaired, bushy-tailed cats were popular in America in the 1800s both as pets and show cats, but they lost ground to Persians. (There is lots of trendiness in the pet world.) Maine Coons are popular once again, particularly with people who like longhaired cats that are more active and outdoorsy than the Persians. (Maine Coons aren't lap cats, but they do like to be in their owners' company.) Like the Persians, the Maine Coons are found in a multitude of colors and patterns, even within the same litter.

167 Somali

The Somali is basically a longhaired Abyssinian, so the breed gives the impression of being a small (and longhaired) cougar. Like their Abyssinian ancestors, the Somali is playful and inquisitive and fond of the outdoors (meaning that, unlike the Persian, the Somali is not a good apartment cat). The Somali has the fairly large ears of the Abyssinian as well as the same affectionate nature and soft voice.

168 Cymric

The beautiful, but somewhat odd-looking, Cymric is more or less a longhaired Manx, with the characteristic Manx trait of having either no tail at all (a "rumpy"), a very short tail (a "stumpy") or a half-tail (a "longy"). The breed was the result of a genetic mutation, and by the 1980s they were being exhibited in shows. Like their shorthaired Manx ancestors, the Cymrics are affectionate and active cats, with front legs shorter than back legs, giving them a curious "bunny-hop" walk.

169 Norwegian Forest Cat

Many breeds have geographically based names that sometimes have nothing whatsoever to do with where the cat originated. The Norwegian Forest Cat—the "wegie," as fans call them—really did originate in the forests of Norway. (In their homeland, they are known as the Skaukatt. Nearby Sweden's version is the Rugkatt, while Denmark's is the Racekatte.) As you might expect, a thick coat and stout body help this cat survive in a cold climate. This large longhaired cat resembles the Maine Coon, though the two breeds are not related. They do share the need to roam the outdoors, both are good hunters who like a certain amount of independence, and both breeds are very affectionate. Wegies have been known to fish and even to swim.

170 Tiffany

Does the name sound elegant? The Tiffany definitely is. Like so many longhaired breeds, this one too is the result of a genetic mutation of a shorthair—in this case, the Burmese. Like their Burmese ancestors, the Tiffany has a sleek seal-brown coat, but long and silky, giving the head a rounder appearance than the Burmese. Like the Burmese, the Tiffany has yellow-gold eyes and is affectionate and playful—and also "talkative" (or "noisy," depending on your point of view).

171 Turkish Van

A cat that likes water? No, we're not pulling your leg. This naturally occurring breed from Turkey hailed from the region of Lake Van (hence the name) and was a popular pet in Turkey, finally appearing in Europe and the United States in the 1950s, where owners were amazed to find that the breed didn't mind being bathed—and actually *chose* to swim. The Van has a long white coat with distinctive patches of red on the ears and tail. (Interestingly, in their native Turkey, Vans were often all white, and the Turks still prefer this to the red-patched type.) Although Vans take to water, they are basically a quiet, indoor-loving cat.

172 Ragdoll

Think laidback and the quiet, lap-loving Persian comes to mind. But no cat is more laidback than the Ragdoll, which was named from the curious trait of going completely limp when picked up. Most Ragdolls look like longhaired Siamese, but they are infinitely more docile than their Siamese ancestors. In fact, the breed seems to have a high pain tolerance, so much so that some overly protective owners feel compelled to monitor them for illnesses and injuries. Given this cat's docility, a quiet life indoors rather than an outdoor life is suited to this cat. One other distinctive trait: this is a very *large* cat. The average male weighs more than fifteen pounds. Ragdolls and Maine Coons are the largest breeds of domestic cats.

173 Siberian

You would expect a cat from the cold region of Russian Siberia to be stocky and longhaired, and this one definitely is, making this breed very similar to the Maine Coon and the Norwegian Forest Cat. This cat is active, a good hunter and friendly toward humans but doesn't have the makings of a good lap cat. Most Siberians have the look of longhaired tabby cats. They are fairly new to America, having been bred in the United States since only 1990.

174 Shorthairs, in general

As noted earlier, the domestic cat is genetically shorthaired; long hair occurs as a mutation. So, obviously, there are a lot more shorthairs around than longhairs, and no doubt there always will be. Without the deliberate breeding of longhair with longhair (thanks to human intervention), the percentage of shorthairs would be even higher than it is. There is an immense variety of colors and patterns in shorthairs, but generally speaking they all have the "generic cat" shape underneath—not heavy-bodied, not thin and lanky. The exceptions are the Oriental breeds, which we'll look at in a later section.

175 American Shorthair

When Americans use the term *cat* in the most generic sense, they are referring to the American Shorthair, and the vast majority of American cats belong to this breed. Alley cats are American Shorthairs, and so is the lion's share (pun intended) of household pets, whose owners usually don't particularly care about things like pedigrees. However, there are pedigreed American Shorthairs, and "the papers" are required to enter them into cat shows. But many cat shows now have a household pet category that allows nonpedigreed cats to compete.

176 Ocicat

You may already know that the ocelot is an attractive spotted wild cat of the Americas (see 414). The Ocicat breed gives the impression of being a very small ocelot (which this breed was named for), though in fact the Ocicat is a genetic fluke that occurred in a cross between an Abyssinian and a Siamese. No one knows why the mating produced some spotted kittens, but it did, and this new breed has many fans. Ocicats have a lot of personality, and they are rare among cats in their adaptability to being walked on a leash.

177 Malayan

This breed developed as a color variety of the Burmese, and the color is the only thing that distinguishes the Malayan from the Burmese. The Malayan has a coat of blue-gray, silver or yellow-brown and yellow eyes. All are playful, friendly cats, but they do seem to be more sensitive to loud noises than other breeds.

178 Scottish Fold

You might say that this breed is the flip side of the American Curl breed (see 183). While the Curl's ears turn back, the Scottish Fold's ears are folded forward, flat against the head. Like the Curl, the Fold resulted from a genetic mutation. On a Scottish farm in 1961 cats with the distinctive fold were born, and all other Scottish Folds are their descendants. There is some controversy about the breeding of Folds, since some people suspect that the breeding can perpetuate hearing problems. But Folds have their fans, who like the cats' sweet nature and the distinctive look of the head. Scottish Folds come in most colors and as both longhair and shorthair.

179 Sphynx

This curious-looking creature was largely unknown to the general public until the Austin Powers movies made a household name of Mr. Bigglesworth, the pampered pet of Dr. Evil. The breed originated in Canada in 1966, when an almost hairless kitten was born. The key word is *almost*: although the Sphynx appears to be hairless, there is in fact a thin coat of very short suedelike fur. The thin coat gives the cat a lanky and bony appearance, with oversized ears to boot, a look that is not to everyone's taste. Even so, the Sphynx has become popular in recent years, no doubt aided by Austin Powers.

180 Cornish Rex

In terms of hair coverage, the Rex is one step above the almost hairless Sphynx breed. Unlike the Sphynx, the Rex does not appear hairless, but has a thin coat—that is also curly. As the name indicates, the breed originated in Cornwall, the region of far southwestern England. In a litter of shorthaired kittens, one kitten had wavy fur and even wavier whiskers. These large-eared, slender-bodied cats are extremely playful and have the curious trait of wagging their tails like dogs when they are happy. Because of their curly fur, Rexes are often referred to as "poodle cats."

181 Devon Rex

Devon is a county in southwest England, near Cornwall, and by an odd coincidence Devon was the locale of a genetic mutation that produced a curly-haired cat—like the Cornish Rex but (genetically speaking) not related. The Devon Rex looks much like the Cornish Rex, though slightly curlier in coat and thinner in body. (Both breeds are known as "poodle cats.") The Devon Rex is so unusual in appearance that one appeared in the out-of-this-world science fiction movie *Dune*.

182 Egyptian Mau

As noted elsewhere in this book, *mau* was the ancient Egyptian word for cat. (And it's no coincidence that *mau* sounds a lot like *meow*.) The Mau breed does resemble the cats depicted in the art of ancient Egypt. It is possible the Maus are the direct descendants of those cats—but also possible that the breed was developed to resemble cats of ancient times. We do know for sure that Maus were imported from Egypt to Europe and the United States in the 1950s. Like the Ocicat, the Mau is spotted, a trait many people find appealing, and they are playful and affectionate.

183 American Curl

Again, another genetic mutation that resulted in a new breed: a cat whose ears curl back away from the face. The mutation occurred in a litter of kittens in California in 1981, and the breed is now recognized by most American cat associations. Curl cats are an acquired taste, but one that is easy to acquire, since the distinctive ears do give them an appealing look. They are quiet and sweet natured, and their very long and full-plumed tails are attractive.

184 Tonkinese

The beautiful Tonkinese is the result of crossing Siamese with Burmese. The breed has the blue eyes of their Siamese ancestors as well as their familiar "points," but these are less defined in the Tonkinese. (The points are barely visible on the very dark Natural Mink variety of Tonkinese.) The Tonkinese is a fairly new breed but has become very popular, in part because these cats are extremely affectionate and playful and more adaptable than most cats to riding in cars.

185 Bombay

Think sleek. This solid black shorthaired breed is so extremely sleek that the gorgeous coat resembles black patent leather. There are no connections at all with the city of Bombay in India, but the breeders chose the name because the cat reminded them of the lithe and jet-black panthers of the Indian jungles. These placid, adorable creatures with their copper eyes are veritable "purr boxes," purring almost constantly when in the company of people they love. The one drawback of their affectionate nature is that they don't cope well with being left alone for extended periods.

186 Havana

Though a deep solid brown (almost black), the Havana (also called Havana Brown) has Siamese ancestry, which is obvious from the long slender build, triangular face and slanted eyes. There is no direct connection with Havana, Cuba; breeders chose the name because the cat's color reminded them of Havana cigars. (Go figure.) Like the Siamese, the Havana is alert and playful and requires a lot of attention, which is usually given, given the cat's talkative nature.

187 Singapura

As you might guess from the name, this breed originated in Singapore in Asia, where this cat is regarded as the "drain cat," an unwanted street cat that seeks shelter in drains and other undesirable locations. They are finding themselves more welcome in the United States and Europe, where their short, silky beige fur and quietness make them appealing pets. They love a quiet indoor life and make few demands on their owners. They don't demand much food either, for Singapuras are the smallest of domestic cat breeds.

188 Japanese Bobtail

Want a really distinctive—and really expensive—cat? Then consider the Japanese Bobtail, a naturally occurring breed from (where else?) Japan, where they have long been considered good luck. True to their name, Bobtails have short (and puffy) tails. Most Bobtails are white, with patches of black or red, or both, on the face, back and tail. The Japanese are particularly fond of the Mi-Ke ("three furs") variety—white with patches of red and black. Bobtails are affectionate and playful and, as you might expect from a breed originating from an island nation, very fond of fish. As noted earlier, they are expensive, since they are rare outside of Japan. (Historical tidbit: When American troops occupied

Japan after World War II, the Japanese got a quick education about cats, learning from Americans that Bobtails aren't "normal" by world cat standards.)

189 Burmese

Think of velvet and you have the basic image of the Burmese. The coat is glossy, short and dense, and found in most solid colors. Though Burmese had Siamese ancestors, you would never guess from their looks or voice, for they are heavier bodied (and less loud mouthed) than the Siamese. Like the Siamese, they do love to play and are generally fond of people, even strangers. They travel better in a car than most cats.

190 Abyssinian

Abyssinia was the old name for Ethiopia in northeastern Africa. Soldiers returning from there to Britain in the 1860s brought back some of these handsome cats, which are probably a naturally occurring breed in Africa. Whether these were the descendants of the ancient Egyptians' temple cats (as the story goes) can't be determined, but they do resemble paintings of them. Abyssinians are usually a rich golden brown, with a darker brown "ticking" that gives the coat a plush appearance. These playful cats usually attach themselves to one special person in the home.

191 Korat

Imagine getting a pair of sleek gray green-eyed cats as a good luck gift at your wedding. This occurred often in the province of Korat in Thailand, which lent its name to this naturally occurring breed. The Korat is a quiet breed, adapting easily to indoor life and avoiding noisy situations whenever possible. This cat seems to like most humans but not other cats, so the Korat owner is wise to maintain a one-cat household.

192 Russian Blue

It really did originate in Russia, and was for a while known as the Archangel Blue, after the Russian port city of Archangel. Russian traders brought them to Britain in the 1800s, and no doubt these cats were pleased to live in a locale warmer than Russia (not that Britain is exactly balmy). The "blue" is, of course, a bluish gray, and Russian Blues give the impression of being deep plush all over with thick fur standing out from the body. These green-eyed cats are shy and quiet and make few demands on their owners.

193 Manx

The name Manx means "from the isle of Man," Man being in the sea between Great Britain and Ireland. The Manx people are rather fond of their distinctive tailless native breed, though no one knows for sure where or how the breed first originated. (One colorful legend has it that the cat was late in getting to Noah's ark, and the tail was cut off as the door shut.) Manx cats are found as completely tailless ("rumpies"), with a small stubb ("stumpies") or with a sort of half-tail ("longies"), but cat shows are limited to include only rumpies, the truly tailless variety. Manx are agreeable and active pets, delighting their owners with their "bunny-hop" gait, the result of their having back legs that are longer than their front legs.

194 American Wirehair

Here is one more example of a breed that began as a genetic mutation. This one began in Vermont in 1966, with a wiry-haired kitten born in an American Shorthair litter. The Wirehairs have proved easy to breed, as wire-haired kittens will be born to a mating of a Wirehair with an ordinary Shorthair. Like the American Shorthair, the Wirehair is found in all colors and patterns and has a distinctive trait—a wiry, wavy coat.

195 La Perm

That's *perm* as in *permanent* wave, which is what these cats appear to have. While the American Wirehair has a wavy but somewhat stiff coat, the fur of La Perm is curly but soft. (As with the Wirehair, a genetic mutation caused this.) The curly hair extends only up to the neck; the hair on the head looks like that of an American Shorthair. (This looks either odd or appealing, depending on your point of view.) Curiously, La Perm kittens are often bald at birth, but in a few weeks they begin growing their curly coats.

196 Bengal

Breeds of spotted cats have become popular in recent years, among them the Bengal, which originated from crossbreeding in the 1980s. Supposedly among the Bengal's ancestors were some street cats of India, so the name Bengal is at least fairly accurate. Bengals resemble wildcats and are fairly large. The very attractive Snow Bengals are blue-eyed and white, with black spots or marbling.

197 American Bobtail

While the Japanese Bobtail has been around for ages, the American Bobtail is a fairly new breed. The parent cat for the breed was a mutation, a bobtailed kitten that an Iowa couple found at a Native American reservation in Arizona. American Bobtails are stout-bodied cats, with a mottled coat that, along with their short tails, resembles that of the bobcats of the North American woodlands. Unlike the stubby tail of the bobcat, however, American Bobtails have a bushy plume to their tails.

198 Munchkin

The name gives you the general idea, but not the whole story, of this cat: short, but not a real dwarf, for the only thing dwarf about the Munchkin is the leg bones. Essentially this cat is normal sized but with short legs, the result of a genetic mutation. There is a lot of controversy about whether it is healthy (or ethical) to deliberately breed such cats, and for that reason the cat fancier associations have been slow to recognize this breed. Yet the Munchkins have their fans, not only because of their distinctive look but also because they are so playful and inquisitive. There are both longhaired and shorthaired Munchkins.

199 European Shorthair

If the American Shorthair is the "generic cat" of the United States, the European Shorthair is what most Europeans think of as the typical household pet or street cat. These cats are obviously related because the American Shorthairs are descendants of the cats brought over by European colonists.

200 Snowshoe

Cross a Siamese with a bicolor American Shorthair and you get this lovely creature with light blue eyes and white paws, from which the name is derived. Snowshoes are stockier than their Siamese ancestors, and also less vocal, but they make affectionate and active pets. This very new breed is still rare, but will no doubt catch on with people looking for an attractive and pleasant companion. So far the breed has not been recognized by most of the cat associations.

201 Chartreux

You might guess from the name that this is a French breed. The Chartreux does have a long history in that country, including being known as the "cat of France" in the 1700s, and was bred even earlier than that by monks of the Carthusian order. (Hence the name; French Carthusian monks were well known for their liqueur called Chartreuse.) This cat had virtually disappeared by the end of World War II but has experienced a kind of comeback, and rightly so, for this blue (gray, that is) cat with golden eyes and a sweet disposition deserves to be better known. As seems to be true of the larger breeds, this one is fairly quiet.

202 California Spangled

This breed is, like the Ocicat, another attempt at producing a "wild" look in a house cat, specifically a spotted wild look. California Spangleds have been available only since 1986, though they are already acquiring a reputation as pleasant, human-loving pets. The name "Spangled" seems an odd choice, frankly, since the breed is only found in muted grays and browns.

203 Pixie-bobs

Can the domestic cat (*Felis catus*) breed with the wild American bobcat (*Lynx rufus*)? The answer is a definite "maybe," and fans of the Pixie-bob breed believe that their lovable six-toed, bob-tailed pets are descended from Pixie, the offspring of a cat and bobcat in the Pacific Northwest. Only one of the cat fancier associations The International Cat Association (TICA) has recognized the breed so far, and a number of people believe the Pixie-bob just happens to *look* like a cat-bobcat hybrid. Whether or not they truly carry bobcat genes, Pixie-bobs are gaining in popularity, impressing owners with not only their size (not as large as a bobcat, but still quite large) but also their willingness to ride in the car, walk on a leash, even learn to fetch. These big, active cats have a future, whatever their ancestry and whatever the cat associations may think of them.

204 Orientals, in general

These breeds have a distinctive look: a long, slender body, long legs, a long narrow tail, a wedge-shaped face, fairly large ears and (often) a fairly long neck—in short, traits you associate with the Siamese. They are shorthaired but distinctive enough to be considered as a separate group. Think of the stout-bodied, round-headed, round-eyed, snub-nosed Persians as one cat extreme and the lanky, wedge-headed, slant-eyed Siamese as the other. In the middle are the moderate-bodied, moderate-headed and moderate-eyed shorthairs. However, as you'll see in the descriptions of the longhairs, many of those breeds have Siamese/Oriental ancestry.

205 Siamese

If there's one breed of cat that the average person on the street recognizes, it has to be the Siamese (though Persian owners might not agree). Siamese are blue-eyed, slender-bodied, with a wedge-shaped face, slightly slanted eyes and the very distinctive "points" of dark brown on the ears, muzzle, feet and tail. Whether the breed actually originated in Thailand (formerly Siam) is debatable, but we do know that the Thai people valued them highly. So have many generations of Europeans and Americans, who find these cats to be graceful, playful and extremely inquisitive. They are also "chatty," so much so that their loud voices (especially of the toms) do not endear them to everyone, even serious ailurophiles. Another less endearing trait—one that many owners overlook—is the frequency of crossed eyes, a trait that ensures the cat cannot enter a cat show. Over the years, Siamese have been "bred thin," apparently on the assumption that owners prefer the lanky body. The Siamese of a century ago had a more solid build than the Siamese of today.

206 A word about "points"

All Siamese cats are basically tan or cream-colored with "points" of brown on the face, ears, legs and tail. Siamese kittens are born "pointless"; the points develop as they age. Over the years, several varieties of points have been perpetuated through breeding. The classic was the seal point (*seal* meaning "very dark brown"), but you can also find blue point, chocolate point, lilac point (light brown, not purple), cinnamon point, cream point and fawn point. Each variety is attractive, and each has fans, though some cat fanciers consider the oldest varieties (seal and blue) to be the only "real" Siamese. Whatever variety they are, all Siamese tend to darken if they spend a lot of time outside.

207 Oriental Shorthair

The coats of the original Siamese cats of centuries ago were not always the familiar cream color with points. Many of them were solid colors, and there were solids among the first Siamese brought to the West. Chalk it up to the fickleness of human taste: cat fanciers decided they preferred the pointed Siamese, so for a long time their solid-color cousins were rarely found. Known as Oriental Shorthairs, they are gaining in popularity. They have the typical Siamese personality—gregarious, active, chatty and willing (some of them, anyway) to walk on a leash. They have the body type of the Siamese: long, lanky, with a wedge-shaped face and fairly large ears.

Let's Have a Show!

208 Harrison Weir's legacy

Harrison Weir was a successful English artist and, as it happened, also a lover of cats. He is credited with organizing an 1871 cat show in London's Crystal Palace that is considered to be the world's first cat show. Weir served as one of the judges in the show, and he also created the standards for all the breeds exhibited. Weir also published the book *Our Cats and All About Them*, which helped promote further interest in cat shows. A footnote to this "first" show: prior to this, cats had not been exhibited for their glamour—rather, "working cats" (mousers, that is) were displayed at agricultural fairs, along with cattle, hogs, sheep and other animals.

209 Alphabet soup time

Most cat owners have no interest in entering their pets in cat shows, but for those who do, seven different organizations in the United States and Canada register purebred cats, create breed standards and sanction cat shows and cat show judges. They are the American Cat Association (ACA), American Cat Fanciers' Association (ACFA), Canadian Cat Association (CCA), Cat Fanciers' Association (CFA), Cat Fanciers' Federation (CFF), The International Cat Association (TICA) and the United Cat Federation (UCF).

210 The oldest U.S. cat club

The oldest cat registry association in the United States is the American Cat Association (ACA), formed in 1904 as the offspring of a cat club in

Chicago. Typical of any human organization, disputes arose among members over various rules, and, inevitably, the dispute led to the founding of another group, the Cat Fanciers' Association (CFA). Generally speaking, the CFA is considered the most prestigious of the various cat registry groups, but (obviously) the rival associations would not agree with that.

211 Why so many?

Why are there seven different cat registry associations in North America instead of just one? That is comparable to asking why there are hundreds of Christian denominations instead of just one. Simply put: members can't agree on everything. The different cat associations mostly disagree on which breeds are registered and which standards should be used in judging the breeds. For example, the Cat Fanciers' Association recognizes a certain number of breeds, while the American Cat Association recognizes a different number, and both believe they have good reasons for including or excluding a particular breed.

212 Not "a guy thing"

Yes, there are *lots* of men who love cats (the author is one), but the old stereotypes and prejudices—dogs are the proper pets for "real men," and so on—linger. Thus, while you will see lots of men at dog shows, it is evident that there are far fewer men than women at cat shows. This is changing as more men "out" themselves as cat fanciers, but part of the prejudice against cat shows (which the author fully understands) is the feeling of many men that cats ought to be kept and enjoyed but not necessarily fussed over and entered in competitions.

213 No performance at cat shows

You may have attended dog shows or horse shows, and if you have, you know right away that cat shows are different, for the cats are not expected to perform in any way. They show up, well groomed and healthy, and get judged, whereas in a horse or dog show the animals would be expected to jump through the hoops (literally and figuratively) to prove they are not only beautiful but sound in the muscles as well. Cats (luckily for them) are required only to sit and be beautiful (which they are very good at), and all the movement and hustle are on the part of their anxiety-stricken owners.

214 The cleanliness obsession at cat shows

If you've ever taken your cat to the vet, this has probably crossed your mind: Aren't there a lot of germs floating around in this place? Suddenly you're aware that your healthy and fanatically clean pet could pick up a communicable disease. This concern is felt by everyone associated with cat shows, which is why the judges and other folks associated with them are as fanatical about cleanliness as the cats are. Antibacterial cloths are used to wipe down the judges' hands; ditto for the tables where the cats are judged. Considering that the cleanest animal in the world is being judged, this is appropriate.

215 The show season

Your nearest symphony orchestra or opera company is likely to be in season in the fall and the winter, and this is also true for cat shows, which mostly take place between September and February. There are several reasons for this schedule, notably that the longhaired breeds' coats will be at their most luxurious during the fall and winter. In the spring and the summer, females are likely to be queening (giving birth and mothering), and thus will be out of commission for awhile.

216 No outcasts here!

There was a time when cat show competitions were for purebred cats only, and the many happy owners of mixed-breed cats could not enter their pets in cat shows, no matter how beautiful and adorable they were. That has changed, and now many cat shows award prizes in the Household Pet Competition. The strict rules applied when judging purebred cats are waived, except that mixed-breed cats entered in shows must be neutered and must not be declawed.

217 "Vetting in"

All the people connected to cat shows are, of course, fanatical about the health of the cats, given that so many cats in close quarters could lead to the spreading of an epidemic. For this reason the cats exhibited in British shows all have to be "vetted in," meaning that a veterinarian checks each cat for fleas and other disorders.

218 The point system

The human participants in cat shows are familiar with the points system used to judge the cats. Each breed has its own list of standards and points, but all have certain common features, such as eyes and coat, among others. Each breed's list of standards and points adds up to one hundred, of course. Happily for the cats, they are not required to do the math or agonize about whether they win an award.

219 Contests for darn near everything . . .

In cat shows, the cages in which the cats are displayed are a standard size (24 × 27 × 27 inches). While there is much fuss about grooming the cats in preparation for the shows, there is also plenty of to-do about the cages themselves—owners decorate them with cushions, curtain, fabrics, bric-a-brac and other ornaments. It won't surprise you that some of the cat shows actually give prizes for the best-decorated cages.

220 "Rusting" of black cats

If you own a sleek black car, you know it isn't going to stay very sleek if you leave it outside where it will experience all kinds of weather. In effect the same thing happens to black cats, specifically the longhaired ones. If exposed to the elements—including sunlight—a longhaired black cat's fur tends to "rust"—not literally the rust that forms on iron, but the effect is the same in that the cat's hair turns a kind of reddish-brown. It's bound to happen to any black longhair who spends a lot of time outdoors. Needless to say, folks who exhibit their pets in cat shows are fussy about keeping black longhairs indoors and away from too much sun.

221 Polishing the cat

If you've attended a cat show, you know that the cats inevitably look sleek and glossy. This is not an accident, nor is it the result of good health or grooming with a brush. Show cats, especially the shorthaired ones, are "polished" with a swatch of velvet, silk or chamois—the cat show equivalent of a "wax job." Owners who fuss over their pets sometimes use this technique at home, too.

222 Pedigreed puberty

If you own a pedigreed cat and want to breed your cat, obviously you will not have him or her neutered. But if you have no intention of breeding—ever—you should have your cat neutered, for reasons discussed elsewhere in this book (see 296–300). The usual rule is to have the cat neutered *before* the cat reaches sexual maturity, but owners of pedigreed cats sometimes wait until *after* that time. The assumption is that the animal will not develop all the attractive traits of the breed if neutered before puberty.

Keeping Them Healthy and Safe

223 The dreaded hairball!

Considering that cats are constantly grooming themselves with their tongues, it isn't remarkable that they get hairballs—rather, it's remarkable that they don't get *more* hairballs. If you've never seen one of these ugly objects, consider yourself lucky. It is just what it sounds like: a ball (or wad, to be more accurate) of the cat's own hair, which lodges in the stomach, unable to pass through the digestive tract. Some cats never get them (my own hasn't—knock on wood); some cats get them rarely and vomit them up with no harm to themselves (though perhaps some harm to your upholstery or carpet). The reason owners need to monitor hairballs is that occasionally they can lead to serious digestive problems, sometimes requiring surgery. Pet store shelves are well stocked with hairball preventatives, and most of the pet food manufacturers now market certain foods as "hairball preventers."

224 The lactose problem

Many cats, like many humans, are lactose intolerant—that is, their digestive systems don't produce the enzymes needed to break down lactose, one of the sugars present in cows' milk. The end result (pardon the pun) is usually diarrhea, for either the person or the cat. This needs to be kept in mind by doting cat owners who like to reward their pets with milk or cream, which all cats love. Most cats have no problem at all with milk, but owners who notice a milk-diarrhea connection ought to do the obvious thing and cut back or eliminate the milk they give to their pets.

225 Bowl and collar technology

If you have more than one cat in your home, you may be aware of the problems of feeding them: one cat may hog the food, one may insist on eating before the others, they may (because of age differences or other factors) require different types of food and so on. In past times, owners worked out their own ways of dealing with these problems, but, of course, the pet product manufacturers have come up with their own clever high-tech solutions. One is a food bowl that links up electronically with a special collar worn by the cats you *don't* want eating from that bowl. If a cat wearing the collar nears the bowl, the bowl emits a tone that makes the cat skedaddle. (Are human beings clever, or what?)

226 Some good ole chemical additives

You may or may not have strong opinions about chemical additives in your food, including vitamins and minerals. Some people are fussy about such things, not even wanting additives in their pets' food. But pet food manufacturers haven't been shy about adding nutritional supplements to cat food. One amino acid that has been added to most cat food since the 1980s is taurine, which has been found useful in preventing blindness and heart disease. As time goes by and we learn more about animal nutrition, it is likely that more additives will be found in pet foods.

227 Claw caps

Until recently, you dealt with your cat clawing the furniture by one of two ways: declawing the cat or learning to tolerate the scratching (and hoping the cat will use a scratching post, but some just won't do it). Now there is an alternative: vinyl claw caps, glued onto your cat's nails (generally by a vet) and replaced every month or so as the old nails grow out. The cat still goes through the motions of clawing (as do declawed cats), but the claw caps keep the claws from doing any serious harm.

228 Cat massage

Massage is very "in" these days, with people sometimes paying high prices for the supposed benefits of getting a relaxing massage from a professional. Humans have a way of pushing their trends onto their pets, of course, so there are books explaining the "right" way to massage your cat. The less trendy among us are more inclined to do what people have done for centuries: rubbing and stroking our cats without giving a thought to "technique" just being aware that the cats enjoy it tremendously, and so do we.

229 Cat meets skunk

Wild skunks are the most easygoing, amiable animals in the world. They can afford to be, for they don't need to bite or scratch their enemies, since their malodorous spray is excellent protection. Occasionally a cat gets sprayed by a skunk, and removing the smell is no picnic. First the cat needs a good water bath (which most of them will resist tooth and nail), then a good thorough soaking in either milk or tomato juice, which needs to stay on the coat for at least ten minutes before being rinsed with water.

230 Butt dragging

It's amusing, or disgusting, or maybe both: a cat or dog scooting her rear end across the carpet, pulling herself forward with her front legs. Simply put, the animal's anus itches terribly, and she doesn't have fingers to scratch it. The itching is caused by worms, so your cat requires medicine, administered either by you or your vet. (But by all means, get your camcorder out while the cat is still dragging, for it makes a great video.)

231 The natural worm remedy (not!)

Folk medicine has long been applied not just to human ailments but to pets as well. According to an old wives' tale (and those wives were *never* wrong, as you know), you could treat (or prevent) worms in your cat by adding bits of garlic or carrot to her food. This doesn't work at all, and some cats will walk away from food that has garlic in it. In regard to deworming your cat, be glad there are plenty of effective worm medicines on the market.

232 Pet insurance

Well, you won't get it through your employer, of course, or through the government. Nonetheless, more and more people are choosing to pay monthly or annual premiums for health insurance for their pets. The reason is obvious: medical care for pets (as for their owners) is getting more expensive as it gets more sophisticated, and there is no Medicare or Medicaid for old (or poor) pets. As veterinary costs rise, and as more people (particularly single folks) own pets, the more likely it is that people will choose to pay for pet insurance.

233 "All-natural"

As noted elsewhere in this book, humans have a habit of involving their pets in their own trendiness. This is evident in the "natural healing" movement, in which people replace or supplement traditional medical care with "natural" remedies, such as herbs. Some pet owners believe that "natural" medicine will benefit their pets, so there is an American Holistic Veterinary Medical Association (AHVMA), with a membership of several hundred vets and other animal care professionals.

234 Pregnancy and litter boxes

So what's the connection? Cats may ingest toxoplasma, a nasty microscopic parasite often found in undercooked meat—and in mice or birds they happen to catch. It usually does not harm cats, but since it is passed through the feces, it is possible for a human cleaning a litter box to take in the toxoplasma. If that human happens to be a pregnant woman, the toxoplasma can cause severe damage to the unborn child. So, as a general rule, pregnant women should avoid litter boxes.

235 Thin-skinned white cats

Many solid white cats are pink-skinned—and, literally, thin-skinned. This has led to occasional health problems and even death from a flea bath. Some of the solutions used to kill fleas can kill the cat as well, even when veterinarians or their technicians give the bath. The pink skin of a white cat is more sensitive to flea baths (and any kind of chemical) than the skin of other cats. If you own a white cat, be aware of this, and don't be shy about reminding your vet that your pet has sensitive skin.

236 The New Testament disease

That is, leprosy—the disfiguring skin disease that causes lesions and inflamed lymph nodes. In cats, the lesions occur mostly on the head, neck and legs. Feline leprosy is, thankfully, very rare among cats in the United States, although for some unknown reason it does crop up occasionally in Canada, Australia and New Zealand. There are no drugs available for the disease, but the skin lesions can be removed surgically.

237 Caught it at the gym, maybe?

Ringworm, as you probably know, is not a worm at all, but a fungus that causes itching and redness on human skin, most commonly on the feet (athlete's foot) or groin (jock itch). Humans can pick up ringworm fungus in warm, moist places like shower stalls, so it won't surprise you that ringworm is most common in warm, humid climates. Ringworm fungus is highly contagious, passed on by skin contact, and humans can pass it on to cats (and vice versa). Ringworm on cat skin isn't always red nor always itchy, so sometimes a vet is needed to determine the condition. It isn't dangerous, just irksome, and, as already noted, it can be passed on to humans, so a cat who has it needs to be treated.

238 Even their insides are finicky

Like humans, cats can be allergic to certain foods, and the allergy is usually manifested in itchy skin. It isn't dangerous, just irritating, and as with human allergies, a certain amount of trial and error is needed to determine which food (or which ingredient) is causing the problem. Luckily for cats, food allergies are rare among them.

239 The flea collar problem

Contact dermatitis (see 286) is a skin ailment of cats, and the most common cause of it—is flea collars. Most cats wear them without any problems, but some cats break out in the neck area, and the only solution is to remove the collar. There are many other excellent flea treatments available now, so flea collar dermatitis is nothing to fret over.

240 Frozen cat

Frostbite is not funny, as your author knows from experience. At extremely low temperatures, human skin can suffer tissue damage, which in mild cases leads to temporary pain and numbness but in more severe cases leads to tissue death. It happens most often to the ears and nose, the areas least likely to be covered. And that is precisely where cats get frostbitten: the areas with the least hair, their ears, nose and paw pads. (For some odd reason the tip of the tail seems vulnerable also.) An obvious bit of advice to pet owners in cold areas: don't let the cat outside if it is extremely cold.

241 Feline sunburn

The vet calls it by the fancy name *actinic dermatitis*, but let's call it what it is: sunburn. Most cats won't burn, but the ones most likely to are white cats with blue eyes. (In other words, cats who correspond to blue-eyed, fair-skinned, easy-to-burn humans.) A sunburned cat shows redness around the ears, eyelids, nose and mouth. With a bad burn, there may be hair loss, peeling and itching. Needless to say, it is more common in summer than in winter. Over time, the "fair" cats who have been overexposed to the sun can develop skin cancers, which is also true for sun-worshipping humans. One obvious way to avoid this is keep the cat inside, especially at midday.

242 The bad news about skin cancer

The good news is that most human skin cancers are benign. The bad news is that most cat skin cancers are malignant, and they are also the second most common cancer found in cats. (Lymphoma is the first.) They are more likely to occur in older cats, and the cats most at risk to develop it are white cats, especially those with blue eyes. The danger of skin cancers is their ability to spread to other organs, usually the lymph nodes first, then the lungs. Vets try whenever possible to remove the cancers surgically. Obviously, as with human skin cancers, the earlier the cancer is found, the more likely that treatment will be successful.

243 The dreaded M word

One word you don't want to hear from your dermatologist during his diagnosis is *melanoma*, a type of skin cancer that begins as a small dark brown or black mole on the body. Melanoma is dangerous for both humans and cats, but humans are fortunate in being able to monitor their skin for unusual growths, while on cats the melanoma may be well hidden underneath the hair. In some cases, an early melanoma may not be life threatening, but, sadly, many cats have died from this cancer.

244 Do cats get warts?

Well, they can get acne (see 249), but not warts. Cats do get a form of a skin tumor called a papilloma, which slightly resembles warts. These are usually benign, and usually found on the face. But actual warts, which are caused by viruses, are not found on cats, which is good news because the viruses that cause warts are contagious.

245 The gum test

"Open your mouth and say 'Ah!'" may be good advice when monitoring a cat's health. A healthy cat has nice pink gums, and if the gums are pale, that may be a sign of severe problems, such as anemia or internal bleeding. One condition that does *not* need to be a concern is the presence of black spots on the gums. These would be strange in a human mouth, but they are perfectly normal for many cats.

246 Why not just say "baldness"?

The technical term for baldness is *alopecia*, and cats are subject to a form of it, though a very different form than the human male-pattern baldness. Feline endocrine alopecia is probably hormone related (as is male-pattern baldness), but the areas where the hair thins are the posterior, underside of the tail, belly and inside of the thighs. The remaining hairs can be easily pulled out, but the areas are never completely smooth. No pain is involved, but it does make the cat look less attractive. Some cases respond to hormone treatments. (There is no "Hair Club for Cats," as far as we know.)

247 Patch baldness

Another type of baldness (alopecia) in cats is preauricular alopecia, meaning "baldness in front of the ears," which is exactly where it occurs. Those areas can become thin haired or even totally smooth. It seems most common in breeds that are normally thin haired in that part of the body, such as the Siamese.

248 "Stud tail"

The name may sound somewhat sexy, but the condition itself certainly isn't. Cats possess a preen gland, a sebaceous gland at the base of the tail. If the gland becomes hyperactive, it can lead to blackheads, waxy debris, and painful boils. It is technically called tail gland hyperplasia, and the common name, "stud tail," stems from it being most common among sexually active male cats, even though it does occur among neutered males and among females.

249 Don't say "zits"

Acne does occur in cats, and fairly often, but it doesn't take quite the same form as in humans. Feline acne takes the form of blackheads on the chin and the lower lip. There can also be redness, swelling and itching involved. Humans with acne have always been advised to keep their faces clean, and the advice applies to cats too, though it is hard to imagine any cat *not* keeping her chin clean. Vets have noticed that it seems more common among cats who sleep on hard surfaces or on dirt than among those who sleep on soft surfaces. Get ready for the treatment: benzoyl peroxide, which is commonly used to treat acne in humans.

250 Even cats get glaucoma

Cats are subject to glaucoma the same way humans are, and it can often lead to blindness. Fortunately, both eyes are not usually affected, and a cat, like a human, can make it through life with only one eye. The problem with cat glaucoma is that the blind eye bulges very unattractively. Some owners opt for surgery, which involves removing the blind eye and fitting the socket with a silicone false eye.

251 The deaf gene

It's truth, not legend: Many white cats are deaf, particularly white cats with blue eyes. This is caused by genetics, and if there is a way to prevent it, no one has found it yet. Since cats have such sensitive hearing, it is sad to think of one going through life without being able to hear, but in fact there are plenty of perfectly contented deaf cats in the world, though their owners need to be a little extra watchful for them.

252 No, they aren't drunk

Here's a mouthful of a name: feline idiopathic vestibular syndrome. It is a balance disturbance that, for some unknown reason, occurs mostly in summer. A cat that is mildly affected may walk with a slight tilt of the head. In more severe cases the cat's balance may be so off that she will lie down and roll around. The syndrome resembles tipsiness—or drunkenness way beyond the tipsy stage. Not only is the cause unknown, but there is no known treatment. Most cats seem to spontaneously recover after a short time.

253 Endo- and ecto-

Most living creatures, including both cats and humans, are subject to invasion by other living creatures. Endoparasites live on the inside of us, and ectoparasites live on the outside. Some of these creatures are harmless; some are extremely harmful. And some are just irritating. One thing is certain for the cat owner: no matter how healthy your cat may be, and no matter how much tender loving care you supply, you will at some point have to give some attention to the various tiny critters that live on or in your cat.

254 Mangy mites

You may know that mange is a skin disease, but did you know it's caused by mites? Mites are not insects, but are tiny members of the Arachnida class—spiders and their relatives. Some mites are easily seen; others are barely visible to the naked eye. Female mites lay their eggs in the skin, and the mites that hatch feed on the skin cells. The resulting skin condition is generally called mange, and the symptoms are hair loss, redness, scaling and itching. It is irritating but not dangerous, and the worst thing about the condition is that mites can be transferred from cats to humans, and vice versa.

255 For the woodsy cat

The author, a former camp counselor, is very familiar with chiggers, also called harvest mites. They are common in woodsy areas, and they burrow into human skin and cause serious itching. Rodents get chiggers and so do cats, especially cats who roam in the woods and fields. They are not dangerous, and the itch eventually goes away. The best thing about chiggers is that, unlike other mites, they can't be passed from one host to another.

256 The good news about ticks

They are nasty little blood-sucking arachnids (related to spiders), and they are very common in wooded areas. The best news is that cats get them less frequently than dogs do. When cats do get them, they may barely be aware of them. Those of us who grew up in the country can spot a "full" (blood-gorged) tick right away, appearing as a big brown lump hanging somewhere on a pet. Some not-too-bright pet owners rush their pets to the vet, puzzled about this mysterious "growth," which could be easily removed just by pulling it off. However, when a tick is pulled off an animal, it sometimes leaves its mouthparts behind, which can lead to infections. The old camp counselors' trick: strike a match, blow it out and apply the hot end to the rear of the tick, which will fall off in a few seconds.

257 Those lousy lice

Again, an affliction that cats and humans share. Technically, it's called pediculosis, louse infestation.

Tiny lice chomp on skin tissue and are contagious via contact, specifically by passing from one host's hair to another host's hair. The nasty little insects are itchy and irritating but basically harmless, and they can be easily gotten rid of with special medicinal shampoos. If you or your cat has ever had lice, be sure to wash all your bedding thoroughly.

258 The great high-jumpers, fleas

It won't surprise you that the most common external parasite on cats is the flea, the tiny insect that can jump hundreds of times its own height. They are bloodsuckers, like ticks, but much more common. Fleas lay their eggs nearly anywhere, including in carpeting and air ducts, and they reproduce very fast. Their bloodsucking can cause health problems (such as anemia), but their bites also cause allergic reactions in many cats and humans, leading to skin problems and other conditions. Happily, we have come a long way in flea treatment, and whereas in the past we relied on powders, sprays and flea collars, newer treatments (Advantage flea control, for example, which is rubbed into a cat's skin) are highly effective.

259 Taking the cat's pulse

It is fairly easy to take your cat's pulse, as long as you remember that the wrist isn't the right spot. The best pulse spot on the cat is the femoral artery, which you can feel on the inside of the thigh. The normal heart rate for a cat is anywhere from 120 to 240 beats per minute while at rest. (Yes, that is faster than the human heart, which is about 72 beats per minute. A small animal's heart beats faster than a larger animal's heart.)

260 Stoned cats

Cats share with humans the tendency to get kidney and bladder stones—*uroliths* is the technical term—and they are not pleasant. Male cats are more prone to them (ditto for male humans), and they seem to be more common in cats who are fed an exclusively dry food diet. The overall condition of stones forming in the urinary tract is called feline urological syndrome (FUL). A cat whose urinary tract is blocked by a large stone can be in intense pain, and no wonder, since it needs to urinate but can't because of the stone blocking the path. A vet's aid is definitely called for, and quickly. Once the stone is removed or passed, the cat's diet has to be altered and medication given to prevent more stones from forming.

261 Ten days of madness

If you've ever seen a cat, or any other animal, with rabies, you won't soon forget it. Rabies, sometimes called hydrophobia, is a swift-moving disease of the nervous system. Normally it is transmitted when an affected animal bites another animal, passing on the disease through the saliva into the wound. A cat with rabies is "wired," extremely vicious and has seemingly swifter movements than a normal cat. After a cat shows signs of rabies, death occurs within ten days, but be aware that the cat is truly dangerous during this time. Needless to say, the disease's seriousness is why every pet should be vaccinated.

262 The rabies race

The alarm "Mad dog!" used to strike terror into people, which is why in the United States laws are passed that mandate rabies vaccinations for all pet dogs. With less fear of rabid cats (and perhaps less community concern for cats in general), cases of rabid dogs declined while cases of rabid cats increased, so that by 1981 there were more rabid cats than rabid dogs in the United States. All the rabid cats were, of course, unvaccinated. Simply put, cat owners are less likely to have their pets vaccinated than dog owners are, even if their local laws require it. This is risky, especially for the owners of unneutered toms, who are prone to wander looking for females, and thus may come into contact with rabid wild animals. Unless there is a shift in cat owners' perceptions of the dangers of rabies, cats will continue to be the winners (and ultimately the losers) in the rabies race.

263 Charity with caution

Cat owners are generally charitable toward all cats, but there are situations where this can lead to trouble. One situation that is potentially dangerous to humans is a cat who appears to be choking. It could be choking on a bone or other object, but choking can also be a symptom of rabies, and touching a cat with rabies is asking for trouble. If you don't know the cat, then you don't know if it's been vaccinated for rabies. Your best bet is to call an animal control center quickly.

264 Feline seizures

A cat with rabies (see 261) is viciously, dangerously mad, but only slightly less frightening is a cat with feline epilepsy, also called rolling-skin syndrome and neurodermatitis. An affected cat may bite at her own back or tail. She may experience hallucinations that cause her to run around frantically, sometimes attacking objects or even her owner. Seizures similar to those of human epilepsy may last for several minutes. The good news for cat owners: the syndrome can be treated successfully with drugs.

265 The string disease

"String enteritis" sounds silly when described, but it is a very serious condition. A cat playing with a thread or string happens to swallow it. If the entire string passes into the stomach, no problem, but sometimes the end of the string gets caught around the base of the tongue. This inevitably leads to severe digestive problems—vomiting, diarrhea and other problems—resulting from the cat's intestinal tract trying in vain to pass the string. A vet should be seen, and the owner should definitely *not* try to pull out the string through the cat's mouth.

266 Just say no (to aspirin)

We humans are accustomed to popping an aspirin (or some other over-the-counter pain reliever) for various aches and pains, and some cat owners foolishly give these human medications to their pets. In fact, some of these medications *can* be given to cats, but it isn't wise to do so without consulting a vet. Human dosages and cat dosages are (to state the obvious) very different, plus a cat metabolizes medications at different rates than humans do. Practically every vet has had to treat a cat for aspirin poisoning. The upshot: "Just say no" to administering human medicines to a cat.

267 Nonwhites of the eyes

Jaundice, a yellow appearance to the skin, is a sign of serious liver problems in humans. Cats too can develop jaundice, though it won't be evident in the skin; instead, the white tissue around the eyes will become yellow. If the cat is jaundiced, it is probably experiencing various other symptoms of liver disease, such as vomiting, diarrhea and loss of appetite. A vet's attention is needed.

268 Shutting down the immune system

Yes, cats do get a form of AIDS. It's caused by the feline immunodeficiency virus (FIV), and it's closely related to the human AIDS virus. As in humans with AIDS, the cat's immune system no longer functions properly, making her vulnerable to all sorts of infections and complications that would normally not be a problem. It can be detected by a test, but as with human AIDS, it is not curable (yet) and no vaccine is available. How it is spread among cats is not fully understood.

269 The sweet sickness

Physicians in ancient Greece and Rome spoke of the "sweet sickness," a disease we know as diabetes. It occurs not only among humans but cats as well, generally cats eight years of age or older. A diabetic cat tends to be overweight for a while, then, as the disease progresses, becomes emaciated. It can be treated, just as human diabetes can, but doing so places demands on the owners, including giving insulin injections once or twice daily, frequently testing glucose levels and monitoring the diet extremely carefully.

270 The Black Death—not dead yet

"The plague," the contagious disease that ravaged Europe in the Middle Ages, is still around and still caused by the bacterium *Yersinia pestis*. Then as now, the germ is carried by flea-bearing rodents, and cats can get the germ by eating infected rodents or by being bitten by fleas that have bitten infected rodents. While the infection is no longer common, it is serious business when a cat or any animal is infected with the plague. Cats can transmit the disease to humans through scratches or bites.

271 Forcing the pill

You've probably heard this before: a dog can be fooled into taking a pill mixed with food, but a cat cannot. It's true, which means you have to take an active role in the medicating if your cat has to take a medicine in pill form. It isn't fun (for either you or the cat), and it requires you to force open the cat's mouth, push the pill far to the back of the throat and then hold the head back until the pill has gone down. It has to be done quickly, otherwise the cat coughs up the pill and you begin all over again. It helps the process the next time around if you end each session with some stroking and soft words.

272 Forgetting you in their pain

Owners who have had to deal with an injured cat are often bewildered, because the cat seems to lash out viciously, as if she didn't know her owner. The cat hasn't forgotten, but the pain temporarily overrides her memory. A cat in severe pain—after being struck by a car, for example—is "no man's friend" and thus requires careful handling, since she doesn't understand you are trying to save her life. Cats can't really be muzzled, so you have to take your chances with the teeth until you can get her to a vet. It's wise to wrap the cat in a large towel or blanket, and wear thick gloves if you have them. The good news about an injured cat is that once the trauma is past, she will be friendly again and apparently will have no memory of having bitten or scratched her bewildered owner.

273 If it's hotter than me . . .

Humans can survive (though not comfortably) at temperatures higher than their average body temperature, 98.6 degrees. A cat, however, isn't likely to survive too long at a temperature higher than the cat average body temperature, about 102.2 degrees. Cats do have sweat glands, but they don't function exactly like human sweat glands; plus, a cat can't (or won't) do all the things humans do to cool down, such as bathe in water or remove clothing. In fact, it's very easy for a cat to have a heat stroke, which can be fatal. A sensitive cat owner wants to avoid situations like a parked car with the windows rolled up, any concrete area without shade or any confined area in direct sunlight. Short-nosed cats, including Persians, seem to be the most at risk for heat stroke.

274 Chasing those stinging things

A cat is as fascinated by a bee or wasp in flight as by any other small, moving object and may swat at the insect and get stung in the process. While a healthy cat isn't likely to die from such a sting (though it is possible), the owner should try to locate the stinger and remove it using fingernails or tweezers. A paste made of water and baking soda can help relieve both the pain and the swelling. Some cats, like some humans, are allergic to insect stings, and this will be evident if the swelling from the sting doesn't go away soon. As with allergic reactions in humans, this immediately requires medical attention.

275 The nervous human's friend

The tranquilizing drug Valium (generic name diazepam) has been around for years, and many a nervous, stressed-out person is thankful for it. It is widely used by veterinarians to treat cats—not for nervousness but for aggression. It is effective with most overly aggressive cats, though in a few cases it actually seems to make the cat *more* aggressive. Note: do *not* try to administer your own Valium to your cat. The dosages for cats are different than dosages for humans, and this matter needs to be handled by a vet.

Household Hazards

276 How the agile are fallen!

Everything has to be given a fancy name and an acronym these days, so try this one on: high-rise syndrome, or HRS. In laymen's terms, HRS involves cats being injured or killed by falling from windows or balconies. As more pet owners move to high-rise apartment buildings, the number of cat deaths rises. Given how surefooted cats are, it amazes people that cats could ever slip and fall. In many cases HRS is the result of a cat snoozing on a rail, then waking and falling before knowing what was happening. Actually, the most surprising news is not that they fall, but that they often survive. (Remember: *nine lives.*) Cats have fallen from as high as eighteen stories and survived. Yes, they do almost always land on their feet, and the legs absorb most of the impact and are often injured—but a fractured leg is better than death. It goes without saying that no cat owner wants a beloved pet to die from a fall, so it makes sense for urban "cliff-dwellers" to keep a close eye on open windows and balcony doors.

277 The worst kind of cat death

Though the poet Thomas Gray wrote a famous poem on the drowning of a pet cat (see 773), cats rarely do drown because they can swim when they have to. If they fall into a pool or large tub that they can't climb out of, then of course swimming won't save them. A cat who has "gone down for the third time" but is still alive can be aided by being held up by the hind legs, which will help get most of the water out of the lungs. Naturally the nearly drowned cat needs a vet's attention as soon as possible. While drowning is unlikely to happen to your cat or any other, it would seem to be the most horrible kind of death, given cats' notorious aversion to water.

278 Getting a buzz off electricity

It looks dangerous, and sometimes it is: a cat gnawing on an electrical cord. Apparently the cat gets an actual buzz from doing this and may be able to chew entirely through a cord without harming herself. But the risk of severe shock is always there, plus she can burn her mouth or nose in the process. A cat who has experienced electrical shock may have difficulty breathing, her gums may appear blue and she may stare glassily. A vet is needed in this situation. If your cat is a chronic cord-chewer, try the squirt-gun method (see 30) or the brand-name spray No (see 31).

279 An antifreeze buzz

Automobile antifreeze, kind of a luminous green, doesn't look or smell good to humans, but cats and dogs must find it appealing—if it is spilled on the ground they will readily drink it. The ethylene glycol in antifreeze will produce a state of drunkenness for several hours, and it can cause severe kidney damage. The cat will experience diarrhea and vomiting, then finally fall into a coma. A cat who drinks enough antifreeze may even die. Needless to say, if you have a cat and you spill antifreeze in your garage or driveway, clean up the spill immediately.

280 The dryer scenario

It's usually just funny but occasionally can be deadly: a cat goes to sleep in a clothes dryer, and someone turns the dryer on and walks away. This is most likely to happen when there are several loads of clothes being done: the dryer is already warm from a previous load, and the cat sees the door open and decides the dryer would be a warm and cozy place for a nap. In comes the next load, on goes the dryer and the cat is taken for a spin. In most cases, the owner will quickly get an earful of noise to let him know the cat is in the dryer. Usually no harm is done (after all, the cat is surrounded by clothing), but in some cases cats have died from suffocation.

281 Are all bowls the same?

Chances are your cat's food and water bowls are made of hard plastic, and your cat probably shows no ill effects. Some of the more persnickety cat fanciers claim that plastic bowls are wrong for cats:

plastic cracks and erodes over time, and bacteria grow in the tiny crevices. Older plastic can become rough enough to irritate the cat's skin. And no matter how often a plastic bowl is cleaned, it can harbor odors. Ceramic is not a good option either, since some ceramic ware contains lead, which is poisonous (over a long period, anyway). So, say some of the experts, the only really safe choices are bowls of glass or stainless steel.

282 Killing the rat-killers

It's sad but ironic: over the years, cats have died from eating rodents that had eaten rodent bait. That is, humans set out bait to poison rats and mice, and the bait ended up poisoning nature's original rodent killers. This fortunately doesn't happen too often today, since older rodent poisons, such as strychnine compounds, are seldom used any more.

283 Cleaning themselves to death

Professional pest exterminators sometimes used chemicals called tracking powders to control rodent populations. These poisons are meant to stick to the feet and fur of rodents, eventually causing death. Regrettably, if a cat walks through an area that has been treated by tracking powders, she may ingest the poison from grooming her feet and fur. You need to be aware of this if you hire a professional exterminator. Of course, you can't decide what types of rodent controls your neighbors use, which gives you a good reason to be on friendly terms with your neighbors so you can keep yourself aware of any potential hazards to your pet.

284 Keeping the lawn (and cat) green

As noted in the last entry, any toxic substance that your cat walks through is dangerous, since the cat will lick herself and her fur in the process of grooming. If your cat plays outdoors, she will pick up any pesticides and other chemicals you spray on your lawn, and those useful lawn chemicals can end up inside your cat. They aren't often fatal, but you need to monitor your cat's activity in a freshly sprayed lawn, particularly since lawn chemicals are "in the air" for a time, leading to possible respiratory ailments.

285 Pot cats

Lots of people grow marijuana for medicinal purposes (wink, wink), and some growers have found that their cats chew the leaves and get the same sort of high that human beings get from smoking marijuana. (It doesn't seem to increase their cats' appetites, however.) Amusing as this might be to marijuana users (sharing a high with your pet), it is also potentially dangerous, as marijuana has been known to cause seizures, sometimes fatal ones, in cats.

286 Evil touch

Would you believe that your cat can get a rash on her mouth because of contact with a plastic food dish? It is rare, but not unknown. Human skin and cat skin are both subject to contact dermatitis, which happens when the skin comes into contact with a substance that causes a rash, usually with itching. The common culprits in human contact dermatitis are plants like poison ivy and poison oak. Individual cats are sensitive to certain plants, and also to some household chemicals, and some cats can't wear a collar because the leather or plastic makes their neck skin break out. And, as mentioned earlier, some cats break out in a rash because of their plastic food dishes. Also, as already noted in 239, flea collars are a prime cause of contact dermatitis.

Lost and Found

287 Reunited, but not often

Animal shelters do more than take in strays and abandoned animals. They also are a place where frantic pet owners go when beloved pets disappear. Sadly, not too many pet-owner reunions take place in shelters. Often the pet simply isn't there, of course, but there are also cases where the pet is there but can't be identified with absolute certainty.

This is the reason that vets and animal control experts highly recommend having the pet tattooed or implanted with a microchip, not to mention wearing a collar with an ID tag.

288 ID them, please!

In the weeks while I was writing this book, I was bitten by a cat and, luckily for me, the cat was wearing a collar and ID tag with the owner's phone number, so I was able to contact the owner and determine whether the cat had had a rabies vaccine. This is only one of several reasons for your cat to wear an ID tag, but the most obvious reason is that if your cat wanders off too far or is injured or, heaven forbid, ends up in an animal shelter, someone will be able to contact you. Collars cost very little; ditto for a small metal tag with the cat's name (or yours) and your telephone number. The great thing about a collar, even if the ID tag has come loose, is that it tells someone who finds your cat that she is *not* a stray and probably has an owner who is looking for her.

289 ID registries

We are all so concerned with privacy these days, particularly in regard to giving out our telephone numbers, so many people are reluctant to have their phone numbers engraved on their pets' ID tags. One option is to use a registry service, which keeps info about you and your pet in their files. If you use such a service, you are given an ID tag with the service's phone number, and if your pet is lost, whoever finds your cat can call the service.

290 The tattoo trend

Tattooing is obviously trendy among humans and is becoming trendy among pets too, but not for reasons of personal adornment or social conformity. For ID purposes, a veterinarian or animal shelter can tattoo a number onto your cat's ear or elsewhere, a number that can be used to identify the cat if she is lost. Some animal shelters now make it a standard practice to tattoo all cats and dogs given up for adoption.

291 Computer in your cat

Politicians like to toss around the idea of having microchips implanted in human beings so that each of us carries around identification (and other sensitive information) on a tiny chip under our skins. It's already being done to lots of pets, both by vets and animal shelters. There is a charge, of course, but the injection of the microchip is almost painless, and there are no side effects (so far). The hope is that if your pet becomes lost and gets picked up by an animal shelter, the shelter can digitally "scan" the cat to retrieve your contact information. The problem with both microchip implants and tattooing is, of course, that both are practically invisible to most observers. Your best bet for your pet, particularly one who spends a lot of time outdoors, is to have her fitted with a microchip *and* make her wear a collar and ID tag.

292 Pet on board

Remember the "baby on board" car signs that were popular years ago? In the same vein, pet stores sell window decals that you place on your home's windows to let the fire department or other emergency personnel know that you have a pet inside the home. The goal is that, if you yourself are absent or injured, emergency workers can tell that there are pets inside who need attention.

The End, Alas

293 Dogs linger, cats don't

Most vets will tell you that older cats don't linger for years the way older dogs do. There are exceptions, of course, but generally when a cat's health starts to slide because of age, she won't be around for much longer. This is especially true of outside cats, who seem to be able to sense that they are about to die and so wander off to a secluded place to "die with dignity."

294 Pet cremation

The cremation of humans used to be rare in America and Europe, but it is becoming more and more common. As it gains acceptance among humans, it is also becoming more common for pets. There are animal crematoriums, and some vets perform cremations. Some pet owners dislike the idea of burying their pets, whether it's on their own property or in a pet cemetery. (And, in the case of apartment dwellers, burial on the premises is not even an option.) Cremation seems a good alternative to burial (or the even worse alternative of putting a beloved pet in the garbage). As with cremated humans, a cat's ashes can be kept in an urn, buried or scattered.

295 A decent burial by country folk

Pet cemeteries are a relatively new phenomenon in the world, if you overlook the ancient Egyptians' habit of mummifying their deceased pets. While most Americans and Europeans choose not to bury their cats in pet cemeteries, there is a long tradition among rural folk of burying a departed cat or dog on the family property, perhaps first wrapping the body in a towel or blanket and then digging a fairly deep grave. People invest a great deal of time and emotion in their pets, so tossing the body along a roadside or (even worse) depositing it in the garbage hardly seems appropriate.

Mating and Motherhood . . . and "Fixing"

296 "Fixing," "spaying," "neutering"

A female pet is spayed, which means her ovaries and uterus are removed. (Interestingly, it comes from the old French word *espeer*, meaning "to cut with a sword.") A male is neutered, or castrated. Either operation can be done as early as six months of age, and some vets will do it even earlier. The word *fix* (not a technical term, and not one vets use) applies to either males or females. Cat owners seem much happier once a cat is fixed.

297 "Whole" cats

A male cat who has never been neutered is called "whole." While we might debate the subject of whether an adult male human can be happy and psychologically sound while living a celibate life, there is no question that a "whole" tomcat faces a lot more challenges and hazards than a neutered tom. The simple fact is that an unneutered tomcat feels compelled to mate regularly, which usually involves a lot of rambling and fighting with other tomcats. Most cat owners solve this in the obvious way: they neuter the cat.

298 Oh, those unneutered toms

The slang word *tomcat* that describes certain actions of human males is rooted in the real behavior of unneutered ("whole") male cats. Tomcats really do roam around in search of a female in heat, and in doing so they sometimes stray far from home. The quest for a receptive female can lead to fights with other whole toms (besides which, whole toms are much more likely to fight over territory or just fight in general). In short, a whole tomcat is more likely to lose some of its nine lives in fighting—just another reason to have the cat neutered.

299 The infamous "spraying"

Some people use the word *spraying* to refer to urinating in general, but in fact only unneutered tomcats spray urine. All cats' urine has a powerful smell, but a whole tomcat's urine has a rank odor all its own. A whole tom will leave its urine not only in the litter box but also on walls, drapes and darn near anything. They are either sexually aroused or marking their territory, or both, and the sprayed urine can make a home uninhabitable. The solution: have the cat neutered.

300 Neutering: the younger the better

You can have your male cat neutered any age past six months, and the general rule is, the earlier the better. Once a tomcat has reached sexual maturity and started roaming and fighting with other males, there is no assurance that neutering will completely eliminate those behaviors. A tom who is neutered before he is eight months old never has the opportunity to roam, spray or fight viciously with other males, so he makes a thoroughly desirable pet.

301 The V word

Vasectomy, that is. It isn't the same as neutering, since neutering essentially desexes a tomcat, especially if done before he reaches puberty. The neutered tom is castrated, whereas a vasectomy only makes the tom sterile. A neutered tom won't usually roam, fight or spray urine, but a tom with a vasectomy will continue to do all those things. The obvious question: Why would a cat owner opt for a vasectomy instead of neutering? Some would reply that a vasectomy is more "natural," since the tom remains more fully male in his behavior. The happy owners of neutered toms would reply that "natural" isn't always a good thing, especially for a house pet.

302 Tomcat "on hold"

Tomcats have a reputation for being promiscuous, but in fact an adult tom, unneutered, never has sex on his mind (unlike male humans). His entire reproductive system stays "on hold"—until, that is, he hears the inimitable caterwaul of a female cat in heat or picks up her scent (usually from her urine somewhere nearby). Either via the ear or nose, or both, suddenly Placid Tom turns into Randy Tom, and he won't rest until he locates the source of the "heat signal."

303 Oh, lecherous males!

Feel free to blush as we ask an embarrassing question: do cats masturbate? Well, male cats do—not with their paws, but by mounting an object like a fuzzy toy or anything roughly the size and texture of another cat. It occurs most often with unneutered tomcats, but occasionally neutered toms will do it as well.

304 Feline puberty

In animal terms, reaching "puberty" means a creature is able to reproduce. Female cats hit puberty between seven and twelve months of age, while toms usually reach puberty around nine months. There are some interesting variations: indoor cats hit puberty later than outdoor cats, purebreds are later than mixed-breeds and Persians and Himalayans are later than most of the other breeds.

305 "Long day" breeders

We note elsewhere (see 308) that the estrus (heat) of the female cat is unpredictable, and that there is no "regularity" involved in cats. Let's qualify that observation with this bit of information: as a general rule, the female cat is more likely to be in heat when the days are lengthening—that is, after late December, when the amount of daylight increases with every passing day. (This is true in the northern hemisphere. In the southern hemisphere, days begin to lengthen in late June.) Veterinarians speak of cats as "long day" breeders, since the females (and the females of several other species) are more likely to be in heat from (roughly) January through September.

306 Heat, phase I

Before the female cat is fully in heat, she is in a stage called proestrus, or "preheat" you might say. During this time her owners might notice that she is more affectionate than usual, wanting to be petted more. On the other hand, she may be more aggressive than usual, more inclined to bite or pounce. If there is a tomcat about, the female isn't quite yet ready for mating, but she is willing to seriously flirt, rolling on the floor in front of the tom. Proestrus is brief, usually no more than a couple of days.

307 Heat, phase II

Some of the signs of heat—estrus—have been noted elsewhere in the book. One sign—probably the most irksome to humans—is the loud and distinctive howling, which the female can maintain for up to three minutes without stopping. Bothersome as it is to us, it serves the obvious purpose of letting the tomcats know she is available. (And remember that the tomcats' ears are much more sensitive than ours, which explains why toms sometimes travel a long distance to locate the amorous female.) While the howling is going on, the female is likely to roll on the floor, which, if a tom is in sight, is another sign that she is sexually receptive. In short, she is making a perfect spectacle of herself—and the tomcats love it.

308 Unpredictable heat

Cats are considered to be unpredictable, which some people find attractive but others find maddening. One thing that is unpredictable is the female's estrus, or heat. Dogs predictably go into heat every six months, with the estrus lasting for twenty-one days, but there is no such predictability with cats. A cat who just went out of heat might be in heat again in days—or weeks—or months. No one knows, and no one can predict.

309 Love bites

Cats, like most animals, have sex strictly for reproduction, and so it only takes place when the female is fully fertile. Part of the brief ritual of mating (calling it "lovemaking" would not be appropriate) involves the male biting the nape of the female's neck before the sex actually takes place. This love bite is actually a kind of fertility test, because the female would not submit to this bite unless she was in full heat. That is, if she submits to the bite, the male can proceed knowing the female is as fertile as she can be.

310 No fang, no mate

During mating, the tomcat always sinks his canine teeth—the fangs—into the neck skin of the female. This isn't optional, and if for some reason the tom is missing one or more of his canines, he won't be able to breed, even though he and the female are otherwise willing and able.

311 Short and businesslike mating

The actual sex act between a tom and a female is over with very quickly, and if the tom enjoys it (he undoubtedly does), the female certainly does not seem to. When the penetration is over, it isn't unusual for the female to hiss at the male and claw at him. She needn't bother, since the male cat (like males of certain other species) seems eager and willing to depart.

312 Stud males and brood queens

As in horse breeding, a male kept for purposes of breeding is called a stud. His female counterpart, the female kept for producing kittens, is a brood queen. As is true of humans, horses and other mammals, a stud cat can father a lot more kittens in his lifetime than any brood queen can give birth to. (He can mate almost constantly, while the female can't give birth constantly.) Both studs and brood queens are chosen for their overall health, appearance and temperament. Neither is, of course, an ideal pet, as the female's caterwauling while in heat is very unpleasant, as is the unneutered tom's knack for spraying urine and fighting. Breeders construct "stud homes," pens situated outdoors or in an indoor area away from the human living area, as the home of stud cats is going to take a lot of wear (and stench) from tomcat urine.

313 Ritualized mating

Cat breeders have, over time, developed techniques for ensuring that the breeding of pedigreed cats is not left to chance. Typically the process goes like this: the queen (who is in heat, naturally) is delivered in a carrier to a special queen pen in the stud house. This separates her, via wire or bars, from the male, though they can sniff each other and the queen can size up her potential partner. Usually the first nose-to-nose encounter involves a lot of hissing and growling on her part, and the wire that separates them is for the male's protection. Eventually she shows she is ready for the male by ceasing the growling and by rolling on the floor and producing a more welcoming sound. At that point she is allowed into the stud's area, but not before a coarse "mating rug" is laid down for the two. The stud recognizes this as "his" rug, one on which he has mated before. It provides the female a warm surface to grip for stability during the brief mating procedure. When the deed is done, the queen is put back in her own pen—but the two are later allowed to repeat the process, on the assumption that pregnancy is more likely to occur with more than one mating session.

314 What's all the fuss about?

The typical owner of a mixed-breed house cat usually has no desire to breed his pet, and a wise owner will have the cat spayed or neutered. It may surprise such owners that there is a whole branch of veterinary science devoted to reproduction—specifically, devoted to getting animals to mate and produce new litters. Breeding is serious business to the obvious people: breeders, who can't sell their purebred cats if the toms and females aren't mating properly. So, just as human infertility clinics do a thriving business, veterinarians involved in animal reproduction manage to stay busy.

315 Sterile tom, false pregnancy

One curiosity about neutered tomcats is that some of them still seek out a female in heat and go through the motions of mating, even though these toms are sterile. Even more curious is that the female's mind and body may both "think" she has been impregnated, and thus she experiences a "false pregnancy." No kittens are growing inside her, and she doesn't gain weight, of course, but she "feels" she is pregnant and may produce milk and seek out a secluded spot to bear the kittens—kittens that don't exist, that is.

316 That embarrassing problem . . .

Humans have gotten rather blunt about discussing problems like male impotence, infertility, and other reproduction issues, and pet owners sometimes assume that only humans experience sexual problems. That isn't the case at all, and as all animal breeders know, you can put a healthy female in heat together with a healthy male, but you can't assume they will mate. Tomcats can experience impotence for various psychological reasons. For example, (don't laugh!) a very young tom will try to mate with an older and aggressive female, who, however lecherous a female in heat may appear to be, won't accept just any tomcat. And tomcats (never mind all the associations with that word) won't mate with every female in heat.

317 Stud jowls

Just as old male orangutans develop distinctive fleshy cheek patches, older tomcats—unneutered toms—develop "stud jowls," a widening at the cheek area that you don't have to be a cat expert to recognize. The widening of the face is accentuated by the growth of the long guard hairs in that region. If you see a tomcat with stud jowls, you can safely assume that the fellow has probably mated with a lot of females in his day and has sired many a kitten.

318 Cannibal toms?

Once a tomcat has impregnated a female, he is pretty much out of the picture, and childrearing in cats is the work of the mother alone. In fact, tomcats have a nasty reputation for killing kittens, and while many people believe toms will eat kittens, this rarely happens. Oddly, toms seem to have a sense of which kittens are theirs, and they are much less likely to kill their own kittens that those of another tom. But . . .

319 Why toms kill kittens

Tomcats deserve their reputation for being promiscuous, "no-commitment" types, and they seldom play any positive role in raising kittens (their own or any other tom's). They do occasionally kill kittens—their own, or those of other toms. Why they do so is not entirely clear. One theory is (brace yourself) that a tom may sexually mount a female kitten and give it the usual mating bite in the neck—the bite that an adult female cat in heat endures easily enough, but which is often fatal to a tiny kitten.

320 Expectant mom

How do you know a cat is pregnant? Well, with a cat that is far along, it is obvious enough, but in the early stages the first real sign is that the nipples change from light pink to darker pink, which occurs around the third week after mating. This isn't as certain a sign as feeling the lower abdomen to see if any tiny fetuses are present. Radiography, which is harmless to the mother and the kittens, gives a very accurate picture of how many kittens are in a litter. At about fifty-five days after conception, a kitten's entire skeleton is visible.

321 Who's the daddy?

Let's learn a new word: *superfecundation*. Based on Latin, it means "overfertilization." In plain English, a female cat in heat can become pregnant by more than one tomcat at one time. That is, a litter of six kittens might have the same father—or different fathers. Tomcats are not even remotely monogamous, but neither are females, and a female cat in heat has no qualms about being mounted by more than one male, even on the same day. If you understand superfecundation, you will have a better understanding of how kittens in the same litter can look so different.

322 The morning-after drug

Unless you really want to breed your female cat, you'd be wise to have her spayed. An unspayed female, even if kept indoors all the time, may manage to get loose and get pregnant. (Conversely, amorous tomcats can be clever and persistent in making their way to a female in heat.) In the situation where a female has mated and the owner does not want her to have kittens, the drug estradiol cypionate (ECP) can be administered within forty hours after mating.

323 The A word

Abortion, that is. It's a controversial subject among humans, but less so as applied to cats. The fact is that sometimes a cat owner finds that a female pet is pregnant, and the morning-after drug ECP (see 322) can only be used within the first forty hours after mating. A veterinarian can inject the female with prostaglandin, which usually induces abortion, and it can be done up to forty days after the cat has mated. This isn't done often because it makes cats sick, and some have died after the injection.

324 Dual pregnancy?

Yes, really: a female cat can carry more than one litter. It doesn't happen in humans, but it sure happens in cats. Here's the sequence: in rare cases, a female cat goes into heat even though she is already pregnant. (It's called superfetation.) When she gives birth to the first litter, sometimes the second litter is born at the same time—smaller and less developed, naturally, and often incapable of surviving. But the second litter may remain inside and be born after the usual amount of time, thus producing both a teat shortage and a milk shortage, since the first litter of kittens is still nursing. Luckily, sometimes another mother cat will "loan out" her teats and milk to the superfluous babies.

Giving Birth and Being a Mom

325 It's called "queening"

The female cat—technically, a queen cat—is quite capable of giving birth all by herself, as is true of most animals. Normally she seeks out a dark, secluded place with adequate warmth. The kittens may arrive headfirst or "breech birth"—either is perfectly fine. The mother severs the umbilical cords with her teeth. The kittens arrive one at a time, not all at once, and there are cases when the mother ceases labor, moves the kittens who have already been born to a new spot, then recommences labor in that spot. It's possible that the kittens in a litter can be born hours apart—or even days.

326 Could we have some privacy?

Cats were giving birth to kittens a long time before cats lived with humans, and they still don't need our aid now. It's tempting for owners to want to keep a close eye on a mother cat as she gives birth, but the mother cat doesn't want or need supervision, and too much intrusion can disturb her to the point where she relocates herself and the kittens. In a few cases, she may get so rattled that she will eat her own kittens.

327 The clean-up

People who have witnessed the birth of kittens admit that it isn't pretty. For one thing, there are no midwives or nurses available, so the mom is doing all the work herself—which includes licking up the afterbirth and cleansing herself thoroughly. The kittens themselves get licked over thoroughly, not just to clean them but to stimulate their breathing. Not attractive to watch, but it's all part of the miracle of birth and, after all, this is how *your* cat came into being.

328 Cannibal moms

As noted, the mother cat eats the afterbirth. She also eats any stillborn kittens. This offends our human sensibilities, but there is some logic to it: the kitten is already dead, so by eating it she is using it as nourishment both for herself and for the surviving kittens. Rarely, a highly nervous female may devour her own kittens, especially if it is her first litter. Cat breeders make a note of such females and do not breed them again.

329 Feline C-sections

Birth by cesarean section, or C-section, is common among women but not so common among cats, although sometimes a difficult birth does require a vet to anesthetize a mother and deliver kittens by incision. This does not harm the kittens, but it does mean the kittens will be temporarily motherless, since the mother has to recover from anesthesia. The surgery tends to throw her maternal hormones off balance, which means she may be unwilling to nurse the kittens, pulling away from them as they try to grab hold and suckle. Usually she comes around and allows them to nurse, but in some cases she never does, meaning the kittens have to be hand-fed or fostered out to another nursing cat.

330 Passing on protection

Cats, like all mammals, produce milk for their young. What gets passed on to newborn kittens is not only nourishment, but protection as well: the mother's milk contains antibodies that protect the kittens from diseases. The kitten takes in the milk, and the antibodies in the milk pass from the stomach into the bloodstream. So the mom cat actually passes on her own immune system to her babies.

331 Blind, deaf and helpless

Newborn kittens are adorable in their way, though not exactly "cute" at first. Their eyes stay shut for several days, and they also appear to be basically deaf at first, so newborns are as helpless as can be. If you've ever watched them closely, their movements resemble a kind of awkward "dog paddle" stroke, as they use their front legs to move themselves to their mother's teats. Though deaf and blind, they can sense mama's body heat and movements. Newborns are able to nurse within an hour or so of birth.

332 Baby-wipes

This isn't the most pleasant subject in the world, but here goes: a mother cat wipes her kittens' rear ends with her tongue, and in the process swallows some of their urine and feces. Sounds disgusting, true, but cats share this behavior with almost all other carnivorous animals. (Humans don't do this, thankfully.) Cats are, of course, absolutely obsessive about cleanliness, so licking the kittens' behinds is a mother's way of cleaning up the kids and cleaning up the nesting area as well. Keep this behavior in mind if you are tempted to rub noses with your proud new mother cat.

333 Nursing territorialism

"This is *my* spot, not yours" seems to be a trait common to humans as well as most animals. Curiously, it occurs among cats as young as two days old. In a litter of kittens there is actually a "teat order": each tiny kitten (remember, they are still blind and deaf at this stage) finds a particular nipple on its mother and from then on the order becomes fixed. Whether some nipples give more (or better) milk is not known, nor is it known how the order is decided. We only know that when kittens take their nursing positions, the lineup isn't random. If you see four kittens—let's call them A, B, C and D—lined up while nursing, you will find them in that order the next day, no B-D-C-A, or C-B-A-D. Odd, but interesting.

334 By the scruff of the neck

We've all seen it, and yes, it is adorable: a mother cat transporting a kitten by carrying it by the scruff of the neck. A cat's skin is fairly loose anyway, and the skin of the neck seems to be a perfect "handle" that nature built in just for the mom cat's use. Interestingly, in adult cats, picking one up by the scruff of the neck is a way of establishing dominance. Apparently it "puts the cat in its place," since it is being treated as a kitten again.

335 The kitten scruff posture

A kitten has its own instinctive response to "scruffing": while being carried by its scruff, it stops wriggling and tucks its legs close to its body—in short, makes itself easier to carry. Nature designed a kitten to know to relax in this situation, no small marvel considering that a mom's canine teeth are lethal weapons to anything the size of a kitten.

336 Hearing first, or seeing?

As noted, kittens are born both blind and deaf. So which comes first, hearing or seeing? The average kitten's eyes open in about a week—the range is usually from six to twelve days. However, the ability to hear is evident about a day or two earlier. Prior to both hearing and seeing, the helpless creatures sense the world primarily through smell and touch.

337 Alas, weaning

Kittens seem to thoroughly enjoy nursing, and so does a mother cat—up to a point, anyway. The mom cat seems to have an innate sense that the nursing has to end at some point and that the kittens have to "leave the nest" and start eating solid food. Around the third or fourth week after birth, the mother actually starts to move away from the kittens when they try to nurse. There isn't a "cold turkey" sort of break, yet the kittens begin to get the idea that mom isn't quite as thrilled with nursing them as she once was, and that it is time to grow up and try something besides milk.

338 Oral Fixation

Once a kitten is weaned, his sucking days are over—but not always. Sometimes older kittens, and even adult cats, can be seen sucking on another cat's teat, on a human's finger or on a piece of cloth. It does no harm, though it strikes the owner as peculiar. The author has known of a few cases where a fully grown cat would "nurse" on the teat of a dog—in some cases, a *spayed* dog that had never produced a drop of milk in her life. In every case it appeared that both the cat and dog enjoyed the arrangement.

339 Playing to prey

Roughly about the time of weaning (three weeks or so), kittens find a new source of pleasure besides nursing, namely play. It begins with gentle swatting at each other with their paws, then progresses to biting, chasing and rolling. (Kittens do bite each other in play, but less often than puppies do.) As their muscles grow and coordination improves, kittens learn the joy of leaping and pouncing and of standing on their hind legs. This is all good pleasurable fun, of course, but also is training for the hunt.

340 Then on to real preying

The predator instinct is inborn, but, as noted elsewhere (see 63), kittens also learn hunting by watching their mothers. So how old is a cat when he can do his own killing? Roughly two months, by which time most kittens can catch and kill a mouse. Here's a curious thing: a minority of cats seem to be afraid to hunt, and those cats are also fearful of humans. In short, a cat who doesn't like to hunt makes a poor pet. Cat owners who are angry at their pet for bringing home birds or mice ought to consider that a good hunter is also a warmer companion.

341 Little boys and their toys

Both male and female kittens will happily chase after rolling objects, just as they will swat at suspended objects like strings and strips of paper. There is some difference in the sexes, however, as males seem to engage more in "object play" than females do.

342 Social skills

A person who grew up in large family generally may have better social skills than someone from a small family. This is, in a way, true for cats, too. Every cat is part of a litter of several kittens, and the general rule is that the longer a kitten stays with his littermates, the more tolerant he is of other cats while growing up. None of this information is very important if you own only one cat and don't want another. But if you're thinking of having two or more cats in your home, it might be useful to learn about the "adolescence" of the cat you are thinking of taking in.

343 Multiple meanings of "litter"

If you ever studied French, you probably know that *lit* is the French word for "bed." Our English word "litter" is rooted in the old French word, and it has two related meanings that apply to cats. A "litter" of kittens reflects the idea that a cat "took to her bed" to give birth. The "litter" in a litter box is a sort of "bed of soil" (or recycled newspaper, pine or whatever you use for litter) for the cat to deposit its waste discreetly.

344 Poor excuses for mothers?

Cats are, of course, excellent mothers in every respect, designed by nature to provide food, warmth, nurture and defense. But if cat moms are warm and loving, they certainly aren't sentimental. By the time her kittens are about fifty days old, a mother seems to realize they are ready for the world. Her work is done, and there is no anxiety about being separated from the kids, nor are the kittens sad at leaving home. However, breeders as a rule don't separate the mom cat from the kittens all at once but generally remove one kitten at a time from the litter, one kitten per day. This makes it easier for mom to return to her premother life.

345 Do they recognize mom?

Alas, no. It shouldn't surprise us that they wouldn't recognize their father, since he was nothing more than a sperm donor (and remember that kittens in the same litter can have different fathers, as described in 321). But it does strike some people as odd that kittens, once grown and separated from their mothers, do not seem to recognize her if they meet her again. This raises a question: would a male cat ever mate with his own mother? The answer is yes, though some experts say there is some "incest instinct" that prevents this from occurring often. In the interest of breeding for specific traits, humans will sometimes create an incest situation, a practice called backcrossing (see 137).

346 The burning house scenario

It's been described so often that it is practically a cliché: a mother cat runs into a burning building to rescue her kittens, carrying them out one by one (by the scruff of the neck, of course), not giving up until they are all safe. What impresses people most is that sometimes the mother loses her own life in the process.

Find 'Em, Feed 'Em, Change Their Litter

Bringing Home a Pet

347 Top dog is now . . . the cat

This was big (but not totally surprising) news in 2003: a survey by the American Pet Products Manufacturing Association showed that more Americans had cats as pets than dogs. According to the survey, more than 60 percent of households in the United States owned pets. The tally was 77.7 million cats, 65 million dogs and (in a distant third) 17.3 million "small animals" (rabbits, gerbils and the like). Gone are the days when cats were considered second place (in numbers, affection and so on) after dogs. Couple this bit of news with another bit of trivia: it's inevitable that there are a lot more feral cats in the United States than there are wild dogs.

348 The puppy-to-kitten shift

Not so long ago, the typical pet shop drew in customers by placing a group of adorable, playful, yipping puppies in its window. That has definitely changed, and pet shop windows today are much more likely to display kittens than pups. Obviously this reflects changing demographics as more and more people own cats.

349 Male or female pet?

News flash (except it's old news): male and female human beings are different—and not just physically. After years of the unisex concept dominating discussions about men and women, we've come back to the commonsense observation that in temperament, attitudes toward relationships and so on, males and females differ. It's true of cats as well, and in some ways their differences align with human differences. Talking about neutered males and spayed females, generally females are more affectionate, more placid and more inclined to stay home. There are plenty of individual exceptions, of course, and all cats retain some of their predator instincts. But, as a general rule of thumb, a female might be expected to be a little more loving and more docile. On the other hand, however, many owners think that toms—neutered or not—demonstrate affection more than females. (Put another way, there are plenty of happy owners of male cats and female cats.) Generally, you can't go wrong with a neutered male or spayed female, but the more you know about the potential pet's parents and their temperaments, the better off you are.

350 Those wonderful petmobiles

Animal shelters are literally overflowing with cats and dogs who need homes, but, alas, not every potential owner bothers to drop by an animal shelter. So some shelters have employed a wise marketing strategy: take the "product" to where the people are via "petmobiles," transporting some pets to malls, civic gatherings and other places where people can get some face time with some adorable animals. Inevitably some adoptions will follow.

351 "Hand raised"

If you know anything about pet birds, parrots in particular, you know the importance of buying a bird that is "hand raised." That bird will make a much better pet since it bonded with human beings early in its life. Some catteries and other cat breeders advertise that their cats are "hand raised," and what is true for parrots is true for kittens as well—kittens who were handled often in their early weeks make more sociable and affectionate pets.

352 The cattery

A cattery is just what you'd think: a place where cats to be sold are raised. It differs from a pet shop in that it sells only cats, nothing else. Catteries are usually the most expensive places to buy a cat, because they specialize in purebreds. The best catteries are absolutely fanatical about hygiene, since any good cat breeder knows how easy it is for disease to spread quickly through a group of cats confined in the same space.

353 "Blue light specials" among pedigreed cats

If you want a cat with "all the papers" (pedigreed, that is), be prepared to pay for it. Thousands of animal shelters across the country give cats away for free or for small adoption fees, but people still find themselves paying stiff prices because they want a particular breed. There is no arguing with taste, of course, and here's a bit of advice if you want a particular breed but don't want to pay a fortune: a cat that is purebred but, because of some minor variation in coat or eye color, isn't "up to standard" can be bought at a discount. Such a cat is called "pet quality." You can't enter the cat in a cat show, but the cat will make a fine (and not-quite-so-expensive) pet, and you can still have the "brag factor" of owning a pedigreed pet with the particular look that you like.

354 Coddling the kitten

You can never predict how a very tiny kitten will react when you bring her home. One who has just been taken from her mom may miss her, and while the owner will quickly fill the mom cat's role, a pining kitten can be made to feel at home by letting her snuggle with a hot-water bottle or heating pad (on a low setting); either one will fill in for the high-temperature body of a mother cat. Some kittens feel safe near the ticking of a wind-up alarm clock, since it apparently reminds them of their mom's heartbeat. (Good luck finding a wind-up clock in the twenty-first century, though.)

355 Humane pet shops

Here's some cheery news: some pet shops actually give away cats instead of selling them. In this situation the shop owner or the manager has made the store a clearinghouse for unwanted strays and kittens. In other words, the shop serves the same function as an animal shelter. It is a win-win situation, for the shopper can get a free pet, and the shop generates some good will and (hopefully) the happy cat owner will in the future buy cat supplies at that store. The real beneficiaries are, of course, the cats.

356 Impulse cats

You've heard the old saying, "Marry in haste, repent at leisure." It would be just as truthful to say, "Buy a cat on impulse, repent at leisure." People who have no previous experience with cats often find themselves fascinated by a cat (or, more often, a kitten) in a pet store, so they buy on impulse, take her home, then discover they know nothing whatsoever about taking care of the creature. Happily, most novices do in time become competent caregivers to their pets, but too many of these "impulse buy" cats end up in animal shelters or abandoned by a roadside.

357 The shelter alternative (cheap and compassionate)

If you want a purebred cat, with the papers to prove it, your only choices are catteries or pet shops. If you don't care about the purity of the breed, the most humane way to obtain a cat, and certainly the cheapest, is your local animal shelter or humane society. The cats there (and many of them are still kittens) face the inevitable future of being euthanized, so you get a pet and save her from death at the same time. The typical animal shelter today charges an "adoption fee," which is really a bargain since the shelter will have already neutered the cat and given her the required immunizations. The author's cat Lucy was a five-month-old kitten when she was brought home from the county shelter, where she had the good sense to be the friendliest cat in her litter. Considering the adoption fee was a mere $15, Lucy has proved to be quite a bargain.

358 Animal shelter "specials"

The staffs at animal shelters know that kittens are much more appealing than adult cats, and, sadly, an adult cat at an animal shelter is more likely to end up being euthanized than a kitten is. This is especially true of cats who are obviously well on in years. For this reason, shelters occasionally run "specials," waiving the usual adoption fees for older cats. Also, at certain times of year when cage space is limited due to an overflow of animals, the usual adoption fees may be reduced or waived.

359 Yes, senior discounts

Senior citizens are accustomed to getting discounts for all kinds of products and services. It even happens at animal shelters, which sometimes waive the usual "adoption fee" for people who can verify that they are over a certain age. This is a nice arrangement, particularly for older adults who live alone and could benefit from a pet's companionship. It probably won't surprise you that many shelters in Florida (with its large population of seniors) have this policy.

360 Purina's nonprofit

The Ralston Purina company (now called Nestlé Purina PetCare) is noted as a maker of pet food, but the company also established a nonprofit program called Pets for People. Managed by local humane societies, Pets for People works to provide free pets to people over age sixty. To no one's surprise, Pets for People and the many programs like it report that most of the recipients of pets report that the quality of their lives has improved considerably after taking a pet into their homes.

361 The vague category of semistrays

One of the old Warner Bros. Looney Tunes cartoons was about a cat with several owners. There are indeed such cats around, unusually unneutered ones, who are not quite strays but not quite attached to a single house, either. In most cases they have been strays for several years, and while they like the food and affection that humans provide, they never quite cease to hear the "call of the wild," so they wander away, either hunting or on the sexual prowl, sometimes returning to "home base," sometimes not. These cats seldom experience enough human interaction to become truly "tame" in the real sense—*unless,* of course, you have them neutered. It's amazing how many semistrays (or even a few ferals) have settled down after neutering.

Finicky Eaters? Well . . .

362 Skip the carbs

Humans require (and like!) carbohydrates in the form of sugars and starches, but cats have no such requirement. This is worth noting when you buy cat food, because canned foods are made of about 10 percent carbohydrates, and dry foods are about 40 percent carbohydrates. The carbohydrates don't do any harm, of course, and your cat can metabolize them easily. But in its natural state as a hunter in the woods and fields, a cat wouldn't take in starches or sugars at all. Also, keep in mind that an excess of carbohydrates will have the same effect on your cat as on you: obesity.

363 Bring on the Fat!

As noted above, cats in the wild wouldn't take in carbohydrates in the form of starches and sugars. They would instead derive most of their energy from fat, which they have a great need for. In fact, adult cats require a diet that is about 10 percent fat to stay healthy, and kittens require even more. So many adults now are obsessing over eliminating fat from their diet that they foolishly try to impose their own diet regimens on their pets, and this is not a good thing. Too little fat can lead to weight loss, susceptibility to infection, slow healing of wounds and other problems. Another point to remember: cats can only metabolize animal fat; they cannot metabolize the fat in vegetable oils.

364 The protein palette

Cats' protein requirements are high, and so their need for variety is high also, because no one source of protein—red meat, poultry, fish—provides just the right amounts of all the amino acids that a cat needs. Humans can get into a diet rut, and, thanks to their owners, cats can too, so owners need to be conscious of varying their cats' diet, selecting an assortment of canned and dried foods that make use of protein from various sources.

365 Serious protein

The ads for kitten food are correct: kittens do have different dietary needs than adult cats. Specifically, a kitten needs one and a half times the protein required by a mature cat. And cats in general have high protein requirements. Proportionate to their body weight, cats require three or four times the amount of protein that humans require. (Humans are omnivores and take in a large amount of plant food, but cats, as noted in 376, are almost exclusively carnivores.)

366 The water-urine connection

One reason that cat urine has such a powerful odor is that it is highly *concentrated*—a lot of waste matter in a relatively tiny amount of water. The urine of humans or dogs is, by comparison, much more watery. Since cats lose less water through urination, they require less than humans do, and they can go much longer without water than a human or a dog can. But like all living things, cats do require water. In fact, a cat's body is about 70 percent water, which is true of you as well. Stating the obvious, the drier the food your cat eats, the more water is required.

367 Dry, but not really

If you place dry cat food on a paper towel and leave it there a while, you'll find later that the paper towel has absorbed moisture. "Dry" food is never as dry as we think. In fact, it contains up to 12 percent moisture, some of which is fat put on as a coating to improve the taste. (Remember, a cat loves and needs fat.) The bad news about dry food is that it is still lower in moisture than a cat's natural foods (mice, birds and other small animals), and cats who are fed dry food constantly are susceptible to feline urological syndrome (see 260). The obvious solution: vary dry food with other foods and keep plenty of water available.

368 That satisfying crunching sound

If you've ever heard a cat chowing down on dry food, you would assume they are enjoying it, and with good reason, because the crunchy quality of dry food is similar to the crunch they would find in the bones of birds and mice. While an entirely dry-food diet has its drawbacks, dry food not only provides the "crunch factor," but also does a better job than canned food of cleansing tartar from the teeth and gums.

369 What's in that dry stuff anyway?

You can't take meat or fish or chicken and magically transform it into tiny bits of dry cat food . . . or can you? The animal protein found in dry cat foods gets there in the form of *meal*—beef meal, fish meal, chicken meal. Soybean meal, also high in protein, is a common ingredient (but so is cereal, which cats in their natural state would have no interest in). Many manufacturers add vitamins and minerals to the mix, and as a final stage in the process, the bits of dry food may be sprayed with a coating of concentrated meat extract, enhancing the nutrition value as well as giving an appealing smell and taste. In short, dry food is meatier than you might have thought.

370 Paying for a lot of water

On the price scale, the most expensive way to feed your cat is with canned food, especially the "gourmet" varieties (with ads designed to appeal to human snobbery). Canned food is also the most appealing, as you can tell when you pop the top of a can of cat food, and your pet comes racing in from the other end of the house. Owners faced with a finicky cat usually find they can easily solve the problem with canned food. While there is nothing wrong with canned foods (though they vary in nutritional quality), be aware of this: about three-quarters of canned cat food is water. It costs more than dry foods and, pound for pound, you're getting less real food and more water.

371 The old food switcheroo

Cats are creatures of habit (as are humans), and yet they need variety in their diet, so owners are sometimes in the awkward position of having to change the cat's diet only to finding that the cat rejects the new food. One solution is to introduce the new food into the diet gradually by mixing a small amount in with the old food. Over a period of several days, change the proportion so that eventually the cat is eating only the new food. (Even better, you may be a lucky cat owner like the author, whose cat appears willing to eat whatever is put in front of her.)

372 Airtight only

Most canned and dry cat foods have vitamins and minerals added, which is the good news, but the bad news is that those supplements can literally evaporate into the air. For that reason, unused food ought to be tightly sealed, preferably in an airtight container. The plastic lids now commonly used to seal canned cat food work well (plus, putting an open can in the refrigerator slows the breakdown of vitamins). People do get careless with dry food, leaving the bag wide open or perhaps just rolling up the end. It's better to fasten the end with a clothespin or, even better, dump the whole bag into an airtight plastic or glass container.

373 Smelly and "light"

It's true of both cats and humans: as they age, their senses of smell and taste both become less acute. Many older adults lose their appetite because they just don't derive as much pleasure from the taste of food any more, and this is also true for older cats. For this reason cat food manufacturers produce foods especially for "senior cats," foods with intensified smell and taste to appeal to the older pets. The flip side of aging is that some cats eat enough but exercise little, resulting in obesity, so the manufacturers now offer "light" cat foods that promise all the nutritional value with fewer calories. (A more sensible alternative: simply feed the older cat less if the cat shows signs of getting chubby.)

374 Dog food, yes, but not regularly

Cats will eat dog food (and vice versa), and it's not uncommon in homes with both dogs and cats for an owner to let the dog and cat both eat dog food. Probably one incentive to do this is that dog food is generally cheaper than cat food. While it won't hurt the cat to eat dog food now and then, making a regular diet of it is bad news. Remember that cats are carnivores while dogs are omnivores, and their foods are formulated accordingly. Dog food, even the canned variety, usually has a fair amount of cereal in it—fine for dogs, who need plant matter in the diet, but not adequate nutrition for your meat-loving cat.

375 Are they really finicky over food?

First, Lang's Law of Feeding Cats: if your cat is really *really* hungry, she will eat whatever canned or dry food you put in front of her. This has (for me) proven to be the most effective way of dealing with a "finicky" cat. Hunger overrides finickiness every time. (It's true for finicky humans, also.) Some cats, of course, are not finicky at all (lucky owners!), while some are extremely fussy, leading their owners to try one brand of cat food after another, usually buying on the assumption that the more expensive brand is more likely to please the cat. This isn't necessarily true, but manufacturers have made a killing from the idea that cats are finicky, as evident in the success of Morris (see 943) and the glossiness of the Fancy Feast food ads.

376 No veggies, thank you

The various mammals belonging to the order Carnivora are meat eaters, but most of them will eat fruits, vegetables and other plant matter. (And, oddly, pandas are classified as carnivores, yet they live almost exclusively on bamboo.) That is, carnivores are not exclusively meat eaters—except for cats, that is. All cats *must* have animal protein and fat to survive, and though house cats might munch on cooked rice at times, cats as a group are truly "meat-only" animals.

377 Do cats like booze?

In a word, no. Numerous stories have circulated about this or that cat with a taste for beer or sherry or whiskey, but most of those rumors are unsubstantiated, and veterinarians have reported almost no cases of drunken cats, though most admit that they've encountered an occasional tipsy dog. The truth is that both cats and dogs show a lot more good sense than humans about intoxicating beverages. And besides, could a cat find anything more intoxicating—and less harmful—than catnip?

378 The pill obsession

People are so nutrition obsessed that they dose themselves constantly with various vitamin, mineral and herb supplements. Many pet owners impose this obsession onto their animal companions, assuming the pet just can't get by without some sort of pill or liquid supplement. While the intention is good, most commercial foods are already well supplied with vitamins and minerals. In the case of some vitamins, such as A and D, there is even a danger of overdosing to the point of toxicity. In a word, be conscious of nutrition (your own, and your pet's) but don't go overboard.

379 The rib test

We have all seen stray cats who looked pitiful with their ribs protruding, and our instinct is to bring them home and fatten them up. In a cat of normal health and weight, the ribs would not be visible to the eye, but you could definitely *feel* them if you rub the cat's torso or pick up the cat. The sign that the cat is obese is when you use the touch test and can barely feel the ribs underneath. You've got a fat cat on your hands, and while the cat (unlike its human owner) doesn't care how she looks, too much body fat can lead to health problems.

380 Chubby castrati

You've probably heard of the castrati, male opera singers of centuries ago who had been castrated (voluntarily) before puberty so they would retain a sweet soprano voice all their lives. Alas, one other effect of prepuberty castration was that the castrati tended to be extremely obese (which, as far as their singing was concerned, was not a bad thing). It appears that neutered tomcats are, in general, more prone to obesity than are unneutered toms. In fact, a neutered tom could eat the same amount as an unneutered one and *gain* weight, while the unneutered tom might *lose*. Not every neutered tomcat becomes obese, but as a neutered pet ages, his weight should be monitored.

381 Slimming down the chub

One obvious solution to slim down a fat cat: feed her less. It's best to do this gradually instead of dramatically. A sudden "starvation diet" can lead to serious health problems. Not only should the cat be fed less but the diet ought to be altered to include less fat and more protein. And, as with humans, proper diet ought to be coupled with proper exercise. Obese cats, like obese humans, typically don't exercise, which can be partly blamed on their owners, who may enjoy a placid lap cat but who ought to realize that every cat does require play and exercise.

382 The anorexic cat

Anorexia has gotten a lot of attention in recent years because so many people—teenage girls in particular—starve themselves, leading to serious health problems because they fear being overweight and looking unattractive. Cats, needless to say, have no concern about looking slim and sexy, but cats can experience anorexia, though exactly why is not known. It seems more common among cats placed in kennels or in hospitals. The cats simply refuse to eat, and sometimes it is necessary to insert a feeding tube into their stomachs. Curiously, the tranquilizer Valium, used to treat aggression in some cats, is also used at times to stimulate appetite.

Litter Matters

383 Inventing kitty litter

Prior to 1948, cats "did their business" either outdoors or in boxes their owners had filled with sand or soil. In 1948, Edward Lowe of Cassopolis, Michigan, hit upon the idea of using absorbent clay. His local store mocked the idea of selling the product, so Lowe started giving it away in bags, and people liked it so much he started selling it out of the trunk of his 1943 Chevy. He eventually sold it under the brand name Kitty Litter, and he became a wealthy man.

384 The litter revolution

Edward Lowe probably had no idea in 1948 that absorbent cat litter would alter the pet world forever. Before his product existed, part of cat owners' daily ritual was putting out the cat for the night. Few owners were willing to bother with boxes filled with sand or soil, and since most cats don't like to be walked, apartment dwellers weren't keen on cats. (After all, if they had a cat, where would the cat "go"?) Cat litter changed everything: You could have a cat without having a yard and without having to worry about what might happen to your cat outside every night. In short, cat litter made it inevitable that more people would be able to own cats.

385 The second litter revolution

Cat litter, as noted above, made it easier to own a cat. Around the late 1970s, a new type of litter made it even easier. This was the "scoopable" type, made of clay containing sodium bentonite. This new litter clumped when moistened, so cat owners (using perforated "scoops" that are now standard equipment for most owners) could easily scoop out the clumps of urine-saturated litter, leaving behind dry litter. It requires changing much less often than the old clay litter and is also less dusty.

386 The anti-scoopable data

Most cat owners aren't going to give up using scoopable litter, but there are some potential hazards (or so the rumor goes). Critics of scoopable litter say that sodium bentonite, the ingredient that gives litter its clumping quality, can cause problems if it enters a cat's lungs or digestive system. Every advance has its downside, and probably in the future there will be a "new and improved" litter that poses fewer health risks for cats.

387 Acidify that smell!

If you think the smell of cat urine is offensive (and it assuredly is), then you know that your cat's ultra-sensitive nose doesn't like it either. If her litter box isn't cleaned out regularly, a cat will do the obvious thing and start urinating somewhere else. Scoopable litters have made tending to litter boxes less of a chore, but you still have to wash out the whole pan thoroughly from time to time. When cleaning it, keep in mind that urine is basically alkaline. So is ammonia, so if you clean the box with ammonia or an ammonia-based cleaner, you will only increase the urine smell. Use something acidic like vinegar or lemon juice, which neutralizes the urine smell.

388 The godsend: baking soda products

Baking soda, so inexpensive and so versatile, is one of those products no homeowner should be without—and no cat owner. Soda absorbs and neutralizes the chemicals present in cat urine, so you can't go wrong by sprinkling a thin layer of soda in the litter box, then pouring the litter on top of it. Arm & Hammer, Tidy Cat and several other companies now sell boxes of "cat box deodorizers," which are basically made of baking soda and some chemicals. Any of these work fine at keeping odors down. If you choose to use regular baking soda, keep in mind that you can buy it in large boxes, not just the small "kitchen size."

389 The "no-perfume" zone

There has been a lot of controversy lately about people complaining that coworkers wear too much perfume and cologne, and some companies have instituted "no-perfume" policies. Your cat is basically a no-perfume animal, and the flowery, spicy scents that we find so attractive have no appeal at all to cats. More importantly, they don't like cleaning products that are heavily perfumed, and if their litter boxes are cleaned with such products, the cat might stop using the box. In short, if you hope to keep the litter box as odorless as possible, trying to make it smell "pretty" will only defeat your purpose.

390 Creatures of habit

Well, humans are, and it shouldn't surprise us that animals are. Certainly cats are, and while they like occasional changes in diet, they definitely do not like changes in their litter boxes. Many a cat owner has discovered that a change in cat litter often results in the cat not using the box at all. Some cats eventually adjust to the change, but others don't, and sometimes the most sensible choice is to return to whatever you were using before.

391 Litter box buffet

It's not pleasant to talk about, but it's a fact: dogs will sometimes eat cat feces out of the litter box. Why? No one seems to know for certain. Dogs are not finicky eaters (well, duh!), and they will sometimes eat other dogs' feces or even their own, and they seem to be curious enough to sample any kind of organic matter. People who have both a cat and a dog in the home find the habit to be an incentive to keep the litter box scooped out as often as possible.

7

Wild Ancestors and Wild Cousins

Way, Way Back in Time . . .

392 The carnivore clan

You probably know that carnivores are animals that primarily eat a diet of meat. In scientific terms, the order Carnivora includes several familiar families of mammals: dogs and their kin, bears, raccoons and their kin, weasels and kin, mongooses, hyenas and, of course, Felidae, the cat family. All these families descended from the same mammal ancestors, which arrived on the scene sometime after the age of the dinosaurs.

393 The carnivore ancestors

Presumably the dinosaurs died out around 65 million years ago (give or take a year), and the age of the mammals began. The earliest mammals were known as *creodonts*, and they apparently lived on fish and were small, not more than a foot tall at the shoulder. So far as we can tell, the creodonts were the distant ancestors of all the carnivores, including the cat ancestor *Miacis* (see 394).

394 50 million years ago

Miacis is the name the scientists give to a creature that lived about 50 million years ago and was the probable ancestor of cats. This creature had a long body and fairly short legs and had retractable claws (a distinctively feline feature), which were apparently used to climb trees. Note that this was a long time before any form of humans walked on Earth.

395 The infamous saber-tooths

Granted, they were much larger than today's house cats, but in some way the ferocious saber-tooth cats are among the ancestors of today's pets (or, at any rate, of cats in general). The sabertoothed tiger (*Smilodon* is the scientific name) lived in Europe, Africa, Asia and North America 35 million years ago. With its huge daggerlike teeth, it could bring down an elephant. Scientists think these cats' combination of large body and small brain ensured they would not last forever. (An interesting tidbit: before the U.S. president Thomas Jefferson sent the Lewis and Clark expedition to explore the American West, it was widely assumed that creatures like saber-toothed tigers still existed in the wilds of America.)

396 From whole foot to tiptoes

Roughly 20 millions years ago, the carnivore *Pseudaelurus* lived, and like modern cats, it walked on its toes instead of flat-footed (see 117). It possessed sharp, stabbing teeth and a very flexible spine—like that of modern cats. The *Pseudaelurus* varied in size between 50 and 200 pounds. Scientists assume this was the true ancestor of cats.

397 The in-between phase

After *Pseudaelurus*, there was *Felis lunensis,* which lived in Europe around 12 million years ago. This species was smaller than *Pseudaelurus* though still larger than today's house cat. Scientists assume that it had a fairly thick coat and the markings of a tabby cat.

398 The original Sylvester

Who was the most recent ancestor of the house cat? Scientists believe it was (maybe) a European wildcat, *Felis silvestris,* or perhaps another wildcat of Asia and northern Africa, *Felis libyca*. Other scientists think these were subspecies of the same basic species. At any rate, this wildcat was (and is) similar in size and shape to today's house cat and had the markings we associate with the "tabby" cats. (And now you also know the source of the name of the cartoon cat Sylvester.)

399 Roaring and non-roaring

The cat family, Felidae, is divided into two genera, Felis and Panthera. Roughly speaking, the Felis cats are the small ones; the Panthera cats are the biggies. But more technically, the Felis cats do not roar (though they can purr), while the Panthera cats do roar (but can't purr). Needless to say, your pet belongs to the Felis genus. Aside from the roar-purr divide, however, the members of Felidae are amazingly alike in shape and overall behavior, and there's no doubt that one of the great attractions of cats as pets is that they remind us so much of graceful and powerful lions, tigers and leopards.

400 Felis, Feline, etc.

The Latin word *felis* lies behind our common word *feline,* and *felis* was indeed the word the ancient Romans used to refer to a cat. Originally, though, it had a much broader meaning—a *felis* could be any yellowish-colored carnivore, such as a weasel or a polecat. By the year 200 or so, the Latin *cattus* was being used in place of *felis,* and *cattus* referred only to cats.

401 Everywhere but Australia

Australia is a unique continent, notably because it is really just a large island, and its isolation from other land masses has resulted in wildlife very unlike the other continents. You probably are aware that many of its mammals are marsupials, mammals that carry their young in pouches. Many of these animals, such as the kangaroos and koalas, are not carnivorous, but there are plenty of carnivorous marsupials. They fill the ecological niche that on other continents is filled by cats. There were no true cats in Australia until the Europeans settled there, and the vicious marsupial "tiger cat" of eastern Australia is not a true cat.

402 *Felis catus* in the wild

You occasionally run across the term *feral* in reference to cats, dogs, pigs and other creatures. It describes a domestic animal that has "gone native"—returned to living in the wild. It could be a "first-generation feral," or it could be the offspring of feral parents. There are plenty of feral cats around of exactly the same species, *Felis catus,* as any pampered house pet. There are probably more feral cats in cities than in the country, and they survive quite well without help from humans. Unfortunately, because they don't get vaccinated, feral cats can easily spread rabies through contact with one another or with skunks or raccoons.

403 "Cats," but not really

Various animals go by "cat" names but aren't related to cats at all. Skunks are sometimes called "polecats," while in Europe the "polecat" is a creature related to the weasel, but neither "polecat" is a true cat. Civets and genets are animals related to the mongooses, and you will hear people speak of "genet cats" and "civet cats," but neither is a cat belonging to the family Felidae.

404 The last to be domesticated

Cat owners may well wonder if any cat can ever be *fully* domesticated. At any rate, the fossil records indicate that cats were certainly among the last of animals to be domesticated. This makes sense: early man found the dog useful as a hunter, the horse for transportation and cattle and swine and sheep as sources of food and hides. Apparently our human ancestors were slow to realize cats' potential as rodent exterminators.

The Small Wildcat Cousins

405 *Silvestris,* still around

As already noted, today's domestic cat probably descended from *Felis silvestris,* and the wild *silvestris* is still very much alive. The various subspecies are described in this section. All of them look a lot like our house pet cats, but, as you will see, their capacity for being tamed varies greatly. Worth noting: all the *silvestris* wildcats possess larger brains than those of domestic cats.

406 The Scottish wildcat

Felis silvestris grampia probably ranged all over Great Britain in earlier times, but by the 1800s it was found only in Scotland, where it still survives, though in limited numbers. The Scottish wildcat resembles a grayish-brown tabby house cat, but its head is broader and its tail shorter than those of most house pets.

407 The Spanish wildcat

Felis silvestris iberia, resembles the Scottish wildcat but its coat is darker. Like its Scottish cousin, it has a heavier build than most house cats. Its attractively striped coat led to its being hunted by fur trappers, a fate that has befallen many wildcats over the centuries.

408 The European wildcat

Felis silvestris europeus once ranged all over Europe before practically reaching the point of extinction. The species is now recovering, notably in Germany, Slovakia and the Czech Republic. It is slimmer and more housecat–like than the Scottish and Spanish wildcats, but like those subspecies has a noticeably shorter tail than the domestic cat. European wildcats are fearful of humans and are not tamable. Their only contact with humans is the occasional raid on a chicken coop, which does not endear them to people.

409 The African wildcat

Felis silvestris lybica ranges over much of Africa but it has become rare. It is grayish-brown in color and has distinctive striping on the legs. Like the other *silvestris* wildcats, its eyes are yellow, never green. If reared in captivity, the African wildcat can become tame.

410 The Indian desert cat

Felis silvestris ornata differs from the other *silvestris* wildcats by having spots rather than stripes. It has a wide range, from southern Russia to central India. It is somewhat smaller than the wildcats mentioned already.

411 Can Felis silvestris mate with Felis catus?

The answer is yes, but you probably would not like the results. This is especially true of cases where a European wildcat tom impregnated a domestic female. European wildcats fear and distrust humans, so any offspring of a European wildcat will quickly manifest its wildness, either by fleeing the human home or becoming so obnoxious that the humans will gladly set it free.

412 The U.S. wildcat

The wildcat that is most likely to be seen (or, more often, *heard*) in the United States is the bobcat, or lynx (*Felis lynx*), which is found from Canada to Mexico. As you might guess from its name, it has a short tail, and, in general, its appearance suggests a stocky, grayish-brown, thick-haired house cat, with spots on the lower half of the body. Its fairly large ears have noticeable tufts on the ends, and males get very shaggy hairs around the cheeks. Bobcats are shy and seldom seen, but their hoarse voices are occasionally heard. It is possible they can mate with house cats, resulting (maybe) in the Pixie-bob breed (see 203).

413 Pet otter?

While Native Americans did not have *Felis catus* house cats before Columbus arrived, there is some evidence that they had tamed a native cat called the jaguarundi. This long-bodied brown cat is still found from Arizona to Argentina. Its lanky body and otterlike head have led to its being called the "weasel cat" or "otter cat." Pre-Columbus, the native peoples of South America tamed it and used it to kill rodents. Whether they really made a pet of it and doted on it the way Europeans and Asians doted on their house cats is not known.

414 The ultimate fur cat

The beautiful spotted ocelot (*Felis pardalis*) found over much of the tropical Americas had the misfortune to be widely hunted for its fur. Public opinion has shifted, and fewer people are wearing furs of any kind, so the wild populations may be on the rise. An ocelot practically lives in the trees, where it hunts by night, seeking out birds, reptiles and small mammals. In earlier times it was found as far north as Arkansas in the United States.

415 Little spotty

Ocelots (see 414) are about four feet long, and their close relative the margay (*Felis wiedi*) is a sort of mini-ocelot, only about two feet long, tail included.

In other words, this beautiful spotted creature is only slightly larger than a house cat. It ranges from Mexico to Argentina, and it is still occasionally seen in southern Texas.

416 Why "tiger," when it's spotted?

The species *Felis tigrinus* goes by several names, including tiger cat, although it is spotted, not striped. Also called the little spotted cat and oncilla, it is barely larger than a house cat. It ranges over Central America and much of South America, and, like several other species with beautiful coats, it has become rare because of fur trapping.

417 High-altitude American

The mountain cat (*Felis jacobita*), true to its name, lives high in the Andes Mountains, sometimes as high as 16,000 feet above sea level. High altitude means cold nights, so this grayish cat has dense shaggy fur. The tail's wide stripes make it look like a raccoon's tail. It is only slightly larger than a house cat.

418 Smallest of all

No, the house cat is not the smallest member of the cat family; the kodkod (*Felis guigna*) of Chile and Argentina is smaller, never weighing more than seven pounds. Like many other wildcats of South America, it has a spotted coat. It lives in trees and feeds on birds and reptiles, but it also has a reputation as a poultry killer, which does not endear it to humans.

419 Made for the desert

We tend to think of wildcats as living in jungles, but the distinctive sand cat (*Felis margarita*) of Africa and Asia is adapted to a desert environment. It needs little water, apparently getting enough moisture from the desert rodents it feeds on. To prevent it from sinking into the sand, its paws have thick hairs between the pads.

420 Webbed feet, yes

"Cats hate water"—no, not all cats, and certainly not the fishing cat (*Felis prionailaurus*) found in the mangrove swamps of India and southern China. This beautiful cat eats snakes and mammals but, true to its name, also eats fish and shellfish found among the mangrove roots. Its toes are slightly webbed, and, of course, it is not afraid to swim.

421 Europe's bobcat

The lynx may be a subspecies of the American bobcat (see 412), or perhaps a closely related species. It resembles its American relative with its shaggy fur, short tail and distinctive ear tufts. The lynx was once common all over Europe but today is absent from most countries. It is still occasionally seen in the more remote sections of northern Europe.

422 The crab-eater

The Iriomote cat was not discovered until 1967, and it's no wonder, for only a few survive on the small Japanese island of Iriomote. The small cat hunts by night, stalking birds and small mammals, and it also ventures to the water's edge to catch crabs.

423 Compressed head

Imagine a thick-furred house cat with a head compressed so that it was very wide and with ears very close to the head. That pretty much describes the Pallas cat (*Felis manul*), which is found in mountainous regions from Iran to western China. These are cold regions, so the cat has very dense fur.

424 Distinctive and tamable

The caracal (*Felis caracal*), sometimes called the Persian lynx, is found over much of Asia and Africa, where it preys on gazelles, small deer and birds. No other cat quite resembles it, thanks to the long black tufts of hair on each ear. The beautiful reddish brown cat, somewhat larger than a fox, can be tamed, and in some regions it has been trained to hunt small antelopes and deer.

425 A truly inappropriate name

Though called the jungle cat, this species (*Felis chaus*) is more likely to be found in the open country and marshlands of Asia and northern Africa. Apparently the cat was to some degree tamable—mummified jungle cats have been dug up in Egypt. The beautiful cat has sleek grayish-brown fur.

The Big Cat Cousins

426 Only the size is different . . .

Because all members of the Felidae family are similar in overall shape, cat lovers are naturally fascinated by the house cat's larger wild relatives. This works both ways: the qualities that we find attractive in house cats are visible in the wildcats, and, vice versa, the regal qualities seen in lions, tigers, leopards and other wildcats that have impressed humans for centuries are found in domestic cats.

427 The big guy, Leo

The lion (*Panthera leo*) isn't the largest cat (tigers are larger), but he has probably made the deepest impression on humans, partly because the male's large mane does give it a "kingly" look. Lions once ranged over not only Africa but also Europe and Asia, but today they are found only in Africa and a small section of India. The lion is the only social cat, living in small groups called prides that are composed mostly of related females and one dominant male.

428 The big spotty

The leopard (*Panthera pardus*) is actually more ferocious than the lion, and it also has a wider range, living in Africa and much of Asia. The leopard usually has a fawn-colored coat with black spots, but the hair colors and spot patterns vary so greatly that in times past people assumed there were several different species. Leopards have no fear of water and are good swimmers. Leopards are often called panthers, particularly in India, and centuries ago they were referred to as simply pards. Worth noting: leopards like to eat dogs (both wild and domestic) and baboons as well, though their favorite prey is antelope.

429 Panther, but really a leopard

The beautiful black panther found in much of Asia is in reality a color morph of the leopard. The base color of the hairs is black, and so are the spots, so the panther gives the overall appearance of being jet black. In fact, you can see the spots clearly at certain angles.

430 The claws-out cat

You probably know that the cheetah (*Acinonyx jubatus*) is the fastest land animal, and that it relies on speed to bring down its prey. You may not know that the cheetah is the only cat whose claws are not retractable. Cheetahs feed in the same areas as lions and leopards, but there is no real competition, since cheetahs tend to hunt at morning and early afternoon when lions and leopards are dozing. Cheetahs chase down their prey and deliver a swift death bite under the victim's throat.

431 The tame one

Cheetahs, as already noted, are distinctive cats, most notably in that they have been tamed (more or less) and trained as hunting animals. Ranging over Africa and much of Asia, cheetahs were long ago tamed in India. Hunters would take them blindfolded to the hunting site and release them when the prey was sighted. Aside from the domestic cat and the caracal (see 424), the cheetah is the only cat to be truly tamed by man. Incidentally, cheetahs, since they are spotted, were often referred to in the past as "hunting leopards," and it was believed (wrongly) that they were hybrids of lions and leopards.

432 Ligers or tigons, but sterile

Scientists tell us that if you strip the hides from a lion and tiger, you can barely tell them apart. In fact, the two species are so similar that they can and occasionally do mate (only in captivity, never in the wild), and the hybrid offspring are called "ligers" or "tigons." These hybrids do not reproduce, however, since they are almost inevitably sterile.

433 The American big spotty

You might call the jaguar (*Panthera onca*) an American leopard because of its beautiful spotted coat. The jaguar ranges over much of South America, as well as Central America and Mexico, living in jungles and swamplands. In earlier times it ranged over parts of the United States. Jaguars were and are widely feared by Native Americans, and with good reason: jaguars do occasionally attack and eat humans. It is the largest cat species in the Americas.

434 The biggest

The tiger (*Panthera tigris*), the largest cat in the world, lives only in Asia. All tigers are striped, and though we assume they are all orangey in color, their color varies widely depending on location. Tigers in Russia and northern China are very light in color, and some are almost white. A male tiger may weigh up to five hundred pounds and stand five feet tall at the shoulders. Tigers do not have the beautiful manes that male lions possess, but older male tigers do have long spreading hairs on their cheeks. Tigers are good swimmers, but unlike most cats, they seldom climb trees.

435 True man-eaters?

As the biggest cats, tigers bring down some mighty large prey, including deer, cattle and wild hogs. (Interestingly, they like peacocks, also.) Alas, they do on occasion kill humans, though usually only old or disabled tigers attack people. Their reputation as man-eaters has led to extensive hunting of tigers, which has considerably reduced their populations.

436 The monkey-eater

The beautiful clouded leopard (*Neofelis nebulosa*) has very large spots on its tan coat. Found over India and much of southeast Asia, it is basically a tree dweller, and among the trees it finds its favorite foods—monkeys, squirrels and birds.

437 Cougar, puma, etc.

This beautiful, tawny-haired American species (*Felis concolor*) goes by several names—puma, cougar, mountain lion, panther, catamount, deer tiger, Mexican lion, to name a few. (Scientists seem to prefer the name puma.) Its range is wide—from southern Canada all the way to the tip of South America. It is found over much of the western

United States, where it has made itself unpopular by preying on livestock, although its usual food is deer. (Fenced-in livestock are obviously less trouble to catch than deer.) After the jaguar, it is the largest cat in the Americas. An adult male can weigh up to 275 pounds.

438 The Sunshine State cat

The official state animal of Florida is the very rare Florida panther. Scientists debate whether the panther is a subspecies of the cougar (see 437) or a separate species. The Florida panther certainly has a distinctive look, for although it generally looks like a cougar, it has a kinked tail, white spots and a distinctive swirl of fur in the middle of its back.

Cats with Humans, Beginning in Ancient Egypt . . .

It Started in Egypt

439 Egyptian mau

Here's a big surprise: the ancient Egyptians' word for cat was *mau*. Yes, the name was obviously based on the sound cats made, just as if today we were to refer to cats as "meows." There exists today a breed called the Egyptian mau (see 182), which may be (but probably isn't) a direct descendant of the ancient Egyptians' pets.

440 Cats and silos

Way back in the sixteenth century B.C., the Egyptians invented the silo—a big tower for grain storage. Good news for humans, but also good news for hungry rodents, to whom a silo was a giant buffet. The grain drew rodents, and rodents drew the small Egyptian wildcats. So naturally the Egyptians appreciated the rodent-eating predators. We really have no idea at what point the rodent killers were adopted as pets, but we can thank the Egyptians for knowing a good thing when they saw it. In terms of the human race at large, it was the beginning of a beautiful friendship.

441 Cat mummies

As you know, the ancient Egyptians mummified the human dead. They thought so highly of cats that they mummified them too—or, at least, upper-class Egyptians could afford to do so. Since the Egyptians believed that the afterlife was essentially like earthly life, they mummified mice to place in the tombs as food for the cat mummies. In 1890, over 300,000 cat mummies were found at one site in Egypt. Most were in cases of engraved wood, with the bodies wrapped in colored bandages. The world's museums display cat mummies along with the human mummies.

442 The cat battle ploy

One of the oddest stories in the history of warfare is set in ancient Egypt. Cambyses, the king of Persia, was trying to conquer the Egyptian city of Pelusia. Knowing the Egyptians thought cats were sacred, he had six hundred of his soldiers march into battle carrying cats. He suspected the Egyptians soldiers would refuse to attack, afraid they might wound a cat. He was correct, and the Persians conquered the Egyptian city.

443 Did the Egyptians really worship cats?

They were accused of it by (of course) non-Egyptians, and there is plenty of evidence that they really did worship cats, since we have paintings and carvings that show priests bowing to cats, making offerings to cats and, in general, treating the creatures as if they were indeed gods. Religion experts make fine distinctions between "venerating" and "worshipping," but the average human being doesn't, in mind or heart, grasp such distinctions. About all we can say for certain is that the ancient Egyptians truly *adored* cats as they did no other animal.

444 The old cat-woman dog-man cliché

The world has changed a lot, but one old cliché still lingers: women like cats, men like dogs. We all know exceptions to these stereotypes, but we all also know there is a bit of truth to them. The cliché goes back centuries, even to the very starting place of domestic cats: ancient Egypt. Tomb paintings of wealthy Egyptians have often shown the happy family at home, with a cat sitting under the wife's chair, a dog under her husband's chair. We can safely assume that husband and wife played with each other's pets, of course, but the stereotype is still there: cats for the women, dogs for the men.

445 Cat-head and lion-head

Among the Egyptians' various goddesses was Sekhmet, who had a lion's head on a woman's body, and thus was not too different in appearance from Bast, another goddess. Bast was sometimes called the Lady of the East (meaning the east side of the Nile River), while Sekhmet was the Lady of the West. Over time the two similar goddesses were thought to be one and the same, both regarded as symbols of fertility, motherhood, hearth and home.

446 Ancient Egyptian humor

In ancient Egyptian art, cats are depicted as sacred or as beloved pets of the household—but not always. Humans have always had a sense of humor, even in ancient times. There survives from ancient Egypt, land of the sacred cat, a drawing on papyrus dating from about 1150 B.C., showing a large lady mouse and her brood, being waited on by a bevy of cat servants.

447 Capital cat crime

You might have heard this story and assumed it was a legend: in ancient Egypt, deliberately killing a cat was a capital crime. This is fact, not legend. Indeed, a person might even be executed—or more precisely, lynched—if he killed a cat accidentally. Needless to say, it didn't happen too often.

448 Deep mourning

People grieve when they lose a pet today, but perhaps not as ostentatiously as the ancient Egyptians did when a pet cat died. The whole family would go into mourning and, as an obvious outward sign of grief, shave off their eyebrows.

449 Cats as retrievers

Say the word *retriever* and people immediately think of several breeds of dog, used to bring back the game that the hunter has shot down. But paintings on the walls of many ancient tombs in Egypt show cats being used as retrievers—specifically, bringing back ducks that had been shot by arrows or slings.

450 The oldest cat art

Precisely when the ancient Egyptians began domesticating cats is in dispute, but the oldest artwork depicting a cat dates from around 1950 B.C. Found at Beni Hasan, this wall painting shows a cat crouching beneath a woman's chair. Roughly about this same time, cat figures began to appear in hieroglyphics, the Egyptians' form of picture writing.

451 Snake hunters

One thing that is often forgotten in histories of the cat is that cats were snake killers as well as rodent killers. Various types of poisonous snakes live in

Egypt, notably the infamous asp (the species Cleopatra used to kill herself). True, a venomous snake can kill a cat as well as a human, but it appears that the ancient Egyptians learned quickly that cats' claws, teeth and swift reflexes made them competent snake killers. And, obviously, the cat's sensitive hearing and sight made them watchful for snakes entering human habitations.

452 The cat charm

Egyptians, like people everywhere, had certain symbols and figures they liked to wear as charms or amulets. One that was commonly worn was the *utchat,* the "sacred eye." It consisted of one large stylized eye, with several small cat figures engraved around it. The connection between cats and eyes was obvious enough, for the Egyptian word for cat, *mau,* not only was the sound made by cats, but also meant "to see."

453 Sacred and four-legged

Travelers to ancient Egypt got the impression that the Egyptians literally worshipped cats. Did they? Aside from the love they showed to their own pets, they did have an even higher respect for "temple animals," the animals kept at the temples of the Egyptians' many gods, one of whom was Bast, the goddess with the woman's body and cat's head.

The temples of Bast had, naturally, cats on the premises, and they were worshipped—or, more accurately, they were honored as the earthly representatives of Bast herself. Bast herself was far away in heaven, but humans could honor her—and definitely did—in the form of the temple cats.

454 Cats in dreams

Styles change—not only in clothes and furniture, but even in dream interpretation. In the twentieth century, it became trendy to believe that dreaming about a cat meant you were dreaming about sex. Not so in ancient Egypt. If you dreamed about a cat, it was a good omen but not related to sex. It was a sign of prosperity to come—specifically, a good harvest. This makes perfect sense: cats were the exterminators of rodents, which were always a threat to human food supplies, especially grains. If you dreamed of a cat, it meant your harvest—and thus your fortune—was in good hands (or good paws).

455 Magic knives

Archaeologists have unearthed numerous ivory knives in Egypt, some dating as far back as 2000 B.C. These are no ordinary household knives; they are engraved with the images of various gods and animals (and gods in animal form). Some of the knives are engraved with the images of cats, naturally. The archaeologists think these were "magic knives," more symbolic than practical, kept around as good luck charms to ward off illness, accidents and other dangers to people. Since cats protected the household from such beasties as rodents, snakes and scorpions, it was natural to engrave the good luck charms with cat imagery.

456 Ra, the Great Tomcat

You might already know that Ra is the name of the Egyptian sun god. (Or, at least, *one of* the sun gods, since the Egyptians had so many gods that their mythology was hopelessly confused.) In a myth dating around 1500 B.C., Ra journeyed to the underworld at night in the form of a cat. There he battled the serpent Apophis, whom he slayed with a large knife, ensuring that Ra could return as the sun the following morning. Numerous paintings have been found showing Ra, the "Great Tomcat," using a knife to slay Apophis.

457 Ruling From Cat City

The Egyptian pharaoh Shishak (mentioned in 2 Kings 11:40 in the Bible) ruled the country from the city of Per-Bastet, or Bubastis, a city especially sacred to the goddess Bast. In fact, the city's name means "house of the goddess Bast." Not surprisingly, one of the pharaohs of Shishak's dynasty actually ruled under the name *Pamiu*—meaning

"Tomcat," a highly appropriate name for a ruler who expects to be protected by a cat-headed goddess.

458 Cats and sistrums

In the many images of the goddess Bast found in Egypt, she is often depicted holding a sistrum, a musical instrument (or, more appropriately, noise-maker) similar to a maraca. Worship in ancient times often involved a lot of ritual dancing and music, and in the worship of Bast, large groups of women would have been dancing and rattling their sistrums. The sistrums themselves were often carved with cat images.

459 Sistrums—or Fiddles?

"Hey diddle diddle, the cat and the fiddle . . ." How did the old nursery rhyme originate? Some say the image comes from statues of cat-headed Bast, holding her instrument, the sistrum. Though the sistrum was not a stringed instrument like a fiddle, its general shape did resemble a fiddle (which came along centuries later), and in some Bast images it almost appears that the cat-headed goddess is resting it on her shoulder, just as a fiddle player would. Centuries after the end of Bast worship and after sistrums fell out of use, people who saw Bast images would assume they were statues of a cat (or cat-woman) holding a fiddle.

460 Herodotus in Greece

The Greek historian Herodotus visited Greece in the fifth century B.C. and, happily for posterity, wrote about what he saw there. He described the worship of the cat-headed goddess Bast (see 453), whom he (and other Greeks) identified with the Greek goddess Artemis (see 475). Herodotus witnessed a Bast festival at the city of Per-Bastet (see 457), attended by some 700,000 men and women. As Herodotus describes it, the "worship" turned into a veritable orgy, with lots of wine being consumed, frequent "lifting of the skirts" and a general "girls gone wild" atmosphere—which makes sense, since cats were associated with fertility and reproduction. According to Herodotus, the Bast festival drew more people together than any other festival in Egypt.

461 From Bast to Isis

Ask people the names of the Egyptian gods, and the one most likely to come to mind is Isis, one of the few gods shown in fully human form. Isis was the devoted wife and mother, and, of course, a fertility goddess. Egyptian mythology was never very consistent, so the various goddesses overlapped, and some people confused Isis with the cat-headed goddess Bast, who also symbolized motherhood and fertility. The popular cult of Isis took over much of the Bast cult, including all the cat symbolism. After Egypt was conquered by the Roman Empire, the

Isis-Bast cult spread all over the empire, even to faraway Britain, where there were worshippers of the Egyptian cat cult.

462 The cat in the moon

Did you know that the ancient Egyptians associated cats with worship of the moon? The cat was sacred to the goddess Isis, who symbolized the moon. The cat too was believed to be a symbol of the moon, partly because cats are more active after dark, partly because the pupil of the cat's eye reminded people of the waxing and waning of the moon. A cat's pupils can change from the narrowest slits to the widest circles—exactly as the moon does.

463 Killing the sacred

Religion isn't always rational or consistent, as evidenced by the fact that cats were sacrificed to the cat-headed goddess Bast. Remember that the ancient Egyptians adored cats so much that deliberately killing one was a capital crime (see 447). Cats were sacred to Bast and were kept in her temples. And yet, illogically, kittens two to four months old were sacrificed to the goddess. This seems remarkably cruel to us (and inconsistent to boot), but to the minds of the ancients, the sacrificed animals were, in dying, joining their own spiritual power to that of the goddess. Bast was taking back what was hers, and in a way we can barely grasp, the sacrificed cats were honored by becoming gifts given to the goddess.

464 The lynching

In ancient Egypt, as we've already noted, killing a cat was a capital offense. Thanks to the adoration that people felt for cats, there rarely had to be any kind of judicial trials, for the people gladly took justice into their own hands, killing an offender without waiting for the slow wheels of the legal process. As you might imagine, this kept the killing of cats to a minimum. A person who killed a cat by accident was in an awkward situation, but he could avoid lynching by running as far as possible from the dead animal and, once someone discovered the body, joining in the loud lamentation.

465 The cat drowning ritual

Egypt was for centuries regarded as the home of occult magic, and archaeologists do stumble upon evidence of this. They have found papyrus fragments inscribed with various occult rituals, among them one in which a priest (or magician) drowns a cat while uttering a spell invoking a curse upon the worshiper's enemies. The spell contains several references to the "cat-faced god," whichever god that might be, possibly the sun god Ra. Once sacrificed by drowning, the poor cat was reverently mummified and sealed up in a tomb.

466 A solar eclipse (gasp!)

We can predict solar eclipses with great accuracy today, so they never catch anyone by surprise. This wasn't so in the ancient world, and the Egyptians, like other ancient folk, took eclipses very seriously. For them it was a time to break out their sistrums, make a lot of noise with them, and pray that Ra, the sun god (and also the Great Cat), would win this battle with Apophis, the serpent monster of the darkness. There must have been an atmosphere of panic during eclipses, since it seemed that, for the moment, the Great Cat was losing out—possibly forever?—to the power of the dark.

467 Ancient images: cats, or big cats?

Imagine you are an archaeologist sorting through the items found at a dig—vases, mosaics and other items. You find images of cats—but how can you tell if these are house cats or larger wildcats like leopards and cheetahs? In some cases, you can't tell, because of the poor condition of the object—pieces broken off, weathered by time or otherwise damaged. But one general rule helps: domestic cats did (and do) have triangular-shaped ears, while leopards, cheetahs, lions, and most other big cats have rounded ears. This is reflected in ancient art—*usually*. Ancient craftsmen had talent, but they weren't always sticklers for details.

468 Freeing the captives

The Greek historian Diodorus Siculus traveled in Egypt around the year 60 B.C., and he is the source of much of what we know about the Egyptians' love of cats. According to Diodorus, when Egyptian troops entered another country, they ransomed any captive cats and brought them back to Egypt. He spoke with Egyptian priests about why they worshipped various animals, and the priests informed him that honor was owed to animals who had rendered man service in the past and present. Special honor, of course, was due to the cat for killing rodents and snakes.

469 Pagan to Christian

Egypt has been a Muslim country for so long that we forget the country followed Christianity long before Islam even existed. As Christianity spread from its home in Palestine, Egypt gradually changed its religion from pagan to Christian. Old habits die hard, and some people were slow to give up worshipping their old gods, including the cat-headed Bast. The Christian writer Clement, writing about the year A.D. 200 in the Egyptian city of Alexandria, mocked the old religion and its worship of animals and animal-headed gods. He wrote of the huge temples, each with an inner sanctum, and in that inner sanctum, curled on a purple cushion was . . . an animal, often a cat. Clement, like many Christian writers, claimed that Christians were wiser in worshipping their invisible God than pagans, who were fools to build a temple to honor a cat or crocodile.

Greeks and Romans

470 Crossing to Europe

How did cats get to Europe? Historians think that the ancient Greeks learned about cats through their trade with Egypt. The Greeks were pleased to see that Egyptians had found a perfect rodent exterminator, and an attractive, clean companion to boot. To the Greeks' dismay, the Egyptians had no interest in sharing cats with the rest of the world, so the Greeks did the obvious thing and stole several pairs and took them home to become the ancestors of Europe's cats.

471 Meet me in Greece

We don't know precisely when the Greek traders brought home cats from Egypt, but we do know they were regarded as a great curiosity at first. A marble sculpture from around 500 B.C. depicts one man with a dog on a leash encountering another man with a cat on a leash. (Dogs have been in Greece for centuries, of course.) It is obvious from the posture of the humans that cats were new enough that people weren't quite sure how dogs and cats would respond to each other.

472 No word without meaning

By the fifth century B.C., the Greeks were using the word *ailouros* to refer to the domestic cat. Ancient words were never "just words," and *ailouros* had a definite meaning—roughly speaking, it meant "moving tail," from *ailos,* "moving," and *ouros,* "tail." Apparently the ancient Greeks were impressed with the expressiveness of the cat's tail—as we are today. While dogs are also noted for having "waggily tails," perhaps what impressed the ancients was that cats seem to move their tails about even when asleep. The word *ailuros* lingers on in our modern words *ailurophilia* (love of cats) and *ailurophobia* (fear or hatred of cats).

473 Leashes and the ancient Greeks

Did the ancient Greeks know something that we don't? In the depictions of cats found on Greek vases and paintings, a cat is often shown on a leash. Today, it is a rare cat owner who can walk a pet on a leash, for most cats resist it heartily. Perhaps the Greeks knew the trick of starting a cat on a leash while still a young kitten. Or perhaps those cats depicted in Greek paintings were simply (like cats today) very unhappy and very uncomfortable with their leashes.

474 The Philosopher

The Greek philosopher Aristotle was so widely read during the Middle Ages that scholars simply referred to him as "the Philosopher." It was widely assumed that if Aristotle said it, it must be so. (Since Aristotle said that the sun and the planets revolved around Earth, we know he was wrong about quite a few things.) He wrote on almost every subject, including plants and animals, and inevitably he had something to say about cats. Regarding the mating of cats, Aristotle observed that "the female cat is peculiarly lecherous, and wheedles the male on to sexual commerce, and caterwauls during the operation." Well, he was partly right: the female does caterwaul, but it's doubtful she is any more lecherous than the male, and tomcats do not have to be "wheedled" into sex.

475 Catty Artemis

In Greek mythology, the goddess Artemis was the twin sister of the god Apollo, and a goddess of hunting, the moon and chastity. Greeks who traveled in ancient Egypt had the habit of identifying the various Egyptian gods with the Greek gods, and the Greeks identified their Artemis with the Egyptians' Bast, the cat-headed goddess of hearth and home. The identification made some sense: cats are hunters (like Artemis) and roam at night (and so are linked to the moon). But the Egyptians never connected Bast, or cats, with the concept of chastity, and Artemis was very much a virgin goddess. Yet, oddly, Artemis the virgin goddess is sometimes regarded as a fertility goddess—which makes no sense at all. But then, mythology hasn't always been logical.

476 Bosomy and catty

The temple of the goddess Artemis in the city of Ephesus was one of the Seven Wonders of the ancient world. Artemis, as already noted, was a virgin goddess—but also a fertility goddess. You can see the fertility aspect clearly in some of her statues found at Ephesus, where she is depicted having dozens of breasts. Some of these images show her body engraved with images of cats, and the cats themselves bear large (and very human-shaped) breasts.

477 Athena the cat

The Greek goddess Athena personified wisdom and handicrafts, and was the favorite goddess of Athens. While the animal usually associated with her was the owl, she also has some cat connections, and in some parts of Greece, cats were considered sacred to her. She was often referred to as *Athena Glaukopis*—Athena Shining-eyed—calling to mind the eyes of a cat shining in the dark.

478 In heat (literally)

The Greek author Claudius Aelianus (c. 170–235) wrote *De Natura Animalium,* "On the Nature of Animals," which gives some insights into what the ancients knew (or thought they knew) about beasts. He observed that a female cat in heat was "extremely lustful," but that she did not enjoy the actual mating, since the male cat's semen was "extremely hot and fiery, and burns the female." Not true, but certainly a colorful explanation as to why female cats do seem to find mating very painful.

479 Greeks go Italian

The ancient Greeks were a seafaring people, and as noted elsewhere (see 470), they acquired cats through trading with Egypt. As Greeks traveled, they took their cats with them, including to their colonies in southern Italy. Archaeologists have found coins in that region, dating from around 750 B.C., showing a man (the colony's founder) seated in a chair, while a cat on hind legs plays with something in the man's hand. Another coin from about the same period shows a man with a cat seated behind him.

480 Roman PR

The Roman scholar known as Pliny the Elder (A.D. 27–79) wrote an encyclopedic work, *Natural History.* In it he describes the domestic cat, which apparently he learned about through Romans living in Egypt. Pliny's writings helped spread the knowledge of these mysterious, fascinating creatures across the wide Roman Empire.

481 Diana as cat

The Romans often identified the goddess Diana with the Greek goddess Artemis (see 475). The poet Ovid, in his famous work *Metamorphoses,* states that during an epic war between the gods and the giants, the gods temporarily fled to Egypt, where they hid in the form of animals. Diana took the form of a cat, which is appropriate, since Artemis was often associated with cats. Ovid's poem reflects the Roman understanding of why the ancient Egyptians worshipped many of their gods in animal form.

482 Etruscan cat decor

The Museum of Fine Arts in Boston has a bowl dating from the sixth century B.C. that was produced by Etruscans who dwelled in Italy. We can safely assume that Etruscans not only had cats but were very fond of them, for the bowl's rim is decorated with the carvings of four cat heads.

483 The Roman dog fixation

The Greeks kept both dogs and cats as pets, as did the Romans, but the Romans never took to cats as much as the Greeks did. While the Romans sometimes set up tombstones for their departed dogs and hoped they would see their dogs in the afterlife, cats were not as highly regarded, especially by Roman men. The Romans kept to the old stereotype—cats for women, dogs for men—although there were lots of exceptions, as noted elsewhere in this section.

484 Roman tomcats

The ancient Romans have a well-deserved reputation for their lax sexual morals, which is evident in their literature. The dramatist Plautus (circa 251–184 B.C.) wrote numerous comedies, and some of them deal very bluntly with sexual themes. Some of his plays, written in Latin, use the term *feles virginaria*. Translated literally, this means "cat of the virgins," but Plautus used a different meaning, "cat who preys on virgins"—that is, "tomcat," the human male seducer of women. Other Roman plays refer to a man who is a *feles pullaria,* "cat of young women," which, again, refers to the seductive male human.

485 From ancient Pompeii to today

Some things never change. If you have a birdbath in your yard, you've no doubt seen your cat hungrily eye the birds in it and probably try to climb it. (A *good* birdbath is unclimbable, of course.) Archaeologists have dug up a similar scene from Pompeii, the Italian city famously destroyed by the eruption of the volcano Vesuvius. A mosaic from the ruins of Pompeii, dating from about the year A.D. 79, shows a spotted cat eyeing three long-tailed birds in a birdbath.

486 Pet name "Kitten"

You might recall the adorable daughter nicknamed "Kitten" on the old TV sitcom *Father Knows Best.* Well, "Kitten" was around as a pet name for a girl long before television. Among ancient Romans, the Latin names Felicla and Felicula were popular among women, and both names mean "little cat" or "kitten." There are tombstones with Felicla or Felicula carved in them, and some of the tombstones even have a figure of a cat carved into them. The names Catta and Cattula—both meaning "cat," of course—were also used for Roman women. And though they were more rare, the names Feliculus, Cattus and Cattius were also borne by some Roman men.

487 *Felis* morphing to *cattus*

The early Romans used *felis* to refer to the domestic cat, but in time the word *cattus* replaced it. When did the change occur? We can't be certain, but we do have a clue, since we know that by the sixth century A.D., one unit of the Pretorian Guards (the emperor's personal bodyguards) was known as the Catti, meaning "cats." We can assume that these soldiers did not see anything negative—certainly nothing *feminine*—in applying the name "cats" to themselves.

488 Soldiers and cats?

Yes, the Roman armies that marched through and conquered much of Europe and northern Africa carried cats with them and kept them at their forts, which has been proven by archaeologists who have dug up cat remains. While Roman men in general liked dogs (see 483), cats were useful for keeping rodents out of the soldiers' food supplies and from gnawing on bowstrings and other leather goods. The Roman troops apparently admired the cats as predators, and perhaps they saw themselves as cats, preying on the "barbarians" as cats preyed on the troublesome rodents.

489 Nautical hood ornaments

Cats have a long association with ships and sailors and were considered lucky to have on ships. In fact, many ships of the Roman Empire had a carving of a cat on the prow. It's also worth noting that many Roman ships bore the name Isis, the Egyptian goddess associated with cats (see 461) and regarded as the protector of sailors.

490 The Roman goddess Liberty

Americans were not the first people to have a Statue of Liberty. To the ancient Romans, Liberty was worshipped as a goddess. Appropriately, the goddess's pet was the most freedom-loving animal, the cat. The goddess Liberty was often depicted holding a cup in one hand and a broken scepter in the other, with a cat lying at her feet.

491 Cat in the afterlife

It's always touching to look at the grave of a child, and certainly this is true of a very ancient gravestone found in France. Dating from around A.D. 100 (when France was the Roman province of Gaul), the gravestone has a statue of a young boy named Laetus holding a cat in his arms.

492 Venus and friend

Venus was, of course, the Roman goddess of love, though it might be more accurate to call her the goddess of *erotic* love—or maybe just the goddess of lust. At any rate, paintings and statues of Venus sometimes depict her with a cat, and perhaps the Romans fancied that Venus was herself somewhat like a cat—cuddly and adorable at times, but aloof at others, and even occasionally fierce and vicious. In short, predictably unpredictable, as love is, and as cats are.

493 Cats versus Ferrets

Ferrets, like all members of the weasel family, are predators with skinny, flexible bodies. They readily go after rodents and rabbits by burrowing into their prey's hiding places. People in the ancient world often used them as rodent exterminators, but ferrets lost favor as cats became more popular—and for the obvious reason that people have never completely trusted ferrets. Families, especially those with small children, feared that ferrets would turn vicious and bite someone (which happened at times, and still does now). Ferrets are still around, but it was inevitable that they would be eclipsed by cats.

Pagans and Christians

494 In merry olde England

Those of us who had English-speaking ancestors may well wonder: when were cats introduced to Britain? We don't know the exact date, of course, but a house cat skeleton was found at a Roman villa in southeast England, dating from around A.D. 100. At this time, England was the Roman province Britannia, and it would be several hundred more years before the island was invaded by the Angles, the Germanic tribe that gradually turned Britannia into Angle-land, or England.

495 Cats and Celts

Those of us with Scotch and Irish ancestry may find this a little embarrassing: the Celts, our long-ago ancestors in the British Isles, were notorious for mass sacrifices of cats. Specifically, huge numbers of cats were placed in giant wicker baskets and slowly burned to death. The other method of sacrifice was swifter but no less horrid: cats were thrown to their deaths from great heights. The early Celts apparently did not think highly of humans either, for they were notorious for using these same methods to sacrifice their fellow man. The Romans were horrified at human sacrifice and stopped it wherever Roman authority spread, and it appears that they lessened (but didn't totally eliminate) cat sacrifice as well.

496 Why did the Celts do it?

Did the ancient Celts sacrifice cats because they hated them? Not necessarily. As noted elsewhere (see 463), even the cat-loving Egyptians sacrificed cats. Why the Celts chose to burn huge numbers of cats is not known. It appears that Celts, like other ancient people, associated cats with fertility, and so a mass sacrifice of cats to the gods of fertility had a certain odd logic to it. We still have a lot to learn about the Celts.

497 Early PETA

People for the Ethical Treatment of Animals (PETA) is a well-known group today, sometimes controversial for its attitudes (such as its antifur stance). No such organization existed in the ancient world, and generally the ancients were rather more callous toward animals than we are today. Even while they doted on their pet cats and dogs, the ancients had no qualms about sacrificing animals, including cats, to the gods. Indeed, animal sacrifice was almost universal in the old days. But as Christianity spread, animal sacrifices halted (or at least weren't as common). Christians worshipped only one God, who did not require the sacrificing of beasts. So in a way the cat, and all other animals, got a boost in status as paganism faded.

498 Christians with cats in tow

While Christians have occasionally been anticat (more about that in the next entries), in the past there was a connection between the spread of Christianity and the spread of cats. Christianity began in Palestine, right next door to Egypt. In its pre-Christian days, Egypt practically embargoed the exporting of cats (after all, they were sacred), but as Christianity penetrated Egypt, the cat embargo was lifted, and cats spread north into Europe along with Christianity.

499 Christians versus cats?

Were the early Christians anticat, as has sometimes been alleged? Not at all, though they did, as noted elsewhere, oppose the sacrifice of cats and other animals. One thing that Christianity inherited from Judaism was the hatred of idolatry—that is, worshipping anything but God, who is invisible. To both Christians and Jews, bowing down to an animal, or a statue of an animal, was a terrible sin, for only God deserved to be worshipped. So, naturally, Christians were appalled at the honor paid to cats in the worship of goddesses like Bast, Artemis and Isis. They were antiidolatry not anticat. Regrettably, in time the antiidolatry attitude would show itself in displays of genuine cruelty to cats. Read on.

500 In faraway Wales

We are fortunate to possess copies of laws mandated in the tenth century by Howel the Good, the ruler of Wales. Howel's law code stated that a newborn kitten was worth one penny, and an adult cat (able to kill mice) was worth four pennies. If a cat was killed, the owner was recompensed four pennies. Just to let you know the relative value: a mature sheep or goat was also worth four pennies, while a goose or hen was worth only one penny. If a couple divorced and had only one cat between them, the husband got the cat, but if they had two cats, the wife got one, too.

501 Illuminated cats

We sometimes refer to the early Middle Ages as the Dark Ages, but the times don't seem so dark if you see some of the beautifully illuminated manuscripts, the handwritten books copied in monasteries. Monks embellished the writing with ornate letters and colors and drawings in the page margins. Some of these volumes, such as the famous Book of Kells, still exist, and they overflow with sketches of real and mythical animals, including cats. Apparently the monks who produced these masterpieces thought rather highly of the natural world in general and cats in particular.

502 Cats and Vikings

Can you picture the Vikings, those ruthless pirates and raiders, enjoying the company of cats? Well, the archaeologists have dug up a number of Viking living sites and found evidence that these fierce folk did keep cats but not necessarily as pets. They mainly kept cats for their pelts. It appears that a cat was allowed to reach the age of about a year—long enough to reach full size, that is—then was killed and skinned. The pelts were (like furs throughout human history) used as articles of trade. (If this is unpleasant for you to read, please be aware that it is unpleasant to write about also.)

503 The Templars

The Knights Templars were a military-religious order established around 1118 to protect Christian pilgrims in the Holy Land. They lived in Jerusalem at first but later spread all over Europe, and in time the order became rich from gifts from wealthy patrons. In 1307 the bankrupt king of France, Philip IV, tried to acquire the Templars' wealth by starting a smear campaign, accusing the Templars of all kinds of crimes—including the heresy of worshipping a cat. The campaign worked, and in 1312 the pope dissolved the order. Several Templars were executed. It was neither the first nor the last time that a group or individual was sullied with the accusation of cat worshipping.

504 Cats and Crusaders

It's worth remembering that the Crusades, the medieval wars between the Muslims and the Christians, resulted in Christians learning about Muslim culture, including becoming aware of the Muslims' love for cats. You might say that the Crusades planted the seeds of the idea that cats were associated with a "bad" religion (Islam). That, coupled with the fact that the old pagan religions associated cats with goddesses like Bast, Isis and Artemis, shows you why the Christian Church sometimes took a dim view of cats. To the Christians of the

Middle Ages, the cat appeared to be the mascot of the old religion (paganism, which was always threatening to resurface) and of the new rival religion (Islam, which was being spread by force at the expense of Christianity).

505 The antiwitch anticat mandate

In 1233, Pope Gregory IX issued a famous (and infamous) decree, *Vox in Rama,* directed toward suppressing heresy and witchcraft in Catholic Europe. This led to the persecution of those who were suspected of witchcraft and, alas, to the killing of countless black cats, since it was widely believed that Satan and his demons consorted in the form of black cats with human beings. There's no doubt that many of the so-called witches were innocent—and there's no doubt that some of them probably did believe they were worshipping Satan. But if there was any truly innocent party, it was certainly the many cats who were exterminated for no other reason than having black coats. (A curious footnote: Pope Gregory IX was a good friend of the gentle, animal-loving Francis of Assisi.)

506 The Celtic rite, revisited

The pagan Celts, as already noted, were infamous for sacrificing large numbers of cats in wicker baskets, who were roasted over a fire while they screamed in agony. The ancient ritual persisted for centuries in some parts of Europe and was conducted by two very different groups. One were the "neo-pagans," who existed within the Christian culture but were still pagans "on the inside," conducting the old religion by night, out of sight of the church authorities. The other cat burners were, at times, the Christians themselves, who associated cats (especially black ones) with Satanism and witchcraft.

507 Several hundred years of "civilized" Europe

Human beings aren't perfect, and every civilization has its dark side. For hundreds of years, Europe was (on the surface) Christianized, yet there was sporadic persecution of cats, which modern people find inconceivable. How could these people have been so callous to innocent creatures like cats? You can blame Christianity for being anticat, but that isn't quite fair, because the truth is that people in old Europe were generally callous toward all animals. "Sports" that we would consider horrible, like bull baiting and bear baiting, were enjoyed by people of all classes. Even intelligent and upper-class folk would watch with interest as animals in a pit or ring tore one another to shreds.

Near East and Far East

508 No Good Book cats

Are cats mentioned in the Bible? Lions and leopards are, yes, but not so the common house cat. However, the brief Book of Baruch, found in the Apocrypha, does mention cats prowling about the temples of pagan gods. Apparently the author of Baruch associated cats with idolatrous religions, which might help explain why ancient Israel did not have a high opinion of domestic cats. Israelites never forgot they had once been slaves in Egypt, nor did they forget that their cruel Egyptian masters had been fond of cats.

Lions and leopards, as already noted, were another matter. In biblical times, both cats lived in Israel, and while they were on occasion a threat to human life, mostly they were admired for their magnificence and swiftness. Samson, the hulking strongman of Israel, killed a lion with his bare hands, and the spunky shepherd boy David (later king of Israel) also felled a lion that was threatening his flocks. It was the prophet Jeremiah who posed the classic question "Can a leopard change his spots?"

509 Even in Israel . . .

House cats are not mentioned in the Bible, but archaeologists found indications that the ancient Israelites kept cats, or at least their non-Israelite neighbors did. A small ivory cat figure, dating from about 1700 B.C., was found at the biblical city of Lachish.

510 Cleanliness next to godliness

As mentioned earlier, the Bible makes no mention of domestic cats (see 508). However, the Talmud, the Jews' huge collection of oral tradition, compiled several centuries after the time of Christ, does mention cats, praising their cleanliness. We can safely assume that if the Jewish teachers praised cats, it's safe to assume that cats were present in many Jewish homes.

511 Muhammad the cat lover

You may be aware that many Muslims today consider dogs to be undesirable animals, signs of the decadence of Europe and America. The antidog tradition goes back centuries, recalling that dogs in the ancient Middle East were loathsome street scavengers, despised by humans. (You see this in the Bible, where dogs are always mentioned disparagingly.) However, Muhammad, the founder of Islam, was fond of cats and had a pet female cat named Muezza. According to legend, the cat was sleeping on the sleeve of his robe, and Muhammad cut off the sleeve rather than disturb the cat's sleep.

512 Run of the mosque

As already noted, the prophet Muhammad was fond of cats, and Muslims have always had a high opinion of cats, which are allowed to wander freely through mosques. During the Middle Ages, Christian warriors from Europe spent time in Muslim countries fighting the Crusades and learned much about Muslims, including their affection for cats. Some historians speculate that anti-Muslim feelings may have been at the root of Europeans' growing antipathy to cats during this period. That is, the people of Europe began to think of cats as "those things that the wicked Muslims are so fond of." (There is a flip side to this, which still lingers today: Muslims in the Near East generally detest dogs, partly because dogs are a favorite pet of "decadent" Americans and Europeans. What a pity that innocent animals have often been the victims of human culture wars.)

513 On the tiger's coattails

Long before the domestic cat reached Asia, the tiger was already there, impressing humans with its strength and grace—and, no doubt, its occasional eating of human beings. As the domestic cat was carried eastward from Egypt, it met with a warm reception, partly because it was a perceived as a "minitiger"—not as powerful (or dangerous) as its mighty cousin but every bit as graceful and mysterious. Asians could admire and fear the tiger, and admire and love their domestic tigerettes.

514 The high road to China

How did cats reach Asia? Probably through trade with Europe, specifically, the trade in Chinese silk. Europeans were happy to exchange cats for silk, and the Chinese eagerly brought the elegant rodent hunters back home. Among the Chinese of centuries ago, the cat became a symbol of peace and family serenity.

515 Silk guardians

We tend to associate cats, in their role of rodent killers, as protectors of grain and other human food. That much is true, but in the Orient cats found themselves as guardians of the silk industry. Rats and mice were a constant threat, not so much for chewing the cloth (though that did happen) but for devouring the silkworm cocoons. China and Japan gave high praise to the precocious mousers that protected a vital part of the economy.

516 Pampered cats in Japan

According to an old tradition, cats were introduced into Japan from China, and the imperial palace in Kyoto had cats by the year 999. However, the upper-class Japanese pampered and fed the cats and did not let them play their usual role of rodent hunters.

Over time, as rodents proliferated, the Japanese assumed the obvious: maybe we should let our pampered pets act as nature intended and benefit ourselves in the process.

Coming to America

517 Pre-Columbus

Scientists frequently find fossils of big cats in America, and the famous La Brea tar pits in California have yielded remains of the *Smilodon,* the famous saber-tooth cat (see 395). But so far no remains of the house cat, *Felis catus,* have turned up. There would be no house cats in America until Europeans brought them over. Most of the smaller wildcats of America are described in chapter 6.

518 The Jamestown gang

Did the first English settlers in North America bring cats with them? Almost certainly. Unfortunately, some of the poor cats met the same fate as their human owners: they died. You might recall that the English settled in Virginia at a site they named Jamestown. This was 1607. The winter of 1609–1610 was known as the "starving time" because many people died of hunger, and the survivors barely scraped by on whatever food they could find—possums, rodents, snakes and, alas, the cats they had brought from England.

519 English meets native

You might recall the old story of Pocahontas, the young Native American girl who saved the life of the English settler John Smith, who was about to be executed by the girl's father, a chief named Powhatan. Sometime before this incident, relations between the Native Americans and the Jamestown settlers had been warmer, and at some point the English had presented Powhatan with one of the domestic cats they had brought from England. Powhatan and the other Native Americans were intrigued by the cat, which resembled the American bobcats but was, of course, amazingly tame.

520 Mayflower cats?

We know for certain that the Pilgrims who sailed to America on the *Mayflower* in 1620 had dogs with them. Did they have cats? Historians who study colonial New England feel certain that the Pilgrims brought cats, since cats were considered indispensable mousers on ships. Plus, for all the Pilgrims knew, there were no domestic cats in America (which was true). It's rather pleasant to think of cats as well as dogs being present at the very first Thanksgiving in America in 1621.

Lies, Folklore, Myths and Legends

521 Sucking an infant's breath

Not so long ago, many families were reluctant to have a cat as a pet while there were babies in the house. Why? A cat, so the tale went, might kill the infant by "sucking its breath." Ridiculous, yes, but rooted in a common occurrence: a cat would be attracted to any milk sticking to a child's mouth, and no doubt many a parent walked into the nursery to find a cat sniffing or licking a baby's mouth and nose. A cat can't literally suck the breath from an infant, of course, but it's probable that a few cases of crib death got blamed on the family cat.

522 Nine lives?

The notion that cats have nine lives has been around for centuries, and it is obviously based on the fact that cats are rather tough creatures, true survivors in a threatening world. They seem to escape inevitable death at times, so clearly they are blessed with more than one life. But why nine? No one is quite sure, except that humans have always considered three to be a "good" number, and thus a lucky one, and nine (three times three) is even better. "Cats have nine lives" is just another way of saying "Cats are very lucky creatures."

523 Good luck or bad?

If a black cat crosses your path, is it good luck or bad luck? Black cats symbolize evil to many people, so in many countries, including the United States, a black cat crossing your path is a bad omen that means evil is nearby. In Britain, however, it is considered a good omen, for it indicates that evil has passed you by.

524 "Contemptible sneaks"

Sneaky is a word associated with cats, and a cat hater often puts it at the top of his List of Reasons to Detest Cats. Cat lovers scratch their heads over this. Yes, cats are sneaky—and why not, since stealth is a necessary element in hunting (as every human hunter knows). They walk silently, stalk patiently, then make a quick and lethal pounce. Perhaps their fabled sneakiness disturbs some people, the type of people who don't want an animal entering (or leaving) a room with no sound at all. For us cat lovers, sneakiness is part of the total appeal of the cat.

525 Lucky Dick Whittington

There really was a Richard Whittington, who served as the lord mayor of London in the early

1400s. He was real, but the cat legends connected with him probably aren't. According to the stories, Dick was a poor country boy hoping to make a fortune in London. He worked for a merchant who was sending a ship to Morocco, and Dick offered his cat to the ship. Morocco was besieged by mice, and since Dick's cat became the country's savior, the king of Morocco paid Dick an exorbitant price for the mouser. Dick built his fortune on this and became a man of substance. Naturally he came, in time, to get his cat back.

526 Plutarch's crackpot theory

The Greek author Plutarch wrote one of the great classics of ancient literature, *Parallel Lives,* brief biographies of notable Greeks and Romans. Plutarch was a brilliant man but, like most intellectuals, had a few crackpot ideas floating around in his mind. Take this one, for example: he thought a female cat produced one cat in her first litter, two in her second, and so on until she reached the magic number of twenty-eight, at which time she ceased bearing kittens. Well, no female cat ever bore twenty-eight in one litter, of course. Plutarch based that number on the old connection of cats with the moon: there are twenty-eight days in a lunar month, so Plutarch figured a female should bear twenty-eight kittens. As I said, a crackpot idea, but an amusing one.

527 The hellhound (and hellcat) goddess

In Greek mythology, Hecate was a sinister goddess associated with the underworld and magic, usually of the evil sort. Sorceresses like Medea were in league with Hecate, and there were all sorts of spells and incantations directed to her in the practice of magic. It was believed that Hecate was active at night (naturally), and that she often appeared at crossroads, sometimes accompanied by hellhounds (whatever they were), and perhaps even had a hell-hound head herself. But, alternatively, Hecate was often said to take the form of a cat—black, of course. Considering what a sinister goddess she was, it isn't hard to see why the Christian Church might form a low opinion of black cats, given their connection with this goddess of night and sorcery.

528 Buddha versus the cat

In a story from Sri Lanka (formerly called Ceylon), a young follower of the Buddha had fallen in love and wanted to give up the monastic life and find happiness with the woman who had captured his heart. The Buddha spun a fable for the man: a female cat saw a rooster in a tree and promised to marry him if he would come down. The rooster refused and continued to live. The Buddha's point: the woman was a devouring temptress as fatal to the man as the cat would be to the rooster. A curious story and not very flattering to either cats or women.

529 Cat as arbitrator

An old cat fable told by the French author La Fontaine (1621–1695) goes this way: a rabbit and weasel go to an old cat to ask him to settle a dispute between them. The cat tells them to sit on a scale so he can "weigh the case." They do so—and while they are near him, he kills them. Well, it *does* settle their dispute, but not in the way they had hoped.

530 Wake me for the funeral

Cats are generally well thought of in eastern Asia, yet there is an old story that casts the cat in a bad light. According to the story, when the funeral procession of the Buddha passed by, all the animals turned out for mourning—all except the cat, who slept placidly through the whole thing. For this reason the cat was not numbered among the creatures under the Buddha's protection. In another version of the story, all the animals were called to the bedside of the dying Buddha, but the cat (naturally) was asleep. Still one more version: the dying Buddha stated that the first twelve animals to reach his bedside would be given immortality, but the snoozing cat was not among them.

531 Fairy godcat?

Think of Cinderella and you can't help but think of her kindly fairy godmother, the magic-working lady usually depicted as grayhaired and matronly. But the Cinderella story in some of its older forms had no kindly lady: the magical being who aided poor Cinderella was a *cat*—not at all surprising when you consider that cats were associated with the occult and magic. (An obvious question, though: did the cat turn Cinderella's mice into horses so he wouldn't be tempted to eat them?)

532 Vampire cats

Asians have generally thought highly of cats but not always. In one old folk tale of Japan, a demonic cat is a sort of vampire. He attacks a young woman, sucks out her blood and then takes over her identity. In his new guise he proceeds to gradually suck the lifeblood from the girl's fiancé, until a servant exposes the cat-woman as an impostor. Incidentally, in Japanese artwork it is very easy to tell real cats from demon cats: the demon cats have two tails.

533 Lilith, the First Mrs. Adam

In old Jewish legends, Adam's had a wife before Eve—Lilith, who was a real demon. Lilith constantly worked mischief upon Adam's human descendants, turning into a vampire cat by night and sucking the blood of the living, especially infants. In most versions of the story the vampire cat is (naturally) black.

534 Russian wisdom

Consider this old Russian proverb: "A man and a dog for the yard, a cat and a woman for the house." Call it sexist if you like, but there's a measure of truth in it, since no one (male or female) can walk a cat the way one walks a dog. Historically cats have been associated with the house (after all, they're supposed to catch mice there) while dogs were expected to accompany the family hunter (the man, naturally) and aid him in bringing home game. Even today there is still some of the old prejudice lingering in the idea that "real men" prefer dogs to cats.

535 Woman as shelter

Who wears the pants in the family? You would expect that the answer would be, "The man, of course." Not necessarily. In one old story, probably from Africa, the cat seeks a bigger creature to protect him. Each time he finds a protector, a larger predator kills off the protector. So he finally puts himself under the protection of a man. But when the man enters home, he is chased from the house by his angry wife. The cat concludes that the woman is the strongest protector.

536 Madonna kittens

Here's a pleasant legend: long ago Italians told a story that at the time that Mary gave birth to Jesus in the stable in Bethlehem, a cat produced a litter of kittens in the same stable. Because of their birth near the Christian Savior, all those kittens—and all their descendants as well—have crosses marked on their backs.

537 The Nativity cat

So why does the tabby cat have the familiar *M* mark on his forehead? Here is as pretty an explanation as you could find: in the stable at Bethlehem, Mary had trouble getting the infant Jesus to fall asleep. None of the beasts in the stable was able to help, but in came a tabby cat, who lay next to baby Jesus. The cat purred contentedly, and the baby fell asleep. Mary was so grateful that she blessed the cat, who ever since has had the *M*—for Mary, or Madonna—on the forehead.

538 Judas and the cat

In the New Testament Gospels, Jesus is betrayed by Judas Iscariot, one of his twelve disciples. In artwork this traitor was often shown as a redhead (mostly to distinguish him from the other eleven disciples) and, oddly, was sometimes shown with a cat at his feet. There is no mention of cats in the New Testament (see 508), so what is the connection with Judas? Probably the painters were providing a visual illustration of the phrase "turn the cat in the pan"—meaning, to change sides or to be a traitor.

539 The doubtful cat man

In the Bible, Thomas was one of Jesus' twelve apostles, the one who did not believe Jesus had risen from the grave until he had actually touched him. (Hence the phrase "doubting Thomas.") According to old legends, Thomas later preached the gospel in faraway India and was eventually martyred there. In one story, Thomas was en route to India as part of a caravan that included an Egyptian merchant. The merchant's beloved cat was asleep in his lap, and Thomas commented on the cat's peacefulness. The merchant commented that his business kept him constantly worried, and that he wished he could find the peace his cat possessed. Thomas told him that he must first find peace with God, and the merchant became one of Thomas's first converts. He gave Thomas the cat as a gift, and Thomas gave him the Greek name Irene, meaning "peace."

540 Hissing Agatha

Saint Agatha was, so the story goes, a Christian virgin who was martyred during one of the Roman persecutions of the faithful. She became a popular saint afterward, and her feast was celebrated on February 5. In many areas of Europe women observed the day by refraining from work. Legend had it that a woman caught working on Saint Agatha's Day would be confronted by the saint herself—in the form of a hissing cat.

541 Jerome's lion—or cat?

Saint Jerome (circa 342–420) was famous for producing the Vulgate, a Latin translation of the Bible. The studious man never married, and he became the patron saint of scholars. In the many paintings and sculptures of Jerome, he is shown writing at his desk, with his favorite pet nearby. Sometimes the pet is a cat, sometimes a lion—based on the legend that he pulled a thorn from a lion's paw and that the lion became devoted to him afterward. We can probably assume that his real pet was a cat, not a lion. Considering how many writers are fond of cats, it is appropriate that Jerome, the patron of bookish types, would have owned one.

542 Francis the animal lover (usually)

Heaven knows how many lawns and gardens are adorned with statues of Saint Francis of Assisi, the rich Italian boy who gave up his wealth, lived as a pauper and was continually in touch with both God and nature. Francis is almost a patron saint for animal lovers, but according to one legend, he almost learned to hate mice. Satan decided that Francis was simply too Christlike, and to test the saint's holiness, he sent a horde of mice to vex him. The mice made his life a living hell, but God and the angels saw the saint's plight and sent him a spunky tomcat named Felix (yes, really), who made short work of the troublesome rodents.

543 The Finnish Finish

Few people are familiar with the mythology of Finland, but some of it can be found in the old Finnish epic the *Kalevala*. We learn from this ancient poem that the Finns (before the country became Christian, that is) believed that a sleigh drawn by cats arrived to fetch their souls to heaven (or elsewhere) at the time of death. Most cat owners would consider that a lovely way to be introduced to the afterlife.

544 Cat-hold or monkey-hold?

Hindus who worship the god Rama have long debated the cat-or-monkey question. It goes like this: does Rama save a person with that person's cooperation, or without it? Some say that the person must cooperate, that he must "hold on" to the god as a baby monkey clings to its mother's back. Others say that Rama does all the work of saving, just as a mother cat picks up the kitten by the scruff of the neck, with no effort on the kitten's part. Many Rama worshippers identify themselves as "cat-hold" or "monkey-hold."

545 The lady in the cat chariot

Norse mythology is concerned with the various gods worshipped in Scandinavia and Germany in the distant past. One of the favorite deities was the goddess Freyja. She and her brother Freyr both symbolized fertility, and since many people in ancient times associated cats with fertility, Freyja was transported in a chariot drawn by cats.

546 "Bless you" in Persian

Elsewhere in this book we've looked at the scientific origins of domestic cats. The ancient Persians had a more poetic view of the cat's origin—no doubt false, but much more interesting than science. According to the Persian myth, the cat was created from the sneeze of a lion.

547 Maine coons . . . and the queen of France

The French court in the 1700s was home to numerous cats (see 700) and the ill-fated Queen Marie Antoinette, who was sent to the guillotine during the French Revolution, had herself been a cat fancier. While Marie and her equally ill-fated husband, King Louis XVI, watched the Revolution unfold, numerous plots were hatched to help the royal pair escape to elsewhere in Europe—or to America. According to an old legend, Queen Marie sent her cats ahead of her to America, and they became the ancestors of the Maine coon cats. Nonsense, surely, but pleasant nonsense.

548 The source of yoga

Some legends are just downright absurd, but here's one that has some logic to it: an Indian prince was frustrated and anxious, unable to find inner peace.

He withdrew to the forest and was taught the elements of yoga by—what else?—a cat. While this never really happened, can you imagine any animal being more qualified than a cat to teach the way to finding peace and tranquility?

549 "Cat on its brain"

Here's an old British weather tidbit: "Cat on its brain, it's going to rain." This expression refers to a cat's nap pose: curled up so the top of his head touches the floor. Assume that this is as scientific as the numerous other bits of cat-related weather folklore.

550 Good angel v. bad angel

There are lots of myths connecting cats to death, particularly impending death. A bit of old Italian folk wisdom holds seeing two cats fighting means imminent death for the person who sees them (or someone dear to the person who sees them). The two cats are believed to represent a good angel and a bad angel (demon, that is) fighting over the soul of the person who is about to die.

551 The reincarnation explanation

Belief in reincarnation is widespread in many parts of Asia, particularly in India. This belief is at the root of an old explanation for why some people are so afraid of cats: in a previous lifetime, that person must have been a rat or a mouse.

552 The flip side of "cats suck a baby's breath"

There's no truth to the old myth about cats sucking babies' breath (see 521), but there's also no truth to the old Russian peasant custom of putting a cat into an infant's cradle in the belief doing so would drive away evil spirits. Both are equally absurd, but at least the Russian myth showed a more positive view of cats.

553 Year of the cat in Vietnam

If you've ever dined in a Chinese restaurant, you've probably seen the placemats explaining the Chinese zodiac, with twelve different animals assigned to each year in a cycle of twelve years. There is no cat in the Chinese zodiac, but there is a rabbit; in the Vietnamese variation of the Chinese calendar, the cat replaces the rabbit. People born in a "year of the cat" are (as you might guess) supposed to be aloof and devious, but also loving. The last year of the cat was 1999.

554 The pussy willow legend

According to one old tale, a mother cat was crying mournfully by a riverside because a human had thrown her litter of kittens into the river to drown them. A willow tree by the river took pity on the mama cat and drooped its branches in the water, and the kittens grabbed hold, saving their lives. As a reminder of that deed of kindness, the willow became the pussy willow, each spring bursting forth with puffy little "kittens" on its twigs.

555 A warm day in China

A cat's nose is usually cool to the touch, but according to a bit of Chinese folklore, it is warm on one day of the year: June 21, the day of the summer solstice, the longest day of the year.

556 Strangers and grooming

Here's a centuries-old bit of cat lore that is (almost) a snippet of poetry: if a cat washes behind his ear, a stranger will appear. Over the year this piece of folk wisdom got refined somewhat: washing behind a left ear meant the stranger was a woman, washing behind the right ear meant it was a man.

557 Purring and spinning

Given people's affection for cats, and especially the sound of a cat purring, some folk tales had to arise to explain why cats purr. One goes this way: a lovely princess loved a handsome prince, but a witch put a curse on the two, and the princess, sealed up in a room, had to spin a large amount of thread in only a few days or the prince would die. But her three cats came to her aid, and she was able to finish with the thread. Afterward, the cats were given the ability to purr, a reminder of the sound of the spinning wheel.

558 Butter Fingers

Or butter toes, to be more precise. Given that some cats like to wander off, there are some old superstitions about how to keep cats at home. One, from Britain, goes this way: when you bring a cat to your home for the first time, smear butter on his paws. He will lick off the butter, of course, and will connect the delightful taste to his new home, ensuring he will always return there.

559 Cat v. crab

Europeans and Americans are familiar with the fable of the tortoise and the hare. The Japanese have their own fable of the fast and cocky critter losing to the (presumably) slower one. As the fable goes, a cat and crab decided to race, and the cat was supremely confident about beating the crab. The crab was slower, but smart: he hooked a claw onto the speeding cat's tail, then skittered across the finish line, just ahead of the cat.

560 Aesop and Venus

Did Aesop, the famous collector of Greek fables, even exist? Possibly not, but the Greeks and Romans attributed their many animal fables to him. Several of those fables concern cats, the most famous being the tale of the cat who prayed to Venus, the goddess of love, to be turned into a woman. Venus did so, and the cat, now an attractive young maiden, married the man of her dreams. Venus, however, suspected that the maiden was still a cat on the inside. So on the wedding night the goddess set loose a mouse in the bedroom, and the lovely young woman showed her true self by chasing after it. Venus changed her back into a cat.

561 Too many options

Another fable of Aesop (whoever he was) concerns a cat and a fox, discussing how clever they are. The fox boasts that he is quite wily and knows several tricks for escaping from dogs. The cat claims she knows only one trick but one that works. At that very moment, a pack of hounds heads toward the two, and the cat scampers up a tree, shouting to the fox that this is her one trick. The fox dithers as he tries to settle on which of his escape tricks to use—and before he can make up his mind, the dogs pounce on him and devour him. The moral: one plan that works is better than a dozen that are never put into action.

562 Weasels into cats

The ferret is a domesticated form of the weasel, traditionally used for killing rodents in the home, and is still kept as a house pet. They are not related to cats at all, and while ferrets have their fans, they have never been as widely adored as cats have. I mention ferrets here because both weasels and ferrets appear in the earliest collections of Aesop's fables, while in later versions of those stories, the cat is often substituted for the weasel or the ferret. In fact, in the very earliest Aesop collections, only one fable mentions a cat. Why the change? Most likely it was due to the spread of cats over Europe. The editors of the fables chose to substitute an animal that was increasingly well known to people, though not as well known in Aesop's time. As the centuries went by, a person was more likely to have a cat than a ferret in his home.

563 Mr. Tibert

In animal fables, the beasts usually had no proper names, and so in Aesop's fables they are referred to as "the cat," "the fox," "the mouse" and so on. But occasionally the cat in a fable did have a name, often Tibert (just as the fox, who appeared in many fables, was sometimes called Reynard). Exactly why and how Tibert came to be the stereotypical name for a cat is not known. The name Tibert is probably the source of the name Tiddles, a common name for cats in Britain.

564 The Hopis and cats

There were no house cats in America until the Europeans arrived, but even so the Hopi Indians of the American Southwest tell a tale about how cats came to live with people. A boy went out hunting in the winter and came upon some unfamiliar tracks in the snow. He found the animal that made the tracks, and brought it home, keeping it confined for several days and feeding it rabbit meat. After that, the animal (a cat, of course) was thoroughly tamed and attached to the homes of human beings.

565 The spotty leopard tradition

"Can the leopard change his spots?" asks the Bible (Jeremiah 13:23). The obvious answer is "No way!" Several folk tales illustrate the same idea that a being never really changes its true nature. In one tale from the Arab world, the king of cats makes the pilgrimage to the holy city of Mecca. This impresses the king of the mice, who is sure that the pilgrim cat is now saintly and peaceful. He pays the king cat a visit and finds him praying—but then the cat immediately springs on the mouse. The moral: All the religion in the world won't change a predator into a nonpredator.

566 The cat in the mosque

In a charming tale from Persia, a cat rests in a mosque, where he resides to keep down the mice population. A mouse happens to appear and the cat immediately pounces on it. The mouse thinks it has a ploy to get free: it asks the cat to speak the name of one of the blessed prophets in order to speed the mouse's journey to heaven. The cat isn't about to open his mouth and thereby set the mouse free, so he speaks the name Jergis—which he can say without opening his mouth. In short, the mouse served as dinner.

567 Follow the power

An ancient Jewish folk tale is based on the story of Moses in the Book of Exodus. In Exodus, Moses and his brother Aaron confront the Egyptian pharaoh, ordering him to release the Israelite slaves. As a sign of divine power, Aaron's rod turns into a serpent. The Egyptian court sorcerers perform the same trick—but Aaron's serpent devours theirs. In the folk tale, one cat at the pharaoh's court saw this and concluded that Moses's and Aaron's god was stronger than the Egyptian gods, so when Moses and Aaron left the court, the cat followed them.

568 The tide chart

Here's one myth that has had a lot of staying power even though it is so absurd as to be laughable: you can tell the tide by looking at a cat's eyes—the pupils are narrow at low tide, wide at high tide. Didn't anyone happen to notice that if a cat is indoors or in a shady spot, his pupils are wide, but the pupils will narrow immediately if the cat steps into sunlight?

569 Wasteful illness

Oh, the legends that mankind has circulated—and not always just the common folk, but so-called intellectuals as well. For example, a supposed medical expert writing in the sixth century claimed that cat excrement caused illnesses in humans—the specific illness depended on the color of the cat's coat. Recall that the ancients believed the human body had four "humors" (liquids): blood, phlegm, yellow bile and black bile. This alleged medical expert claimed that a black-coated cat's excrement would cause a disorder of humans' black bile; a yellow-coated cat, a disorder of the yellow bile and so on. Nonsense, but quite amusing. The author may have been thinking of people who are allergic to cats. It would be centuries before people realized it was cat dander—and certainly not excrement—that caused the problems.

570 Heavy optics

How can cats see in the dark? Ancient authors had some very amusing explanations. The physician Alexander of Tralles, writing about the year 600, stated that cats and bats and other night creatures had a brighter "optical spirit" within their eyes, allowing them to see at night. Humans and other day creatures, on the other hand, had a heavy optical spirit, which allowed them to see by day but not at night.

571 Muhammad's stripes

Numerous legends are told of the prophet Muhammad and his affection for cats. A favorite one is: the stripes on the coats of cats came to be when Muhammad stroked a cat with his holy hands. Supposedly that same cat saved Muhammad from being bitten by a venomous snake, and in gratitude the prophet blessed the cat with the ability to always land on his feet.

572 The real source of "catamaran"

Many dictionaries will tell you that the Tamil language of India is the source of this name of a type of boat. But there is a more interesting folk etymology that might or might not be the real source of the word: according to one theory, *catamaran* was rooted in the Italian term *gatta marina,* meaning "marine cat." The *gatta marina* was a boat that would not tip over, just as a cat would always land on his feet.

573 Afterlife indicator

Want to know whether a person who just died has gone to heaven or hell? According to an old Welsh superstition, the cat belonging to that person does know. Supposedly the cat, with his sensitive nose, can sense the spirit who comes to take the person's soul away and knows where the spirit is headed. If the cat climbs a tree immediately after his master's death, the person has gone to heaven. If not . . .

574 The Japanese black patch myth

Japanese people were and still are very fond of cats, which is clear in many Japanese paintings of cats. Many Japanese people believed that a black patch on a cat's back was an indication that the soul of an ancestor inhabited that cat, and thus the cat was sacred. If such a cat came into your possession, naturally you treated him with great reverence and perhaps even sent him to a special temple to dwell with other sacred cats.

575 Siamese royal burial

Siamese royals thought so highly of their beautiful and distinctive cats that a live cat was buried along with his owner's corpse. However, the cat didn't die, as the tomb was equipped with a hole for the cat to escape through, and the cat's reappearance in the land of the living was the sign that the soul of the buried person had passed on to heaven.

576 Demon vision

Both cats and dogs have been thought to have the power to see things people can't, including demons and ghosts. In an old Jewish superstition, the afterbirth from the first litter of a black cat was burned, made into a powder and rubbed into the eyes of a human—supposedly bestowing upon that person the cat's power to see demons.

577 A cure for blindness

Related to the last item is this superstition from medieval Europe: supposedly a blind person could be cured if a black cat's head was burned, turned into a powder and blown into the eyes of the blind person three times a day. Unlike the last item, this rather foolish theory could be proved—or, rather, disproved. No doubt some people did try it, and we can only hope they used the head of a black cat that had already died.

578 Cats at Agincourt

If you know English history, you know that the 1415 Battle of Agincourt was one of England's great moments, with the valiant King Henry V leading England's army to victory over the French. One legend (or maybe fact) related to the famous battle has it that the English army carried cats to protect their supplies from rodents. The French had no such protection, and the night before the battle, rats gnawed the bowstrings of the French archers, so the French had no arrow power at the battle.

579 Light reservoirs

Yes, we all know that cats' eyes shine in dim light (see 99), and in the prescientific era, people had lots of fanciful explanations to explain why. One favorite: the cat's eye at night was emitting light that he had stored up during the day.

580 Cats and old maids

You might remember that in the wonderful TV sitcom *The Beverly Hillbillies,* the Clampetts, who were from the Ozark Mountains, were the most superstitious folks in the world. Well, in fact, there are a lot of amusing superstitions that originate from the Ozarks, including some having to do with cats. According to one, if you have black cats in your home, all your daughters will turn out to be old maids.

581 From the land of Dracula

The region of Transylvania in eastern Europe was home to the infamous Vlad Dracul, a prince so sadistic that legend transformed him into a vampire. The region was the source of a rich vampire lore, as well as some other curiosities, such as killing and burying black tomcats in fields on Christmas Eve as a way of keeping evil spirits from harming the crops. In various other parts of Europe there were similar practices of burying cats—usually black ones, and usually toms—to ensure bumper crops.

582 The kinky Siamese

Why does the Siamese cat have the trademark bend, or kink, in his tail? The legend goes like this: a princess of Siam was bathing in a river, and she needed a safe place to put her gold rings while she swam. Her faithful cat obligingly twisted his tail so she could place her rings on it while she frolicked in the water. Ever afterward, Siamese cats have had the royal kink in their tail to keep their mistress's rings from falling off.

583 Mither o' Mawkins

In medieval Scotland, the legendary head witch was known as the Mither o' Mawkins—that is, Mother of Mawkins, and a *mawkin* or *malkin* is a cat (or a rabbit). You might recall that in Shakespeare's *Macbeth,* one of the three witches calls out, "I come, Graymalkin." She was calling out to a gray cat, and the audience would have known that every witch had to have cats, which were always the "familiars," or companions, of witches.

584 The Filipino cat head

Cats are, as is noted often in this book, carnivores, but an individual cat may have a fondness for some kind of nonmeat food. Many cats are fond of coconut, probably because it contains a lot of fat. (And, coincidentally, the edible part of the coconut is often referred to as the "meat.") According to an old tale from the Philippines, cats like coconut meat because the coconut originated from the head of a cat. (But that would make cats into cannibals, wouldn't it? No one ever said there was any logic to these old tales.)

585 Wind the clock—first

It used to be a nightly ritual for untold numbers of people: before retiring for the night, wind the clock and put out the cat. Well, not many clocks need to be wound any more, and, thanks to cat litter, there is no pressing need to put cats outdoors. But in times past the two tasks were closely connected. In fact, a superstition arose that you had to do them in the right sequence: wind the clock, then put out the cat; if you reversed the order, bad luck would befall you.

586 Theatre lore

Theatrical folks as a group can be rather worldly and are hardly a religious lot, but they too have their superstitions, as seen in the curious phrase "break a leg." According to one old theatre superstition, a cat living on the premises is good luck, but it is very *bad* luck for a cat to walk onstage during a play. Cats, unpredictable creatures that they are, have no doubt done this many times, causing actors to attribute bad performances that night to the cat's appearance on the stage.

587 Basking in the sun

Dozens of folk tales from around the world seek to explain why cats love to bask in the sun. One of the more colorful ones is from Romania. In this story, a cat chases a mouse aboard Noah's ark. They cause such a commotion that Noah throws both of them overboard. The cat manages to swim back to the ark (yes, cats can swim), and she stretches herself out in the sun to dry. All of her descendants (every cat in the world, that is) do the same thing.

588 Basic black

A 1727 book, *History of Cats,* offers one explanation of why black cats are considered sinister: "The color black works well against cats in unsophisticated minds. It heightens the fire of their eyes, which is enough to make people believe they are witches at the very least."

589 Like a needle in a haystack

The province of Brittany in France is kind of an oddity—never fully French, with a native language (Breton) that is more like Gaelic than French. The natives have their own traditions and folk tales, among them one concerning cats: the Bretons say that every black cat has a single hair that is perfectly white. The person who finds this hair should pluck it out and carry it as a charm, for it will bring wealth.

Feline Words and Phrases

590 In a word, cat

The English word *cat* dates back centuries, with roots in the Latin *cattus,* which may ultimately be from Africa, in the Berber word *kaddiska* and the Nubian word *kadis*—all of which have the same meaning: "cat." The various European words for *cat* are pretty similar: French, *chat;* German, *Katze;* Italian, *gatto;* Spanish, *gato;* Swedish, *katt;* Dutch, *kat*.

591 Pussycat

In the first place, a female cat is technically a *queen,* not a *pussycat*. In earlier times, people referred to any cat as pussycat. Obviously vulgar slang has had the effect of making people connect pussycat to mean "female cat." Linguists tell us that the old Germanic word puss referred to the female body's sexual area, so in one sense, the word hasn't changed much at all. But it is anyone's guess as to how the word came to be connected with cats.

592 Why catty?

It never fails: a few people are exchanging slurs and snide remarks about someone else, and another person interrupts with "Meow!" Translation: you folks are being really *catty*. Where did it come from, this notion that needling and gossiping maliciously were somehow catlike? Hard to say. In your dictionary, there are probably several different meanings for the word *catty,* such as "stealthy" (makes sense), "aloof" (sure) or "agile" (highly appropriate). But the usual meaning is "slyly spiteful." Who knows why. Your real cat has (thankfully) no ability at all to gossip or criticize.

593 Are kittens kittenish?

Of course they are. Unlike *catty* (see 592), *kittenish* seems rooted in reality, for kittens really are playful and frisky, and occasionally coy as well.

594 Scaredy cat

Are cats cowardly by nature? Some people think so. Certainly it's true that a dog is more likely to attack something bigger than itself than a cat is. (But then, remember dogs are genetically *herd* animals, attacking on the assumption they have buddies nearby.) Own a cat for years and you'll see her attacking lots of things smaller than herself—mice, birds, lizards. The general rule about cat fighting is: a cat prefers to run when faced with a big attacker, but if cornered, they don't lie down and whimper. Cats seem to be practical by nature: attack and kill small things, flee the big ones if you can, fight off the big ones if you have to and go down fighting.

595 Cat-and-mouse

This old expression has a couple of meanings, both similar. It can refer to tormenting something before finally defeating it, an idea rooted in the fact that cats play with their prey before finally killing it. The other meaning is of a kind of pursuit with near captures and escapes before the final capture, as in "she liked to read cat-and-mouse mystery novels."

596 "Belling the cat"

One of the many fables attributed to the Greek storyteller Aesop (who may not have even existed) concerns a meeting of mice. They are concerned about a cat, naturally, and one mouse has an ingenious idea: tie a bell around the cat's neck so they can hear when the cat is coming. A wonderful idea, with one problem: which mouse is going to put the bell on the cat? The job would be suicide, of course, so no one volunteers. The phrase "belling the cat" is still in use, referring to any idea that "looks good on paper" but is useless in the real world.

597 Fighting like Kilkenny cats

Behind this old phrase lies a story that is a sad example of the mistreatment of cats. "Fight like Kilkenny cats" means "fight until everything is lost"—the idea being that the combatants were fierce and courageous, but to the point of stupidity. Here's the story: in the 1790s, when the Irish were rebelling against their English overlords, some soldiers in the town of Kilkenny amused themselves by tying two cats together by the tails, then throwing them over a clothesline. The cats would claw each other unmercifully, usually leading to the death of both cats. Some of the authorities heard of this cruel "game" and sought to stop it. The soldiers, hearing of the approach of the authorities, cut the tails of the cats on the clothesline, and the bleeding cats scurried away before the authorities arrived. The soldiers explained the two tails on the clothesline by claiming that the cats had literally devoured each other, leaving only their tails.

598 Cat (but not a pig) out of the bag

We commonly use the expression "the cat is out of the bag" to mean "disclose the truth," but like most old folk phrases, it is rooted in something very concrete. Specifically, "cat out of the bag" had its origin in country folk playing a trick on city dwellers. (This is a refreshing reversal of the usual situation of the country bumpkin being hoodwinked by the city slicker.) A farmer would go to the market in town, carrying bags containing (so he said) young suckling pigs for sale. The not-so-bright city shopper would buy a "pig," only to learn when he arrived home and opened the bag that his pork dinner was in fact a cat. The expression "pig in a poke" comes from the same scenario; *poke* is an old term for *bag*.

599 Catnaps

As noted earlier in this book, cats really do sleep a lot, generally about sixteen hours per day, though most of it is light, not deep, sleep. Also, cats' sleep periods are much, much shorter than the typical eight hours that humans sleep at night. Thus, a human nap of short duration is referred to as a cat nap.

600 The Cheshire cat, pre-Alice

The phrase "grinning like a Cheshire cat" was around long before Lewis Carroll made the Cheshire cat a character in his book *Alice in Wonderland*. Cheshire is one of the old shires (counties) of England. Why exactly the cats of Cheshire are more likely to grin than other cats is anybody's guess. (There is no breed of cat called Cheshire, in case you were wondering.) An English dictionary of 1785 (long before Lewis Carroll's time) indicates that the phrase was in common use, though no one knew the source of it. Some linguists think the phrase might have originally been "cheeser cat," meaning a cat that liked cheese (as most cats do) or a cat who chased the mice that threatened to eat the cheese.

601 The proverbial cat's paw

In an old tale, a monkey wants some chestnuts that have been roasting in the fire, but rather than reach into the fire himself, he convinces a gullible cat to reach in for him. The story passed into language in the term "cat's paw," someone used as a dupe by another. "Cat's paw" should amuse anyone who knows cats well, for the story is certainly not based on reality. No cat would let herself be used so shamefully. If the story had been more realistic, when the monkey asked the cat to reach in for the chestnuts, the cat would have replied, "Get them yourself, I'm napping, and, besides, cats don't eat chestnuts!" (For an entirely different meaning of "cat's paw," see 640.)

602 Sourpuss

The word applies to a human who is gloomy or grumpy, or both. Most of us have known cats, particularly older ones, who would qualify as grouches, but in fact *sourpuss* has little to do with cats but a lot to do with *puss,* a slang word for face, from the old Irish Gaelic *pus,* meaning "mouth." A sourpuss is a person with a sour face.

603 Cat Fit

Fits of anger or frustration or anxiety must fascinate us, because there are lots of phrases to describe them: hissy fit, duck fit, conniption fit, cat fit and so on. Cats don't, strictly speaking, have fits at all, but a human having a fit does sometimes bear a resemblance to a cat hissing or clawing or meowing (or all of the above) at another cat or some other enemy.

604 Pajamas/whiskers/meow

"You're the cat's pajamas" was a slangy compliment in the early 1900s, ditto for "cat's whiskers" and "cat's meow." Part of the fun of slang is that it is basically meaningless, so looking for the origins of such silly expressions probably isn't worth the time people invest in the quest. However, we do feel fairly certain that "cat's pajamas" was coined (or at least popularized) by cartoonist Thomas "Tad" Dorgan (1877–1929), who is also credited with "twenty-three skiddoo," "applesauce" ("nonsense"), "dumbbell" ("stupid person") and (my favorite) "busy as a one-armed paperhanger."

605 "Cat got your tongue?"

We ask this of someone who seems unable or unwilling to answer our question. The source of the expression is mysterious, since a cat would have nothing to do with human muteness (or stupidity).

One possible explanation: the person won't respond to your question, so you're now asking him—very sarcastically—"Why don't you answer me? What happened to your tongue? Did the cat run off with it?" It's a roundabout way of saying, "Answer me, for Pete's sake!"

606 Catawampus

There is no such animal, but in the past the word was used to refer to a fictional fierce creature of the wild, presumably something resembling a cat. No doubt parents could frighten children with warnings such as "Don't wander too far out there or the catawampus will get you!"

607 Catamount

This isn't a particular species of cat, just a sort of generic name for whatever the local wildcat happens to be. The word is a contraction of *cat-a-mountain* and was often used in the old days of the American West to refer to cougars.

608 Cat burglar

Cats are quiet, sneaky and excellent climbers, so a "cat burglar" is a person who breaks in stealthily, usually through an upper-story window or skylight. A cat burglar could also be called a "cat man" (or perhaps, in our politically correct age, "cat person").

609 Catcall

In days past, there were small whistlelike instruments that made a sound like a cat, and they were used at concerts, political gatherings and other events to express disapproval from the audience. Some people simply made the call with their mouths, and *catcall* came to refer to any kind of disapproving or disruptive sound at a public gathering.

610 Caterwaul

As you might guess from the spelling, this word comes from the Old Dutch and means "cat wail." The original meaning referred to the very distinctive cry of a female cat in heat—or a tomcat who senses a female in heat is nearby. Later the phrase had two meanings related to the original one: to make any kind of disruptive noise or to go around in lecherous pursuit of women.

611 Cat Fight

When two cats fight, they do so viciously and noisily, so "cat fight" has come to refer to any nasty dispute between two people—two *women,* in particular, probably because women are less inclined to use their fists and more inclined to bite and pull hair—as cats do.

612 Pussyfoot

Cats are notorious for walking silently, which is exactly the meaning of *cat-foot* (see 634). But *pussyfoot* carries a rather different meaning, for it doesn't have to do with literal walking but with figurative walking—tiptoeing around a subject in order to avoid offending someone or to avoid committing oneself to a position. For example: "Every time I try to have a serious discussion with George, he pussyfoots around the subject." Pussyfoot is also the name of several types of plants with flowers that resemble (vaguely) a cat's foot.

613 Nondrinking pussyfoot

Back in the Prohibition era in America, a certain law enforcement officer named W. E. Johnson had a reputation as being a gung-ho prohibitionist. Considered sneaky for his pursuit of bootleggers, Johnson got the nickname "Pussyfoot," and the name quickly came to refer to prohibitionists in general, prohibitionist policemen in particular.

614 Catbrier

Various species of briers all over the world have been given this name. The "cat" part of the name refers to thorns that hook tenaciously in the skin, as cat claws would.

615 "Has a cat got a tail?"

This is one of those no-brainer remarks, in the same vein as "Do fish swim?" If you asked a friend, "Are you nervous about your kid getting his learner's permit?" your friend might reply, with a bit of a smirk, "Has a cat got a tail?" The line must give some amusement to the many proud owners of Manx cats, who would probably reply, "Well, not *all* cats have tails."

616 "Nothing itches like a cat's back"

Every cat lover knows the surefire way to get a cat to stay close to you: scratch its back. While most pets respond to stroking, cats in particular seem to find it just heavenly, as you can tell by their closed eyes and purring.

617 "He has his back up"

If someone at work told you that the boss "has his back up today," you would be wise not to cross your boss. The phrase comes from the familiar arched back of a defensive cat. Humans don't literally arch their backs (or hiss or spit—usually), but most humans have seen a cat in this posture, and it is a memorable sight.

618 Cats and dogs on Wall Street

With so many people investing in stocks these days, the average person probably has heard of "bull" and "bear" markets. Well, in an earlier age, investors heard of "cats and dogs"—stocks newly issued, usually low-priced and high-risk. If you invested in "cats and dogs," you were a gambler (or an idiot, or both), the opposite of the more cautious investor who opted for the reliable blue-chip stocks. Exactly how "cats and dogs" came to apply to stocks is anybody's guess.

619 "Tickle a cat"

As much as cats seem to enjoy life, they do not laugh, and this is at the root of the old saying that something is so funny it would "make the cat laugh" or "tickle a cat." Presumably if something could make the cat laugh, the poor humans would be dead from laughing so hard.

620 "Enough to make a cat speak"

For the most part, cats are quiet creatures, if you can overlook females in heat and toms fighting each other in an alley. Since cats are mostly quiet and they don't actually talk using words, the phrase "enough to make a cat speak" was formerly in common use. It could refer to something remarkable, as in "The sight of that tornado was frightening enough to make a cat speak." Or, more often, it could refer to having one's tongue loosened by liquor, as in "Bob is a quiet fellow, but at the party he drank enough to make a cat speak."

621 "Raining cats and dogs"

What's the source of this old phrase referring to a heavy rain? One possibility is humans' delight in sheer nonsense—that is, witnessing a rain so heavy that instead of raining mere raindrops, it appears to be raining something much larger, say, cats and dogs. But some language scholars think the phrase is rooted in the association of cats with witches, whose spells were said to cause terrible storms.

622 Cat ice

Means thin ice—that is, the ice on a lake or a river that would crack if a person walked on it. Apparently the idea was that the ice was so thin that a cat might—or might not—be able to walk on it, but certainly no human could.

623 "When the cat's away"

"When the cat's away, the mice will play"—so the proverb goes in English, but the idea is so common that there are similar proverbs in many other languages. The idea is that when the figure of power or authority is absent, the underlings will goof off and make mischief. It is doubtful that real mice "play" when the cat is absent, but they would certainly help themselves to whatever food was available.

624 "A cat may look at a king"

Animals, unlike people, are totally unimpressed by ranks, titles and other human ways to show who's important. Hence this old phrase, a summation of egalitarianism and democracy: "A cat may look at a king." Put another way: we're all mortal, so don't go putting on airs just because other folks kiss up to you.

625 "Before a cat can lick his ear"

A cat is an expert at grooming, and a flexible skeleton and a long tongue help in this respect. Even so, a cat can't lick his own ear, which is the source of this old phrase meaning, simply, "never" or "not gonna happen"—as in "I'll be president of this company before a cat can lick his ear."

626 "Something the cat dragged in"

This old phrase refers to something—or, more often, *someone*—in a less than presentable condition, that is, dirty, disheveled or otherwise unattractive. Every cat owner knows the source of the phrase: your pet brings in a bird or mouse or lizard that she has caught, and though still alive, the captured prey is a little worse for wear.

627 "Not room enough to swing a cat"

When describing a small house or a small room, it was common to say, "There wasn't room enough to swing a cat in that place." Colorful, but why would anyone want to swing a cat anyway? Scholars who study word and phrase origins think the "cat" in the phrase wasn't an actual cat but, rather, the whip known as a cat-o'-nine-tails (see 637). The idea seemed to be that a place was so cramped that a normal adult wouldn't have enough room to wield a whip in it—as if doing so would be a normal practice in the room.

628 "Care killed the cat"

A cat has nine lives, so tradition says, but even though a cat is hard to kill, care—that is, worry—will kill it. The old expression "care killed the cat" goes back to the 1600s (and probably earlier), and playwright Ben Jonson used the line "care'll kill a cat" in one of his comedies. The idea seems to be this: cats, tough creatures that they are, can die from fretting and worrying, and likewise human beings (who only have *one* life each) can be destroyed by worry as well.

629 "Sick as a cat"

You've probably heard both "sick as a dog" and "sick as a cat." Neither animal is particularly sickly by nature, but these old expressions probably refer to either animal's habit of vomiting, which is an animal's way of coping with digestive upsets. One obvious difference between cats and dogs is that cats, unlike dogs, never vomit up food and then re-eat it.

630 Catting

Believe it or not, in the old days *to cat* meant "to vomit," as in "Joe has the stomach virus, and he's been catting all night." Obviously the phrase is rooted in humans' observation of cats vomiting (the same idea at the root of "sick as a cat"—see 629).

631 "Put the cat among the pigeons"

This means, naturally, to stir up trouble, cause a ruckus. The source of the phrase is easily understood: a flock of pigeons stands cooing and along comes a cat eager for a fresh squab dinner. Inevitably the pigeons take flight with a lot of loud cooing and violent wing flapping.

632 "Living under the cat's foot"

No one uses the word *henpecked* any more or the phrase "living under the cat's foot," which has the same meaning. The idea was that a spineless husband let his wife dominate his life. So what is the connection with a cat's foot? Probably the image of a cat that has caught a mouse but hasn't yet chosen whether to kill it. The poor frightened mouse is under the cat's paw, never knowing if the cat will let it go (only to catch it again, of course) or finally kill it. The mouse is alive, but extremely unhappy and uncomfortable.

633 "Nervous as a cat"

Are cats really nervous animals? You certainly wouldn't get that impression if you see a cat stretched out placidly in the sun or curled up at the foot of a bed. But every cat owner knows that a seemingly comatose cat can spring to life in a split second upon hearing a sudden loud noise. Cats' reflexes are lightning fast, and no doubt the sudden switch from dead-to-the-world to claws-out-and-ready-for-attack gives some people the impression that they are nervous by nature, never fully relaxed. The truth is that a cat's reflexes follow the old motto of the Boy Scouts: "Be prepared."

634 Cat-foot

Cats are notoriously silent in their walk, so the verb *cat-foot* means (obviously) "to tread silently," though it is doubtful that any human could tread as lightly as a cat can. The word *pussyfoot* (see 612) has nothing at all to do with walking.

635 Cathouse

This word has been used since the 1800s to refer to a house of prostitution. We can only assume that it is rooted in the idea that cats in heat are promiscuous.

636 Catlap

Leave it to the Scottish, who are famous for making one of the most potent drinks in the world, to coin this word meaning "weak drink." Presumably a cat wouldn't drink anything strong (like Scotch whiskey, maybe?) but sticks to something lighter like milk or water. (Or maybe cats have better sense than to drink alcohol, especially alcohol sold at outrageous prices.)

637 Cat-o'-nine-tails

It was a kind of whip, used for punishment in a time when corporal punishments were meted out often for a variety of offenses, especially if the offenders were soldiers or sailors. The whip had, naturally, nine cords, sometimes tipped with bone or metal to leave a nasty gash on the offender's back. The "cat" part of the name had nothing to do with a cat's tail, but with the type of wound that would resemble the scratch made by a cat's claw.

638 Cat owls

Owls are the only birds whose eyes both face forward, and so their faces remind us of the faces of people—and of cats, too. This is especially true of the many "horned" varieties of owls, those with tufts of feathers that resemble ears. The various horned owls are often referred to generally as "cat owls." We can assume that the shared resemblance of cats and owls lies behind the old rhyme "The Owl and the Pussycat." Here's an unpleasant bit of trivia that won't please owners: some of the larger "cat owls," such as the great horned owl of the United States, will occasionally make a meal of a cat.

639 Cat scratch fever

A virus infection caused by a scratch can result in chills, fever and a swelling of the lymph glands. Though it isn't necessarily a cat who gave the scratch, people who don't like cats probably enjoyed assuming cats were the cause of it.

640 Cat's paw

The more familiar meaning of "cat's paw" is covered in entry 601. Here is the second meaning, a nautical one: Sailors use "cat's paw" to refer to a sea that is almost, but not quite, perfectly calm. Very light air barely ruffles the surface of the water, as if a cat's paw was lightly touching the water.

641 Cattail

Several marsh plants have this name, notably the *Typha latifolia,* whose wide flat leaves were long used for making mats, chair seats and other furnishings. The name comes from the brown, velvety bloom at the top of the plant, which vaguely resembles a cat's tail but really is closer in appearance to a sausage.

642 Catwalk

You'll find them in ships, industrial plants—and theatres. A catwalk is any kind of narrow walkway through a tight passage, a walkway where the general public would never find itself. Cats, agile creatures that they are, would feel perfectly at ease on anything that a human considered a "catwalk."

643 Cat whisker

Not literally a whisker, this is the name given to a very fine wire found in the crystals of old radios and electronic circuits.

644 Call it "Cat Creek"

One of the best-known mountain ranges of North America is named for cats—the Catskill Mountains. The early Dutch settlers in southern New York state gave the name Kaaterskill ("cat creek") to one of the glens in the area. The name eventually applied to the hills of the region and over time changed to its modern form, Catskill. Presumably the Dutch named the range after the wildcats in the area, not for their own domestic cats.

645 The catty stone

The name cat's-eye is given to several gemstones, which all have in common a luminous band that reminded people of a reflection in the eye of a cat.

(Or, alternatively, the band in the stone reminded people of the slitlike pupil in a cat's eye.) The most common cat's-eye is a form of quartz, and the luminous band is composed of asbestos fibers. Chrysoberyl cat's-eye is a beautiful yellow, with a band of light blue.

646 Chatoyancy

Here's a fancy French word, and if you know that *chat* is French for "cat," you may have a clue what *chatoyancy* means: "shining like a cat's eye." The word refers to a quality of certain gemstones, not only cat's-eye but moonstone and many others. Something that is *chatoyant* possesses a changeable luster and has a narrow band of white light. If you change the position of the stone, the band of light seems to move across the surface.

647 "Useless as tits on . . ."

From the standpoint of natural functions, nipples on male mammals are pointless (see 125). Hence the old folk expression that a certain person or thing is as "useless as tits on a _____"—where the blank is filled with the name of any male mammal, such as boar hog, bull and (probably the most popular) tomcat. "Useless as tits on a tomcat" has the added zing of the alliteration of the *t* in *tits* and *tomcat*.

648 "Cat on a hot tin roof"

The playwright Tennessee Williams immortalized this phrase in the title of one of his dramas, even though the cat in his play was a woman, not an actual cat. The meaning of the phrase is obvious enough: an extremely uncomfortable or unpleasant situation. A cat on a hot tin roof would not be able to stand still for more than a second.

649 "Kitten to a hot brick"

If someone becomes comfortable quickly with a person or situation, we say that he "takes to it like a kitten to a hot brick." Why on earth would a kitten like a hot brick? The idea here is not of a surface too hot to walk on (an idea found in "cat on a hot tin roof" in 648) but, rather, the old custom of taking a motherless kitten and keeping it warm by placing it on a hot brick—with a layer of cloth between it and the brick, of course. The brick's heat was a substitute for the warmth of mama cat's body.

650 Cat's-Faces

Pansies, those delightful little flowers that give us purple and yellow blooms in cool weather, have been given a number of fanciful names, including both "monkey's-faces" and "cat's-faces." Suffice it to say that the human imagination seems to run wild at times.

651 Collectively speaking

Independent individualists that they are, cats could never form a *herd* or *pack* or *flock,* words that apply to creatures that are really "together" in some real sense, functioning as a unit. A herd of cattle might stampede in one direction, but if a group of cats happened to be running in the same direction, you can bet it wasn't a "herd mentality" at work. Nonetheless, there are some words that apply to groups of cats: you can speak of a *clowder* of adult cats (especially old ones) and a *kendle* of kittens. (Don't confuse kendle with *litter,* which refers to kittens born at the same time from the same mother. A kendle is any group of kittens, not necessarily related by birth.) Neither clowder nor kendle is used much, and appropriately so, for we seldom think of cats in group terms—and neither do cats.

652 "More than one way to . . ."

The usual form of the phrase is "there's more than one way to skin a cat," but the earliest form is probably "kill a cat." Neither phrase is very tasteful to us cat lovers, since they both reflect a pretty low view of the value of a cat's life (or skin). The simple meaning is, of course, that one plan or method failed to work, but there are other methods available. Why, in the distant past, someone coined the phrase is anyone's guess. Certainly we can assume that the folks who coined it (and repeated it) were none too fond of felines.

653 "High as cat's back"

You don't hear this old phrase much any more, but it was in common use in the American South not so long ago, and it meant "expensive." For example: "I can't afford to shop at that place, their goods are high as cat's back." The image attached to this expression was a hissing cat with its back arched way up high. True, there are plenty of things in the world much higher than that, but the phrase was commonly used nonetheless. Incidentally, it was always "high as cat's back," never "high as a cat's back."

654 Cat music

This old term referred to really bad music—discordant, out of tune. It's based on the habit of cats sitting on a fence who make their horrible "night music," no doubt a chorus of females in heat and their rival males staking a claim to the ladies.

655 "Catting around"

Like many other cat-based words and phrases, this one is sexual, and it has the same meaning as "sleeping around" (or at least "looking for someone to sleep with"). It is true that a female cat in heat isn't averse to multiple partners (and ditto for tomcats!).

656 Cats don't copycat

It's a mystery how the word *cat* came to be incorporated into *copycat,* for cats certainly aren't inclined to copy behaviors, or anything else for that matter. In times past, people used the word *ape* to mean "imitate," since apes and monkeys often do imitate what they see. (The phrase "monkey see, monkey do" carries the same meaning.) We can only assume that the *cat* in *copycat* simply means "person," and that the alliteration of the letter *c* in both *copy* and *cat* sounded very catchy. Certainly a cat, independent creature that she is, has no interest in copying anyone or anything.

657 The Don Quixote wit

"If you lie down with dogs, you get up with fleas"—so says the old proverb, which means that our actions have consequences, usually very predictable ones. The Spanish author Miguel de Cervantes (1547–1616), creator of the classic novel *Don Quixote,* uttered a cat-related proverb with the same meaning: "Those who play with cats must expect to be scratched." Whether this was original to Cervantes or was simply a repetition of an old Spanish proverb is not known.

658 Selfish, yes, and not ashamed

Are cats selfish? Of course they are, and we love them for it. We would detest a friend or family member as selfish as a cat, but we don't mind selfishness so much in a beautiful, purring beast. Consider this old proverb from Britain: "In the cat's eyes, all things belong to cats." One can easily imagine that cat's reply to that: "Well, of course. Just as it should be. You got a problem with that?"

659 "A cat has no conscience"

You hear this truism a lot from both cat haters and cat lovers. What exactly does it mean? That cats kill prey, snitch food off a table, claw furniture and so on, without exhibiting shame upon getting caught? Well, of course they don't—*they aren't human.* A few dog owners have told me that "a cat has no conscience" is supposed to contrast cats against dogs, who can at times look almost humanly contrite after they've soiled a rug, broken a vase or done something unpleasant. Well, it isn't a cat's fault if her beautiful (and very expressive) face lacks the right muscles for looking embarrassed and repentant.

660 Cats without claws

"He had no more chance than a cat in hell without claws." This old expression has nothing to do with theology (not that a cat would be in hell anyway) but instead is about being in a difficult situation. A cat without claws is nearly defenseless (as every owner of a declawed cat should know), so a cat in a difficult spot (hell) would surely need claws (not to mention a fire extinguisher). The old expression was often shortened to "a cat-in-hell's chance."

661 "Having kittens"

It means "in a tizzy"—extremely upset or anxious, as in "Mike's been having kittens ever since his son learned to drive." This curious phrase dates back to the time when people took Satan and witchcraft as serious threats to humanity. It was believed that a woman enduring a difficult pregnancy might be in pain because there were kittens in her womb scratching to get out. These kittens were the offspring not of a human father, of course, but of a demon, who had seduced the woman in the form of a cat. Sounds silly to us, but in the prescientific age, it provided an explanation for a woman's pains during pregnancy.

662 "Cats in the belly"

This phrase is similar to "having kittens" (see 661) and the old belief that a woman experiencing a difficult pregnancy might actually be bearing kittens (the spawn of a demon who had taken the form of a cat) instead of a human fetus. In a time when abortions were extremely risky to women, some were performed on the pretext that what was being killed was not human at all but, rather, a demonic animal. We can safely assume that those who performed such abortions had never actually aborted any cat fetuses.

663 "Curiosity killed the cat"

We all know that cats are insatiably curious, always eager to explore a box, a bag, a closet—anything. Inevitably some cats are killed when they venture into someplace dangerous. However, those who study word and phrase origins think there may be another explanation behind "curiosity killed the cat." The cat in the phrase may have been a human "cat"—that is, a malicious, gossipy woman. Such a woman is presumably "curious" in the sense of being nosy about other people's business. So eventually her curiosity would kill her—or, more likely, kill the poor souls who happen to live with her.

664 "The cat who swallowed the canary"

If you say someone looks like "the cat who swallowed the canary," you could mean that the person looks guilty—or (more commonly) supremely satisfied. A real cat would look satisfied after swallowing a canary, of course, and guilt would never enter its mind. Probably the deeper meaning of the phrase is that the person has done something he knows he shouldn't have done and is pleased with it, even though he *should* look and feel guilty.

665 The laughing mouse

Mice and rats are not stupid—they know cats are killers, and they fear them. So consider this old proverb from Africa: "If the mouse laughs at a cat, there is a hole nearby." Put another way, a mouse wouldn't presume to mock a cat unless the mouse knew it could make a quick getaway. We can safely assume that real mice don't actually do much laughing, no matter how near the mouse hole may be.

666 "Until a dog comes by"

Americans are big on equality and naturally have a great store of old folk sayings about deflated egos. Consider this one: "A cat is mighty dignified until a dog comes by." This is true about cats, of course (particularly if the dog is large, aggressive and obnoxious), but like all animal proverbs, it is basically a commentary on human behavior. The gist: the little guy can act mighty proud and domineering, but only until someone bigger puts him in his place.

667 "Honest as the cat"

Some people hate cats because of their habit of snitching meat—and "meat" might also include pet birds and fish. Well, why not? To a cat, if the meat is available, it is there to be eaten, even if you had intended to have it for *your* supper. Essentially, no cat can be trusted if meat is within reach. Hence the old proverb about someone who is "honest as the cat when the meat is out of reach." In other words, that person can be trusted only when there is nothing around to tempt him.

668 Alley cat v. tomcat

Yes, there is a double standard regarding promiscuous men and promiscuous women. A man who sleeps around feels little shame in being known as a "tomcat"—in fact, he might be very proud of it. But most women (and a lot of men, too) don't mean it as a compliment when they refer to a loose woman as an "alley cat." Since there are both male and female alley cats, it's anybody's guess as to why "alley cat" came to refer primarily to women. The one notable male (human) alley cat is the subject of the popular "The Alley Cat Song" (see 833).

669 "Cat in the clock"

In olden days, clocks were fairly large items—not just the bulky grandfather clocks, but mantel clocks as well. Presumably if a cat got inside the clock, she would make quite a racket, and her caterwauling mixed with the various noises made by the clock. Hence an old proverb from Flanders: "The cat's in the clock," which referred to a bickering family.

670 "Fight like cats and dogs"

Cats and dogs in the home can learn to tolerate each other, even like each other, but let's be honest and admit that the phrase "fight like cats and dogs" is rooted in reality. Left to their own natural tendencies, without humans bringing them under the same roof, the two species would either avoid each other entirely or fight. A related phrase is "live a cat and dog life," which refers to frequent bickering in the home, particularly between a husband and a wife.

671 Puss caterpillar

The orange-brown "woolly worms," common in the southeastern United States, are known by a variety of names, including "puss caterpillar," which comes from their being fuzzy like a cat. Technically these relatively fast-moving creatures are the larvae of the flannel moth (*Megalopyge opercularis*).

672 "The wrong side of every door"

According to an old proverb, "A cat is always on the wrong side of every door." Well, not *every* cat is like that *all* the time, but every cat owner has had the experience of hearing his pet meow insistently, begging to be let out or in, for no reason we humans can fathom. The ultimate unsatisfied cat is the obnoxious Rum Tum Tugger from T. S. Eliot's *Old Possum's Book of Practical Cats,* who even utters the line "I'm always on the wrong side of every door." The Rum Tum Tugger and his "aggravate the hell out of humans" attitude was one of the most appealing characters in the musical *Cats* (see 827).

673 Catgut—not!

The strings of violins today are mostly synthetic materials, ditto for surgical sutures, but in times past these were indeed made from the intestines of animals—but not cats, despite the name of the material: "catgut." The usual material was, in fact, sheep intestines. So why "catgut"? One theory is that the sound of the instrument reminded some people (perhaps those with no musical taste) of a cat making some of its less appealing noises. At any rate, cats' intestines were never used in making violin strings.

674 "Mog" and "moggie"

Americans haven't yet found a good (and short) term to refer to a nonpedigreed cat, but English people commonly use *mog* or *moggie*. Apparently Moggie is another form of Maggie, a nickname for Margaret, and a *maggie* or *moggie* originally meant "a slatternly woman." Over time the word was extended to apply to alley cats of either sex (since alley cats sometimes look a little slatternly, or worse) and, in time mog came to include any mixed-breed cat, including the beloved (but nonpedigreed) cat of hearth and home. Neither mog nor moggie has any negative connotation, and many English people are perfectly happy with their purring mogs.

675 The "no cats? bad people" tradition

Human beings have loved—and hated—cats for centuries. The love tradition comes through in a number of proverbs, all centered on the basic idea that a house really isn't complete without a cat on the premises. One example is the Irish proverb "Beware of people who dislike cats." And here's a similar one from Portugal: "A house without either a cat or a dog is the house of a scoundrel." While we cat lovers would never call a cat hater a scoundrel (to his face, anyway), the idea has crossed our minds many times. . . .

676 The Felix-Feline connection

A famous cartoon cat is named Felix (see 902), and some people may wonder if *Felix* and *feline* are based on the same root word. The answer is no, although both words have Latin roots. *Feline* is based on the Latin *felis,* meaning simply "cat." *Felix* and such related words as *felicity* (happiness) and *felicitate* (to make happy) are based on the Latin *felix* meaning (of course) "happy." Only one letter distinguishes felix from *felis,* but the meanings are quite different. But most felines give the impression of being extremely *felix,* so perhaps it is well that the words are so similar. And you couldn't go wrong by naming your pet tomcat Felix.

677 The gib-cat

We think of *tom* as the traditional word for a male cat, but *gib* seems to be older. Exactly how gib came into use is not known, though it may be a shortening of the name Gilbert. At any rate, in times past it was common to refer to your pet as gib, a name about as generic as today's "kitty." Over time, gib came to be used for male cats only, and, later, evolved to mean "a *neutered* male cat." In one of Shakespeare's plays a character claims he is as "melancholy as a gib-cat."

678 Catfish

Even people who love the taste of catfish will admit that these fish—of the suborder Siluroidea—aren't exactly pretty. The hundreds of species of catfish got their name from the barbels, the "whiskers" around their mouths. Like cats' whiskers, the barbels serve as feelers. One other trait catfish share with cats: they hear well (by fish standards, anyway). Catfish don't have claws, of course, but the spines on their fins have caused nasty scratches on fishermen. Interestingly, as much as cats love the taste of fish, many of them do not like catfish.

Notable Cat People and Their Opinions

679 The cynical Mr. Twain

One of America's best-loved authors was Samuel Clemens, better known by his pen name, Mark Twain. Though known as a humorist, Twain had a cynical view of human beings. He was fond of cats, and you can see both emotions in this quote: "If man could be crossed with the cat, it would improve man but deteriorate the cat." Twain gave his own family cats some truly off-the-wall names (Blatherskite, for example), and he also gave the world one of its funniest cat stories, the chapter "The Cat and the Painkiller" in his classic novel *Tom Sawyer*.

680 "Papa's" kitties

He loved to play the macho man by big-game hunting, attending bullfights and doing other "guy things," but at home he was a devoted cat fanatic. I'm talking about Ernest Hemingway (1899–1961), one of the most popular novelists of the twentieth century. While "Papa" Hemingway was an incurable womanizer and treated his wives shabbily, he doted on his cats. The monument to his ailurophilia is the Hemingway museum in Key West, Florida, which is still home to the descendants of his bevy of cats. The museum's kittens are sometimes offered for sale, and they are not cheap, partly because of the celebrity connection with Hemingway, partly because many of the cats have extra toes, sometimes as many as seven toes per paw.

681 India v. India

Here's a sign of the hypersensitive, turbulent times we live in: the name of a U.S. president's cat sparked protests in another country. When George W. and Laura Bush moved into the White House in 2001, protesters in India claimed to be "offended" at the name of the Bushes' black shorthair cat, India. This uproar did not, fortunately, prove to be a major glitch in United States–India relations. The cat was, unlike many other pets dubbed India, *not* named for the blackness of India ink. Rather, she was (so her owners say) named for Texas Rangers baseball player Ruben Sierra, nicknamed "El Indio." Given George W.'s love of nicknames, India has her own: "Willie." India has kept a lower profile than the Clintons' cat, Socks, probably because India has to share the spotlight with the dogs Spot and Barney.

682 Socks

Before the Clintons took in the black Labrador dog Buddy as a pet, the only official pet of the Bill Clinton White House was Socks, a black-and-white domestic shorthair, with the trademark smudge of black on his nose and chin. Socks had been given to daughter Chelsea back in 1990. There had been no resident cat in the White House during the Reagan or George H. W. Bush terms, so cat lovers were pleased to have a First Cat (even if some weren't all that fond of the Clintons). But many cat lovers (this author included) raised a cynical eyebrow when the Clintons acquired Buddy. Were they pandering to the popular perception that a "real" American family ought to have a dog?

683 After Albert, what?

Queen Victoria had the longest reign of any English monarch (1837–1901), but sadly she spent much of it mourning for her dear husband, the handsome and high-minded Albert. But she wasn't without affection, and she continued to dote on the cats she and Albert had always adored. Her very special cat was White Heather, who outlived her famous mistress but continued to be a pampered resident of Buckingham Palace in London.

684 Sir Winston

There is no doubt that one of the greatest men of the twentieth century was the British statesman and author Winston Churchill (1874–1965), the prime minister during the tense times of World War

II. He and his beloved cat Nelson both endured the German bombing of London during the war. (Nelson was named for the British naval hero Horatio Nelson.) Churchill also owned a cat named Jock who slept with him and ate at his table. Faithful Jock stayed at the great man's bedside through his final illness.

685 Lady Margaret

Winston Churchill (see 684) wasn't the only British prime minister to adore cats, for the formidable "Iron Lady," Margaret Thatcher, had quite a few cats in her household. During her time (the entire decade of the 1980s) at the official residence of the prime minister, 10 Downing Street in London, reporters commented on the number of cats roaming the halls there.

686 Camelot kitten

Few people remember it now, but John F. Kennedy and his family briefly had a cat at the White House. He was Tom, a gray shorthair and the adored pet of little Caroline. Apparently little Tom wasn't happy at "Camelot," so he was given to the care of Jackie Kennedy's personal secretary, who lived in Georgetown. Sadly, Tom died of liver disease within a few years. We are happy to report that he is one creature connected with Camelot about whom there was never a breath of scandal.

687 Sir Isaac

One of the greatest scientists of all times, Sir Isaac Newton (1642–1727) is remembered for his studies of physics, particularly gravity. (Remember the story of Newton and the apple falling on his head?) The amazing man was also a cat lover, and he may have been the inventor of the cat flap, the small opening at the bottom of a door that allows cats to come and go as they please.

688 Nurse Nightingale

It's always nice to learn that people who show great love for their fellow humans can also be very fond of cats. One of the great humanitarians of history was Florence Nightingale (1820–1910), the Englishwoman credited with improving the science of nursing and of making hospitals more sanitary. The amazing Miss Nightingale had a whole bevy of cats, mostly Persians, who often accompanied her on her travels. With her sensitivity to human suffering, she was well aware that pets (cats especially) made good companions for sick people, especially those with chronic illnesses.

689 Lincoln the indulgent

Abraham Lincoln was a wily politician but, at home, was sometimes an overly indulgent father, and during his years in the White House visitors commented on how he let his children—and their numerous pets—take over the place. Naturally there were cats among them, and his son Tad seemed especially partial to cats. Among Lincoln's many nuggets of homespun wisdom was his observation that "no matter how much cats fight, there always seem to be plenty of kittens." He probably would have applied the cat proverb to his own stormy relationship with his temperamental wife, Mary.

690 Pasteur's admiration

Science and human health both took a great leap forward thanks to French chemist Louis Pasteur (1822–1895), who made world-changing discoveries about germs and vaccinations. Pasteur had a profound effect on animal health as well, finding methods to prevent rabies and other lethal illnesses. Probably more than any other individual, Pasteur helped mankind understand the importance of cleanliness in preventing the spread of disease. Naturally he had great admiration for the cleanest of animals, the cat.

691 Paderewkski's stage fright

The renowned Polish pianist Ignace Paderewski (1860–1941) awed concertgoers worldwide, but in his early days he was subject to stage fright. The story goes that he was afflicted with a severe case of butterflies in the belly just before a concert in London. All aflutter inside, he sat down at the piano and, to his and the audience's surprise, a cat jumped into his lap. This surprise was a delightful icebreaker and set Paderewski at ease. The cat stayed in his lap, purring, during the opening piece. In later years, Paderewski claimed that the cat was what calmed him during this first major concert.

692 The "gather ye rosebuds" Fellow

The English poet Robert Herrick (1591–1674) gave the world the very quotable poem that begins "Gather ye rosebuds while ye may." (The poem's actual title is "To the Virgins, to Make Much of Time.") Herrick was only a part-time poet, actually living out his life quietly as a minister in a small town in Devonshire, England. Like a lot of writers—and other people living quiet lives—Herrick doted on his household of cats.

693 The Huxley literary formula

The British author Aldous Huxley (1894–1963) was known for some fine novels and essays, notably *Brave New World*—and for being one of the first celebrities to experiment with the drug LSD. Huxley was fond of cats, and when a young man asked his advice on becoming a writer, Huxley suggested that he get himself a supply of paper, pens and ink—and two cats. Huxley, like countless other authors, couldn't imagine being a real writer without having a cat in the household.

694 Scott of the Antarctic

Robert Scott was the courageous British naval officer who explored the continent of Antarctica and hoped to be the first man to reach the South Pole. He failed—the Norwegian explorer Roald Amundsen got there first, in 1911. Even worse, in 1912 Scott and his explorartion party perished in the Antarctic cold. A four-legged member of the Scott expedition was an unnamed tomcat, who had his own hammock (complete with blankets and a small pillow) on Scott's ship. The poor cat was swept overboard in a storm and drowned, which at least spared him the horrible fate of Scott and his party.

695 The original Egyptian sex kitten

Perhaps the most famous woman of ancient times was the Egyptian queen Cleopatra, the mistress of both Julius Caesar and Mark Antony. Cleopatra reigned over a cat-loving country, so it is no surprise she was fond of cats herself. Like many public people, the queen was obsessive about her looks, and it is said that she modeled her distinctive eye makeup on her cats' faces.

696 The "no ordinary cats" lady

Colette was the pen name of Sidonie Gabrielle Colette (1873–1954), a French author probably best remembered today for stories that were used as the basis of the popular movie *Gigi*. Colette had a colorful life, with several husbands and a background as a music hall dancer. She absolutely adored cats, always keeping several and writing about them in her stories. Colette claimed (correctly) that "there are no ordinary cats." She also observed, "The only risk you ever run in befriending a cat is enriching yourself."

697 Silent Cal and cats

Calvin "Silent Cal" Coolidge (1872–1933), the thirtieth U.S. president, had a reputation for being painfully quiet, perhaps even a bit chilly emotionally. But in private he was a doting husband and pet lover, and while he occupied the White House (1923–1929), several dogs, cats, raccoons and other creatures had the run of the place. One of the cats would, amazingly, let the pet canary hop about on it. Coolidge was sometimes seen sitting as his desk with one of the cats or the raccoon draped about his neck like a fox fur.

698 America's sweetheart, still active

Doris Day, the lovely blond "girl next door" who charmed movie audiences in the 1950s and 1960s, hasn't made movies in a while, but she is still active in another way, on the behalf of animals. Day has lent her time to the Doris Day Pet Foundation and various other pet organizations. She has also risked arrest at times, liberating animals she saw suffocating from the heat in parked cars. Naturally Day owns numerous cats and dogs, all of which were rescued from animal shelters. Day claims, "You haven't lived until you've lived with a cat."

699 The inimitable Boz

"Boz" was the nickname of one of the great authors of all time, Charles Dickens (1812–1870), the creator of *Oliver Twist, A Christmas Carol, David Copperfield* and other classic novels. Dickens was not an easy person to live with (which seems to be true of many writers), but he doted on his cats, including a cat he named William—who produced a litter of kittens and got renamed Williamina. (Clearly the great author didn't know much about determining the sex of cats.)

700 Who ruled Versailles?

France's King Louis XV (he ruled from 1715 to 1774) enjoyed life at the royal palace of Versailles, and part of the luxury was the many cats there, in particular his favorite white Persian, whom he would not allow anyone to tease. Gray angora cats lounged around the gambling tables, playing with the tokens. Sadly, the next king, poor Louis XVI, who went to the guillotine, was not at all fond of cats, though his wife, the ill-fated Marie Antoinette, definitely was.

701 Mr. Will

George F. Will, the newspaper columnist and political commentator, is known for being fond of baseball—and cats. In one essay, Will noted, "A cat does furnish a room. Like a graceful vase, a cat, even when motionless, seems to flow." Will has also written that "even wellfed cats are predators, apparently for the pure pleasure of the craftsmanship involved."

702 Mr. Lewis's step-cats

C. S. Lewis (1898–1963), a quiet professor of English literature, penned a popular science fiction trilogy, the well-loved *Narnia* series for children, numerous books of literary essays and many still-popular books on Christianity. Like many literary types, Lewis adored cats. In one of his letters he noted, "Yes, it *is* strange that anyone should dislike cats." When Lewis finally married late in life, he referred to his wife's pets as his "step-cats." Like many cat owners, he learned not to get ruffled when a rambunctious cat scattered his papers all over the floor.

703 Cardinal and cat

If you've visited England, you likely toured the magnificent palace of Hampton Court, which King Henry VIII "appropriated" from his lord chancellor, Cardinal Wolsey. Wolsey was, technically, a high official in the church, but he lived like a prince at Hampton Court (before Henry took it over, that is), eating and dining well and keeping a mistress. But he enjoyed simple pleasures too, including a favorite cat who ate dinner at his table and was nearby as he celebrated mass.

704 Lemonade Lucy's gifts

First Lady Lucy Hayes, the wife of the nineteenth U.S. president, Rutherford B. Hayes, is remembered for prohibiting the serving of alcohol at White House social functions—hence her nickname, "Lemonade Lucy." Lucy is also remembered (among cat lovers, that is) as the recipient of a unique gift: a pair of Siamese cats—the first Siamese cats brought to America. Brought over in 1878, they were a gift from the American consul in Bangkok, Siam (now called Thailand). Did Mrs. Hayes and the president have any idea that the Siamese would become one of the most popular breeds in America?

705 Mr. W. H., and Friend

English literature buffs know that William Shakespeare dedicated his fine sonnets to a Mr. "W. H." Literary scholars have spilled a lot of ink speculating over who this was, and many have said he was Henry Wriothesley, the Earl of Southampton. (If he is the real W. H., then Shakespeare was either dyslexic or had a reason for reversing the initials.) The handsome Wriothesley (it's pronounced "risley," by the way), like many aristocrats of his time, found himself imprisoned in the Tower of London for a while. While he was there his faithful black-and-white cat shared his prison cell, not the first or the last example of a prisoner being allowed the comfort of a feline friend.

706 Philip's Felines

The Roman emperor Marcus Julius Philippus, known to history as Philip the Arabian, reigned from 244 to 249. He was ousted by one of his army commanders, Decius, who became the next emperor and is remembered for his severe persecution of Christianity. Philip was no persecutor, and there is an old tradition that he may secretly have been a Christian himself. We do know for certain that he was very fond of cats, often letting them eat from his own table while he dined. When Philip was killed in Decius' coup, Decius also ordered all of Philip's cats destroyed.

707 The original "dunce's" pets

Our word *dunce* comes from the name John Duns Scotus (1266–1308), a Christian theologian who was anything but a dunce. In fact, his writings were so complex that only someone as intellectual as himself could have grasped the meaning. Scotus was an admirer of Saint Jerome (see 541), the Catholic scholar who kept a pet cat, and Scotus did likewise, with his gray cats Caritas (meaning "love") and Fides (meaning "faith") often stretched out on his desk while he wrote.

708 Sir John

One of the greatest minds in the reign of England's King Henry VIII was John Cheke (1514–1557), who was made the tutor to Henry's son, the future King Edward VI. Young Edward thought so highly of this master of Latin and Greek that he had him knighted. Upon Edward's death, Sir John was imprisoned in the Tower of London by the new ruler, Mary I, who did allow him the comfort of having his cat Leo with him. The story goes that Leo, apparently a very large cat, roamed around the Tower vicinity and brought back rabbits and other prey, which his master was allowed to cook for dinner.

709 Queen and cardinal

One of the most colorful characters in European history was Queen Christina of Sweden (1626–1689), who was renowned for her luxurious court and for her patronage of learning and culture. Christina converted to Catholicism, gave up her throne and moved to Rome, where she in time became the friend and later lover of an Italian cardinal, Decio Azzolino. The cardinal and his circle of cultured friends, including the composers Scarlatti and Corelli, introduced the former queen to the joys of cats. Among the cardinal's gifts to the queen was a large white longhaired cat named Alessandro, who was allowed to wander through the Riario, Christina's palace in Rome.

710 Rousseau and cats

Not Jean-Jacques Rousseau, the philosopher, but Henri Rousseau the French painter (1844–1910), remembered for his exotic, dreamlike paintings of jungles, deserts and other settings. Rousseau painted both house cats and jungle cats, although his lions and tigers are more dreamlike than lifelike. In several portraits he included the sitters' pets, and one of his most famous portraits is of a man with a handlebar mustache, a fez on his head and his rather stupefied-looking cat by his side. Some believe the sitter was the French author Pierre Loti, who was fond of cats.

711 The Russian author-artist

Alexander Pushkin (1799–1837) was one of Russia's great authors and also a lover of cats, which are mentioned in many of his writings. Pushkin was not only a professional writer but an amateur artist as well, and he loved to sketch his cats. He appeared on a Russian postage stamp in 1994, accompanied by one of his beloved cats.

712 Petrarch's mummy

The great Italian poet Petrarch (1304–1374) is remembered for the many sonnets and other poems he wrote in praise of a woman named Laura, a woman who may have existed only in his imagination. While he may have given his love to an imaginary human, he also loved his very real pet cat. In fact, he was so fond of his cat that after the cat died he had the body mummified, Egyptian-style. He kept the preserved cat over his doorway, supposedly to keep away evil spirits.

713 Bob "Spay or Neuter" Barker

He's been around a long time, and he's been preaching the same message for years: "Have your pet spayed or neutered." He's Bob Barker, the longtime host of the TV game show *The Price Is Right,* and he never fails to sign off each show without his "spay or neuter" message. Considering the huge number of abandoned puppies and kittens born each day, it is a valid message.

714 The unconventional Cocteau

The French author and filmmaker Jean Cocteau (1889–1963) was a multitalented man who led a life that was, to put it mildly, unconventional. Like many creative people, he didn't like rules or authority, and naturally he was attracted to cats and their air of independence. Cocteau claimed one reason he preferred cats over dogs was that "police cats don't exist."

715 Cats vs. philosophers

Some choice! One who sided with the cats was a noted philosopher himself, the French thinker Hippolyte Taine (1828–1893). Taine was fascinated by the role of genetics in human life, and he toyed with the idea that each person has one dominant trait on which his life and work hinges. He was also fascinated by art and wrote widely about it, and like many artsy people, he loved cats. Having rubbed shoulders with most of the (supposedly) superior people of his day, he concluded, "I have met many thinkers and many cats, but the wisdom of cats is infinitely superior."

716 Cat autobiography

E. T. A. Hoffmann (1776–1822) was a German author of fantasy stories, some of them forming the basis of the famous opera *The Tales of Hoffmann*. He wrote a curious novel, *The Life and Opinions of the Tomcat Murr,* the autobiography of a cat. Naturally Hoffmann was very fond of cats, and, as the book proves, understood them quite well. Regarding cat communication, Hoffmann wrote that the cat has "the incredible gift of expressing the one word 'meow' in many ways—joy, pain, delight, abduction, fear, desperation—in sum, all the sensations and passions." (In other words: "meow.")

717 Cat-loving misanthropes?

Is there any truth to the rumor that animal lovers don't like people? Maybe in some cases, but certainly not in the case of Albert Schweitzer (1875–1965), the noted organist and missionary doctor in Africa. Schweitzer, definitely a people lover, was renowned for his work at the famous hospital for lepers at Lambarene, and he won the Nobel Peace Prize in 1952. But the doctor was a devoted cat man, delighting in the company of his cat Sizi. A Schweitzer pearl: "There are two means of refuge from the misery of life: music and cats."

718 Cosby and the kittens

One of Bill Cosby's best comic routines has to do with a family debating over which TV show to watch. (Obviously this routine originated in the days when most families had only *one* TV.) In the routine, Dad wants to watch the western *Gunsmoke,* but the kids want to watch *Froofy the Dog*. The kids finally win the battle when they air the rumor that the *Gunsmoke* episode is going to feature the drowning of kittens. (In case you were wondering, there never was a *Gunsmoke* episode in which kittens were drowned.)

719 Calvinist cat

John Calvin (1509–1564) was one of the leaders of the Protestant Reformation in Europe and lent his name to the theological system of beliefs called Calvinism. Calvin married a young widow named Idelette, who had a favorite cat named Henriette. Since Calvin was a studious man, he took to the cat quite well. (See 752 for more about the cat-scholar bond.) Unfortunately, Idelette and the cat died in the same month, and poor Calvin never remarried or owned another cat.

720 St. Patrick the cattish

There really was a Patrick, a missionary to the Celts of Ireland, although the story that he drove the snakes from Ireland is purely legend. What is not legend is that Patrick was fond of cats, and he passed on his affection for them to the Christian monasteries that began cropping up in Ireland in the wake of his preaching. Logically, cats were the perfect animals for monasteries: they caught mice, they provided warmth and affection to men who had taken vows of celibacy and they were generally quiet, lending themselves to these places of study and meditation. Patrick was on to something.

721 The literary dictator of London

Samuel Johnson (1709–1784) is chiefly remembered as the subject of one of the great biographies of all time, *The Life of Samuel Johnson,* by his friend and admirer, James Boswell. Johnson was the literary dictator of London in his time, a sociable man who gathered in taverns with his fellow authors to discuss politics and social matters. While he clearly preferred socializing to staying at home, he did enjoy some domestic pleasures, including his faithful cat Hodge. In the biography, Boswell claimed that Johnson liked to buy his cat oysters as treats.

722 The Ivanhoe guy and his cats

Sir Walter Scott (1771–1832) was the most popular novelist of his day, world famous for his exciting historical novels such as *Rob Roy, Kenilworth* and *Quentin Durward*. Literary tastes change, and except for the classic *Ivanhoe,* Scott is rarely read today, which is a shame. Scott's success allowed him to build Abbotsford, a fine estate in Scotland. He ruled there—although visitors to Abbotsford claimed that his co-ruler was his cat, who lorded it over the dogs there, giving each an occasional slap on the head to remind them who was boss. Scott observed that "cats are mysterious kind of folk; there is more passing in their mind than we are aware of."

723 The funny Mr. Amis

The English author Kingsley Amis (1922–1995) wrote several comic novels, including *Lucky Jim, Jake's Thing* and *I Like It Here*. He also wrote a large volume of comic verse, including a poem on how he was trying (but failing) to teach English to his cat. Amis had the usual attraction for cats that authors have, and he claimed that he was "suspicious of a household that doesn't have a cat." He owned several cats himself, including Sarah Snow, a white cat who sat in his lap while he wrote.

724 The unmanned Abelard

Pierre Abelard (1079–1142) was a controversial theologian living in Paris. Although he was supposed to be celibate, he seduced a young woman, got her pregnant and paid the price by being castrated by order of the girl's uncle. The girl, Heloise, retired to a convent, and Abelard, to a monastery. They continually wrote each other. Each had the company of a cat: Abelard's was named Astrolabe, the same name given to the child Heloise bore.

725 Mr. Bentham and Langbourne

The English philosopher Jeremy Bentham (1748–1832) contributed a useful phrase to philosophy, "the greatest good for the greatest number," that served as the touchstone of his own philosophy, called Utilitarianism. In this system, Bentham tried to scientifically assign "points" to various pains and pleasures. Ranking high on his own list of pleasures was his beloved cat, Langbourne. He thought so highly of Langbourne that he invested him with titles, such as Reverend Sir John Langbourne, D.D. Incidentally, Bentham's stuffed and preserved body is actually on display at the University of London. Langbourne's is not.

726 Canterbury cat

He was known as "the Profound Doctor"—and he liked cats. He was Thomas Bradwardine

(1290–1349), and he served briefly as the archbishop of Canterbury, the head of the English church, before dying of the plague. Bradwardine was both a scientist and a theologian, and was also the chaplain of King Edward III. The king tolerated Bradwardine's affection for cats, not minding that the chaplain's cat Culbert rubbed itself against worshippers' legs while Bradwardine was celebrating mass.

727 Headless Charles

King Charles I of England (1600–1649) has the distinction of being the only English king to suffer capital punishment. He couldn't get along with his Parliament, and his armies and those of Parliament were soon at war. Charles's was defeated, and he lost his head, literally. Charles had been fortunate in having a faithful wife, Henriette, and also a faithful cat, a black one who he believed made him lucky. As it happened, the day after the black cat died Charles was arrested, and, shortly afterward, he was beheaded.

728 Bingham of Hawaii

Hiram Bingham (1789–1869) was an American missionary in Hawaii, one who accomplished two major tasks: reducing the Hawaiian language to writing and then translating the Bible into Hawaiian. In the twenty years he lived among Hawaiians, one of his closest nonhuman companions was his faithful brown tabby, which he named Barnabas after a Christian missionary in the New Testament.

729 The French chef

Julia Child is one of the icons of French cooking, made famous through her cookbooks and her TV series *The French Chef*. Born in the United States, she became enchanted with French cuisine while living with her diplomat husband in Paris. She relates a story that a cat named Minette Mimosa lived in her first Paris apartment, and the cat quickly endeared herself to the Childs by killing three mice while the family was at dinner. "We both adored her."

730 O'Rourke's theory

The humorist P. J. O'Rourke has written such popular books as *Give War a Chance* and *Parliament of Whores,* proving himself to be an insightful observer of contemporary culture. He has his own theory about why cats seem to be more popular than dogs today: people want pets who somehow mirror themselves, and most people no longer view themselves as doglike—that is, loyal, devoted, responsible, obedient. On the contrary, people today are much more like cats: "Cats are irresponsible and recognize no authority, yet are completely dependent on others for their material needs. Cats cannot be made to do anything useful. Cats are mean for the fun of it."

731 Poor Mrs. Carlyle

Thomas Carlyle (1795–1881), born in Scotland, was one of the great Victorian authors, penning several notable biographies and historical works—and making life miserable for those around him, including his long-suffering wife, Jane Welsh Carlyle. Poor Jane had to put up not only with her husband's surliness but also with the family's obnoxious cat, who wreaked havoc with the furnishings. She complained that the selfish cat was friendly only at mealtime, when it could cajole "Mr. C." into giving it table scraps. Mrs. Carlyle instructed her housekeeper to manage somehow to make the cat "disappear."

732 Catty Strachey

The English author Lytton Strachey (1880–1932) was notoriously witty—and malicious to boot. In books such as *Eminent Victorians,* he liked to cut famous people down to size, and he was equally adept at doing it face to face also. Unpleasant as he was, he did have the virtue of liking cats, an affection that found its way into some of his writings, as in a poem in which he wondered, "what mystery it is that lies /Behind those slits that glare and gleam."

733 The original Christopher Robin

A. A. Milne (1882–1956) created the Winnie-the-Pooh stories for his son, the real-life Christopher

Robin. Apparently the younger Milne developed a love for cats sometime in his life, and as an adult, he was a guest on a British radio show on which he was asked what he would like to have with him if he were marooned on a desert island. His answer: a pregnant cat.

734 Adlai the wise

The politician Adlai Stevenson (1900–1965) twice ran for president—unsuccessfully—against the very popular Dwight Eisenhower. It seemed the American public preferred "Ike," the smiling, genial war veteran, to the more intellectual Stevenson. But Stevenson did serve one term as governor of Illinois, during which time he vetoed a cat leash law passed by the Illinois legislature. Stevenson's explanation of his veto included some insightful comments, such as: "To escort a cat about on a leash is against the nature of the cat. . . . It is in the nature of cats to do a certain amount of unescorted roaming."

735 The 10 Downing Street cat

You may know that 10 Downing Street is the official residence of the prime minister of the United Kingdom. This London home has had numerous cats over the years, perhaps none more famous than Wilberforce, a large white-and-black shorthair who moved to 10 Downing Street in 1973, a gift from the Royal SPCA to the Prime Minister Edward Heath.

He stayed on through the ministries of three other prime ministers, including the cat-loving Margaret Thatcher (see 685). Wilberforce, who was named for the philanthropist-politician William Wilberforce, "retired" in 1988, after a long career as a highly competent mouser.

736 Lucky (but catless) Lindy

America's Man of the Year in 1927 was Charles Lindbergh, the gutsy pilot who flew the *Spirit of Saint Louis* in the world's first solo transatlantic crossing. In this daring venture, the plane's weight was of vital importance (the less weight, the less fuel required), so "Lucky Lindy" had to abandon his plan to take along his beloved black cat, Patsy, who had been on several of his previous flights. Perhaps it was just as well, for who knows what would have happened if Patsy's weight had been added? Both the cat and Lindy might have ended up at the bottom of the Atlantic.

737 T. R.

Theodore Roosevelt, better known as Teddy, was one of the more colorful U.S. presidents, remembered as a macho outdoorsman who enjoyed big-game hunting. But T. R. was also fond of pets, including a gray cat named Slippers, who was the unofficial White House cat. The story goes that Slippers, who obviously wasn't impressed by human pomp, sprawled out on the floor during a state dinner, while stuffy ambassadors and their escorts daintily made their way around him.

738 M. Chateaubriand

The French author Francois Rene de Chateaubriand (1768–1848) was fascinated by the wild and exotic, and his novels and poems were often set in locales far from his native France. Perhaps this was due to his spending much of his life as an ambassador in the stuffy courts of Europe. Wherever he went, Chateaubriand usually had some of his cats in tow, and he clearly admired their beauty and mystery. He wrote, "The cat pretends to sleep the better to see"—not the first or last time that a cat owner raised the suspicion that a sleeping cat is more aware of his surroundings than it might appear.

739 Cardinal Richelieu

Armand Jean du Plessis (1585–1642) is better known as Cardinal Richelieu, the chief minister of France's King Louis XIII and just as autocratic and pleasure loving as the king he served. Though he was technically a high official in the Catholic Church, Richelieu was as worldly as could be, living in grand style. Among his more innocent pleasures was his bevy of cats, including a black angora with the very un-Christian name Lucifer. Richelieu had no children (none that he acknowledged, anyway), and he left some of his vast wealth for the continuing care of his cats. But the powerful cardinal had made a lot of enemies in his day, and his will proved to be meaningless, for after his death his beloved cats were massacred by Swiss soldiers.

740 Balzac's greeter

The French novelist Honoré de Balzac (1799–1850) was fond of cats, particularly of one special cat who would greet him outside his home at his accustomed arrival time. More curious than this was that the cat also seemed to know when Balzac was coming home later than usual and as such wouldn't go out at the usual time. This isn't the only example of a cat sensing his owner's presence or absence, and behaving accordingly.

741 Leo and Micetto

Pope Leo XII, who reigned from 1823 until his death in 1829, was fond of cats, especially his beloved red-gray cat Micetto, whom he raised from kittenhood. The cat had the run of the Vatican, and while he was small the pope carried him in one of the wide sleeves of his papal robes. People who had audiences with the pope could recall seeing Micetto peering out at them—no doubt puzzled by human formality, as cats often are.

742 Charles de Gaulle and his Chartreux

In the twentieth century, Charles de Gaulle (1890–1970) stands out as the most impressive

Frenchman. A World War II general and later the president, de Gaulle devoted his entire life to the glory of France (and the glory of Charles de Gaulle as well). Naturally this lover of France had to have a distinctively French cat, and so he did: his beloved Chartreux.

743 Bitter Bierce

The American writer Ambrose Bierce (1842–1914) was a gifted but very cynical observer of human beings, as seen most clearly in *The Devil's Dictionary*, published in 1906. The "definitions" make no attempt to be objective, and only reflect Bierce's own nasty attitude to nearly everything. Bierce defined the cat as "A soft indestructible automaton provided by nature to be kicked when things go wrong in the domestic circle." Whether Bierce himself was a cat kicker or merely commenting on the common practice is not known.

744 Mr. Poet Laureate on cats

Robert Southey (1774–1843) was a friend of the poets Wordsworth and Coleridge and was himself an accomplished poet, holding the post of Poet Laureate for the last thirty years of his life. Like Wordsworth, Coleridge and numerous other writers of the Romantic period, Southey was inspired by nature, including cats, and his wife, Edith, made sure the household had plenty around. Southey wrote, "A kitten is in the animal world what a rosebud is in the garden."

745 Granddad Darwin

The scientist Charles Darwin, famous for his theory of evolution, had a famous grandfather, Erasmus Darwin (1731–1802), who was both scientist and poet. He combined his interests in *The Botanic Garden,* a long poem on flowers and other plants. He was fascinated by all of nature and, of course, he was intrigued by cats. On one occasion he wrote, "To respect the cat is the beginning of the aesthetic sense"—that is, if you appreciate the cat's beauty, you probably have a good sense of beauty in general.

746 Anne Frank's cat

The Diary of a Young Girl, published in 1953, was the diary of Anne Frank, a young Jewish girl who died in a German concentration camp in 1945. A best-seller for many years, the diary told of her years in hiding in Amsterdam, when she and her family lived in constant fear of arrest by the Nazis. Among her companions was the cat Mouschi, who proved to be a bit of a problem when the peat that ordinarily served as his litter was unobtainable. Anne reported being doubled up with laughter when Mouschi improvised by urinating on some wood shavings in the attic, with the urine trickling down into the family's living space: "It's a well-known fact that cats' puddles positively stink." (No arguing with that.)

A Litter (Pun Intended) of Cat Haters

747 Ike and Felines

"I Like Ike" ran the campaign slogan for Dwight Eisenhower, and most people apparently did like the thirty-fourth U.S. president. A World War II hero with his warm fatherly smile, Ike was a pleasant soul whom most Americans could admire. But in his eight years in the White House (1953–1961) Ike made it clear that he wanted no cats around. The story goes that he told his staff to shoot any cats on the premises. (Whether any cats were ever shot is doubtful.) Eisenhower serves as a good illustration of the saying that writers like cats while soldiers like dogs. As noted elsewhere in this book, there were notable exceptions to this truism.

748 No lullaby for cats

Musicians and composers as a group tend to like cats, but one exception was Johannes Brahms (1833–1897) famous for his four symphonies, his *German Requiem* and numerous songs, concertos and piano pieces. Poor Brahms not only didn't like cats, he actively disliked them. Some people claimed that he would actually shoot arrows at any cats he saw near his home.

749 Cowardly Henry III

France's King Henry III (1551–1589) is remembered for two things: being under the thumb of his domineering mother, Catherine de Médicis, and persecuting French Protestants. (He had helped his mother plot the notorious St. Bartholomew's Day Massacre, in which thousands of Protestants were murdered.) The effete king was deathly afraid of cats and would faint if he saw one. No doubt Frenchmen (and French cats as well) breathed a sigh of relief when the king was assassinated.

750 The cat-hating emperor

The mighty Napoleon Bonaparte, the emperor of France who fancied he could rule all of Europe, was notoriously *not* fond of cats. On one occasion during a military campaign, he called out loudly from his tents, and his aides rushed to him, perhaps expecting to find an assassin menacing their leader. The pathetic little man was, the story goes, thrusting about with his sword, fearing a cat had gotten into his tent.

751 Alexander the cat fearer

Alexander the Great, the amazing man who conquered an empire and then died in 323 B.C. while still young, was (so legend says) afraid of cats. Supposedly the fearless Alexander would even faint if a cat got near him. Truth, legend or exaggeration? Alexander isn't the only example of a domineering person who couldn't stand cats.

12

In Books, Music and Art

752 Shhh! author at work

Why is that so many bookish people—scholars, writers, librarians—are fond of cats? In a word: *silence*. Cats are basically quiet creatures, if you exempt the ones in heat, or the ones chasing the ones in heat. They don't like noise and avoid it at all costs. Bookish people like quiet—at least while they are working and usually afterward as well. Prolonged thought requires few distractions, and cats, despite their occasional bursts of playfulness, are happy to let their bookish masters work in peace, lying nearby to provide a touchable piece of fur. No wonder Saint Jerome, the saint of scholars, is so often depicted with a cat (or is it a lion?) nearby (see 541). The book you are now reading was written by an author who, most of the time, could reach over and stroke the cat napping by the computer.

753 The mystery cat industry

If you read mystery novels, you surely know the name Lilian Jackson Braun, who has created the series of Jim Qwilleran novels, each with a title beginning *The Cat Who. . . .* Qwilleran is a newspaper reporter who owns two cats, Yum and Koko (named after two characters in Gilbert and Sullivan's *The Mikado*). Just a sampling of the titles: *The Cat Who Saw Red, The Cat Who Played Brahms, The Cat Who Talked to Ghosts, The Cat Who Came to Breakfast*. It goes without saying that Braun is a devoted catoholic. She is correct in her statement that "cats never strike a pose that isn't photogenic."

754 Back from the dead, and mean

The horror fiction master Stephen King gave his readers a very frightening dog in the 1981 novel *Cujo* and followed up that success with a horrifying cat in his 1988 *Pet Sematary*. The cat begins as an adored family pet named Church, but poor Church is flattened by a truck on the highway, and his family uses the mysterious power of the pet cemetery to resurrect Church, only to find that their lovable house cat has turned into a vicious hellion. (The cat's snarling face, along with the deliberate misspelling of the title, certainly helped draw people to the book's cover.) The novel was made into a scary (but generally *bad*) movie in 1989.

755 The Amory trilogy

One of the best-loved cat books of the twentieth century was *The Cat Who Came for Christmas,* published in 1987 by the humorist Cleveland Amory. In the story, Amory rescues a scraggly, injured white cat on Christmas Eve. He has no intention of keeping him, but naturally he gets attached to the white creature, whom he names Polar Bear. The cat and the book proved so successful that Amory followed up the bestseller with two sequels, *The Cat and the Curmudgeon* and *The Best Cat Ever*.

756 The All Creatures guy

You have probably heard of James Herriot, the author of the best-selling *All Creatures Great and Small* and its sequels, all relating the tales of a veterinarian in Yorkshire, England. In fact, James Herriot is the pen name of Scottish-born James Alfred Wight, who died in 1995. Wight/Herriot included a lot of cat stories in his popular books, and one of his last books was *James Herriot's Cat Stories*. His *Moses the Kitten* is probably his best-known cat tale.

757 Gallico the cat lover

The author Paul Gallico (1897–1976) was a prolific writer, producing such children's classics as *The Snow Goose* and adult novels like *The Poseidon Adventure*. Gallico also loved to write about cats (see 856). In his highly quotable book *Honorable Cat,* he analyzed the appeal of cats as pets, why some people hate them and so on. Gallico observed that a cat "is not for the pompous, the conceited, the stuffed shirt or the unmitigated tyrant."

758 One best seller after another

Life's Little Instruction Book became popular, but who would have predicted that *A Cat's Little Instruction Book* would be such a hit? This small book by Leigh W. Rutledge contains such nuggets of wisdom as "No matter what you've done wrong, always try to make it look like the dog did it" and "Worry about courage, cleanliness, and hairballs." The author apparently based the wisdom on his own household—and its twenty-eight cats.

759 Becker and Binky

One of the surprise best sellers in recent years was *All I Need to Know I Learned from My Cat*. The author, Suzy Becker, based the book on her observations of her black-and-white cat Binky, a female cat adopted from an animal shelter. The book dispenses such timeless advice as "Take some time to eat the flowers." A mix of common sense and playful silliness, it clearly caught the public's fancy.

760 Giant purr and midget mew

Eleanor Farjeon (1881–1965) came from a talented English family of poets and artists, and she herself wrote numerous poems, among them a hymn, "Morning Has Broken," that became a hit pop song a few years after her death. Miss Farjeon was, as "Morning Has Broken" would suggest, a true nature lover and also a lover of cats. You can see some of her affection in the first stanza of "A Kitten": "He's nothing much but fur / And two round eyes of blue, / He has a giant purr / And a midget mew."

761 Wordsworth and kittens

The great English Romantic poet William Wordsworth (1770–1850) was, like most of the Romantics, intoxicated by nature, as you can see in some of his classic poems, including "I Wandered Lonely as a Cloud" (the famous daffodil poem). Wordsworth and his sister, Dorothy, who resided with him for many years, were both fond of all kinds of pets, including cats. While in his thirties he wrote "The Kitten and Falling Leaves," with the lines "See the kitten on the wall, / Sporting with the leaves that fall." The only problem with Wordsworth's poem and any other poems about cats: they never quite do justice to the real pleasure we experience in watching a cat. Words fail us.

762 Miss Lessing

The contemporary English feminist novelist Doris Lessing has written insightful novels about the relations between men and women. She has also written about the relationship between humans and cats, as in one story, "Particularly Cats," which is full of wry observations on her various cats, such as one finicky eater who was "as fussy over her food as a bachelor gourmet," and another who "still is beautiful, but, there is no glossing it, she's a selfish beast."

763 The Jungle Book man

The British author Rudyard Kipling (1865–1936) won the Nobel Prize in Literature for his poetry, but he is probably best remembered for *The Jungle Book,* which features several big cat characters, such as the panther Bagheera and the fierce tiger Shere Khan. He also wrote the wonderful story "The Cat Who Walked by Himself," in which Man and Woman tame all manner of animals but don't quite succeed in taming the cat. The cat finally agrees to live in the humans' house and catch mice, but he is never completely tamed. He is "the cat who walks by himself." As you might expect, Kipling was very fond of cats.

764 Just call him Saki

The British writer Hector Hugh Munro (1870–1916) wrote his many clever short stories under the pen name Saki. Among Saki's stories is "Tobermory," whose title character is a cat who can talk. Some of the human characters tease Tobermory about his having an affair with a lady cat who lives at the stable. Then it dawns on them that the cat, climbing around in windowsills as cats are inclined to do, is all too aware of *their* affairs.

765 Skelton's curse

The English poet John Skelton (circa 1460–1529) was a real character, technically a priest in spite of fathering a few out-of-wedlock children, and someone who liked to hobnob at the king's court but who constantly made enemies because of his outspokenness and biting wit. Skelton's poetry covers a lot of subjects, some serious, some not. He had a knack for mingling the two, as in his poem "A Curse on a Cat," in which he lambastes a cat for eating his pet bird: "O cat of churlish kind / The fiend was in thy mind / When thou my bird untwin'd."

766 Glanvil's apt description

A certain Bartholomew Glanvil was the author of *De Rerum Natura,* a book on nature written in 1398. In it he offers a long description of cats. For the reader's benefit, I modernized the spelling somewhat for this excerpt: "The cat is in its youth swift, pliant, and merry, and leapeth and resteth on all things that are before him. . . . And he is full sleepy, and lieth slily in wait for mice." Sound like any cats you know?

767 Shy Miss Dickinson

She's considered one of the great American poets, though she was practically unknown in her lifetime (1830–1886). Emily Dickinson lived a retiring life in New England, traveling little and seeing few people besides her family. So many of her delightful poems focus on everyday things that intrigued her, including the sights and sounds of her garden, descriptions of which she could compress so beautifully into four-line stanzas. Inevitably she encountered cats, as we see in "She Sights a Bird": "She sights a bird—she chuckles— / She flattens—then she crawls— / She runs without the look of feet— / Her eyes increase to balls." The poem has a happy ending, but not for the cat: the prey, a robin, manages to get away.

768 Cat in the Poe house

Edgar Allan Poe (1809–1849) gave the world some enchanting poetry and some truly chilling horror stories, none more memorable than "The Black Cat." The tale is narrated by a man who is clearly going insane, as he proves by cutting out the eye of his beloved cat, Pluto. He also murders his wife and bricks up her body inside a wall, assuming no one will ever find her. But (sorry to give away the ending of the story!) the murder is revealed when the man and the police investigating his wife's disappearance hear screams from behind the wall that turn out to be the pitiful cries of Pluto, who was also bricked up in the wall.

769 The lowercase cat

Please note: when referring to the cat mehitabel created by Don Marquis (1878–1937), never capitalize her name. The cat was a character in a series of stories allegedly typed out by a cockroach named archy (also lowercase), who couldn't hold the shift key down to make capital letters. The entertaining archy and mehitabel stories, with Marquis's own delightful drawings, portray the cat as a basic alley cat who never quite succeeds in being the lady she would like to be. Both archy and mehitabel claimed to have been reincarnated, with mehitabel affirming that she had been a cat belonging to Cleopatra—or Cleopatra herself.

770 Bushy and Pancho

Bushy is a Maine Coon cat and Pancho is a stray, and both belong to Alice Nestleton, the heroine of the mystery novels of Lydia Adamson. Alice is both a part-time actress and a cat sitter, and inevitably (as happens in mystery novels) she gets drawn into murder cases that always involve cats in some way, of course, and are always solved at the end of the novel. You will notice a definite pattern in some of Adamson's titles: *A Cat in a Manger, A Cat of a Different Color, A Cat by Any Other Name, A Cat with a Fiddle.*

771 Sandburg and Fog

The beloved American poet Carl Sandburg wrote one of the world's most famous cat poems—though it really isn't about cats. It is "Fog," published in 1916, and brief enough to quote here: "The fog comes / on little cat feet. / It sits looking / over harbor and city / on silent haunches / and then moves on." People who have never heard the name Carl Sandburg have certainly heard of fog coming "on little cat feet."

772 "Sphinx of my quiet hearth!"

The Victorian poet Rosamund Marriott Watson certainly understood cats, as is obvious in her brief poem "To My Cat." Consider just a few phrases from it: "Half loving-kindness and half disdain . . . serenely suave . . . Sphinx of my quiet hearth! . . . companion of mine ease . . . with somber, sea-green gaze inscrutable." Certainly the lady grasped the essence of catness.

773 Cat elegy

The English poet Thomas Gray (1716–1771) wrote very serious poetry, including the well-loved "Elegy Written in a Country Churchyard," but he could be playful, as in his "On the Death of a Favorite Cat, Drowned in a Tub of Goldfishes." In the poem, the cat, Selima, is attracted to the fishes' gold color, but she slips into the water and drowns, which Gray playfully uses to teach the lesson that those (humans, that is) who seek gold are flirting with disaster. Considering how flippant the poem is, we can assume Gray was not a cat person.

774 Bad press

Textbook authors are human, and they have their own prejudices about things. Consider this excerpt from an 1809 book titled *Natural History for Children*: “The cat is a very false and faithless and thievish animal which neither by caresses and good feeling nor by blows and imprisonment can be so tamed that it will not scratch and steal. It is and always remains a malignant deceiver.”

775 Bad press, II

Consider another example from a supposedly “scientific” textbook published in 1833: “How it scratches and bites and robs and steals! There is no worse thief than the cat. For that reason many people cannot endure it, and some find cats so repellent to their natures that they fall in a faint if a cat so much as comes close to them.” (Well, too bad for them.)

776 Mad Mr. Smart

Christopher Smart (1722–1771), known as Kit, was a gifted English poet who, sadly, ended up spending much of his life in an insane asylum. Even when there, he wrote some brilliant poetry, much of it on Christian themes. During one of his periods in the asylum, he wrote a poem praising his one companion, his beloved cat, Jeoffry, who “is the servant of the Living God duly and daily serving him.” The poem is alternately playful and devout, sometimes both, and Smart clearly adored cats, "For there is nothing sweeter than his peace when at rest, / For there is nothing brisker than his life when in motion." If there is an Ultimate Cat Poem, this is it.

777 Wilde cat

Oscar Wilde (1854–1900) was an Irish-born wit, perhaps most famous for his farcical plays like *The Importance of Being Earnest* and also the strange novel *The Picture of Dorian Gray*. But Wilde was also enchanted by cats, so much so that he penned a long poem, *The Sphinx,* in which he praised the feminine (and feline) traits of the mythical sphinx.

778 Mad and gentle Cowper

Poor William Cowper (1731–1800) spent part of his life in insane asylums and much of the rest of his life fearing he would go mad again. Oddly, his poetry is sane and gentle, a celebration of the small pleasures in life, including pets and wild animals. He wrote hymns, translated Homer's epics and wrote poems that still charm readers with his kindly view of the world. In his poem "The Retired Cat," Cowper wrote of a cat who climbed a tree and "Lodg'd with convenience in the fork, / She watched the gardener at his work."

779 The Macbeth sisters

William Shakespeare's tragedy *Macbeth* has numerous references to cats, mostly because the play features the three "weird sisters," the witches who prophesy that Macbeth will become the king of Scotland. Shakespeare's audience (and ours, for that matter) would have expected the witches to have dealings with cats. In the famous first scene of the play, the three hags gather on the heath, with one responding to the call of Graymalkin, a cat. In the equally famous scene where the witches make their brew in the cauldron ("Double, double toil and trouble"), they speak of the mewing of the "brindled cat."

780 Mr. Swine-borne

The British author Algernon Charles Swinburne (1837–1909) was admired by many but called "Mr. Swine-borne" by others, thanks to his boozing, womanizing and outspoken remarks against religion and morality. But he could on occasion write tender poetry, including his "Ode to a Cat," in which he praises the cat's "wonderful wealth of hair" which "pays my reverent hand's caress / back with friendlier gentleness."

781 Are you ready to order?

Tony Lawson and his wife produced *The Cat-Lovers' Cookbook,* filled with clever illustrations and recipes for such dishes as Meow Sushi, Kitty Pizza and (of course) Chicken Soup. While the recipes are mostly intended for cats, not their owners, the "Tandem Cooking" section of the book has recipes that both pet and owner can delight in.

782 Chaucer and his pilgrims

If you can manage to overlook the archaic language, *The Canterbury Tales* by Geoffrey Chaucer (1343–1400) are still a delight to read. Chaucer's famous work is the account of religious pilgrims journeying from London to Canterbury. Along the way they entertain one another with stories, many of which mention cats. One is "The Manciple's Tale," which makes the observation that even the most pampered cat—who is fed delicacies and sleeps on a silken bed—will revert to her true predatory self whenever a mouse scampers by.

783 Keats and cats

Poor John Keats died before he even reached age thirty (he lived from 1795 until 1821) yet still he managed to produce a large body of work, including some of the most-read and most-quoted poems in the English language, such as "Ode to a Nightingale" and "Ode on a Grecian Urn." Keats also wrote "To Mrs. Reynolds' Cat," praising a cat's mouse-catching ability, "velvet ears" and "latent talons." But this particular cat has seen better days, for "thy tail's tip is nick'd off."

784 Gloomy Mr. Hardy

The English poet and novelist Thomas Hardy (1840–1928) is remembered for such novels as *Tess of the D'Urbervilles, The Return of the Native* and *Far from the Madding Crowd* and his many excellent poems, all of which show that their author had a rather pessimistic view of human life, though on occasion some wit and warmth sneak through. Hardy shared the typical writer's affection for cats, as seen in his poem "Last Words to a Dumb Friend"—the "friend" is a cat, of course. Some of Hardy's affection for cats, as well as his gloomy view of things, can be seen in these lines: "Never another pet for me! / Let your place all vacant be; / Better blankness day by day / Than companion torn away."

785 Philip the perfect

Sir Philip Sidney (1554–1586) was regarded by the English people of his day as the perfect Renaissance man—an accomplished poet, scholar, soldier and a gentleman. He is remembered today as the author of the love sonnet cycle *Astrophel and Stella* and for his *Apology for Poetry,* a long essay on the art of the poet. Sir Philip, among his many other virtues, delighted in cats, as seen in these lines: "I have (and long shall have) a white, great, nimble cat, / A king upon a mouse, a strong foe to the rat."

786 Desmond Morris

The English author Desmond Morris is a noted author on the subject of cats and is the proud owner of a black cat named Jambo. Morris, who oversees the care of mammals at the London Zoo, has written *Catwatching* and *Catlore,* two popular books on his favorite animals. Morris has made the observation that "artists like cats, soldiers like dogs"—a truth to which there are many exceptions and yet, as various entries in this book have shown, is true more often than not.

787 Christina Rossetti

Miss Rossetti (1830–1894) was a gifted poet and the sister of two other noted writers, Dante and William. Unlike the swinging, loose-living Dante, Christina was quiet and religious, and many of her poems made their way into Christian hymnbooks. This shy, withdrawn woman was, naturally, very fond of cats, as seen in her poem "On the Death of a Cat, a Friend of Mine, Aged Ten Years and a Half," which begins with the lines "Who shall tell the lady's grief / When her cat was past relief?" This elegy for a cat somehow manages to be both tragic and playful.

Literature for Kids (of All Ages)

788 Mary Calhoun, cat industry

Children's author Mary Calhoun has almost built an industry on her popular cat books, many of them centering on a spunky Siamese cat named Henry, who appears in *Henry the Sailor Cat, Hi-wire Henry,* and *Cross-country Cat.* Calhoun's Henry books owe their charm in no small part to the watercolor illustrations of Erick Ingraham, who gets to show the indomitable Henry doing things like skiing on snow. Calhoun is also the author of *House of Thirty Cats.*

789 Socks, pre-White House

The acclaimed children's author Beverly Cleary is best known for *Ramona the Pest,* but she also published the very funny *Socks,* a 1973 story of a cat (named Socks, of course) whose life is radically (and amusingly) altered when his owners add a baby to the family. Somehow poor Socks manages, in time, to get over his jealousy, and (this won't surprise you) by the book's end, he and baby are good friends.

790 Cricket, cat and mouse

The Cricket in Times Square by George Selden is a perennially popular children's story about Chester Cricket, who by accident is uprooted from his country home and forced live in the "wilds" of Manhattan. But all is not lost; he is adopted by Mario, a young boy, and offered the companionship of Harry Cat and Tucker Mouse (who make a curious pair). While the book is filled with fascinating characters, cat lovers who read the book as children (and now read the book aloud to their own kids) seem to think that Harry Cat is the most interesting character in the story. Not that cat lovers would be prejudiced, of course. . . .

791 Cats in heaven? no doubt

Elizabeth Coatsworth wrote excellent books for kids, including *The Cat Who Went to Heaven,* about a stray calico cat taken in by a Japanese artist and given the name Good Fortune. The cat proves true to the name, which is fortunate, as the poor artist is on the verge of starving. For the companionship and inspiration given to the master, the cat is welcomed into heaven by Buddha. Published in 1930, the book is still touching, and it provides some interesting insights into Asian culture, including how Asians view the domestic cat.

792 Koko and the kit

Francine Patterson wrote two books on her remarkable pet gorilla, Koko, who has proven adept at learning and communicating via American Sign Language. Koko seemed to be attracted to pictures of cats, so Patterson gave the gorilla a tiny gray kitten that Koko named All Ball (it was tailless) and showered with affection. The photos of the hulking (but gentle) gorilla coddling the wide-eyed kitten surely helped sell Patterson's books, *The Education of Koko* and (for children) *Koko's Kitten.*

793 Cat diva

Opera Cat, a popular children's book of recent years, tells the tale of Alma, who is the pet of Madame SoSo, an opera singer. Alma herself secretly practices singing and longs to perform onstage. Her big break comes when Madame SoSo gets a bad case of (you guessed it) laryngitis. This amusing story by Tess Weaver, illustrated by Andrea Wesson, obviously tips its hat to all the clichés about cats being noisy and very *un*musical.

794 Feline paradise

Cynthia Rylant's 1997 book *Cat Heaven* is a delight for adults as well as its intended audience, kids. In a brilliantly colored cat heaven, cats are cared for by a kindly God and snuggle in the laps of angels, but are also given ample time to frolic. They can even remember their lives on Earth and, of course, their human caretakers. The book was obviously written to provide comfort to anyone who has ever lost a beloved pet. The same author also wrote an earlier book, *Dog Heaven,* but cat owners (who are unbiased, of course) seem to think that *Cat Heaven* is a better book.

795 Nativity kitty

Cat in the Manger, illustrated by Michael Foreman, follows a familiar formula: telling the story of the birth of Jesus through the eyes of an animal. In this case, the narrator is a mouse-catching barn cat who happens to witness, on a chilly night, her turf invaded by Joseph, Mary and, soon, the newborn Jesus. Like the better sort of children's books, the art in this one appeals to adults as much as it does to kids.

796 The classic Puss in Boots

The tale of a poor miller's son who inherits nothing but a cat has been around for centuries, going back to the Italian storyteller Giovan Straparola, who published his version of the story in 1550. Charles Perrault published the story in 1697 with the title *Le Maitre chat ou le chat botte*—"The Master-Cat, or, the Cat in Boots." In all the versions of the story, the miller's cat turns out to be quite clever (and a superb mouse catcher, of course), helping his master become a wealthy man. The story isn't read as often as it used to be, but certainly the title was perpetuated in the name of an old brand of cat food, Puss 'n Boots.

797 Three Little Kittens

The famous poem "Three Little Kittens" is so old and familiar that many people probably assume it is an anonymous nursery rhyme. In fact, Ellen Lee Follen was the author of this whimsical piece about the three little kittens who lose their mittens, resulting in their not getting pie until they find them again. But then the pie soils the mittens, and the three have to wash their mittens and hang them out to dry.

798 Esther Averill, cat woman

The children's author Esther Averill has written numerous books, many of them about a gang of spunky cats living in New York City's Greenwich

Village. The Cat Club includes Madame Butterfly, Macaroni, Mr. President and the black cat Jenny Linsky, whose owner is a sea captain. Jenny is at the center of many of these books, which include *The Cat Club, Captains of the City Streets, Jenny's Birthday Book, The Hotel Cat* and *The Fire Cat* (named Pickles, who lives in a fire station).

799 Cats in painter overalls

The Color Kittens was published more than fifty years ago by Little Golden Books, but the delightful book about kittens Brush and Hush is still popular. Dressed in painters' overalls and caps, the two kitties with their buckets of paint are determined to make "all the colors in the world." The story was written by author Margaret Wise Brown, with classic illustrations by Alice and Martin Provenson.

800 Barnyard adventure

The Shy Little Kitten was another popular children's tale in the classic Little Golden Book series. While *The Color Kittens* (see 799) was really about color, not cats, *The Shy Little Kitten* is about a very real farm kitten who happens to wander off from her mom and siblings and in the course of the day encounters a frog, a squirrel and a puppy. First published in 1946, the story was by Cathleen Schurr, and the adorable black-and-white kitten and other critters were drawn by Gustav Tenngren.

801 Trillions of cats

Millions of Cats, first published in 1928, is still a delight to read. Written and illustrated by Wanda Gag, this children's book tells of an elderly couple who want a cat, specifically, the most beautiful cat in the world. The husband goes out on a quest to find such a cat and ends up returning with "hundreds of cats, thousands of cats, millions and billions and trillions of cats." The couple can't keep them all, of course, so they end up keeping one scrawny white kitten—who, to the pleasure of the old couple (and the reader) turns out to be the most beautiful cat in the world.

802 In two words: Beatrix Potter

The English author-illustrator Beatrix Potter centered her many classic children's books around the creatures she knew at her country home: rabbits, ducks, squirrels, hedgehogs and (naturally) cats. While she is best known for *The Tale of Peter Rabbit,* she also wrote *The Tale of Tom Kitten,* published in 1907. In the tale, three rambunctious kittens have various adventures, upset their mother's dignified tea party and manage to be both mischievous and adorable—as real cats so often are.

803 When mom's away, the cat will play

Theodore Seuss Geisel (1904–1991) is better known by the pen name Dr. Seuss, and one of the most famous Seuss creations was *The Cat in the Hat,* published in 1957. The lanky cat in his famous red-and-white stovepipe hat shows up to entertain two bored children while their mother is away, creating chaos (isn't that what cats do?) but thoroughly enchanting kids and their parents. A whole generation of kids grew up on the rhymed antics of the cat and the kids, spawning (of course) a sequel to the book, numerous Cat in the Hat toys and, in 2003, a live-action movie starring the comic Mike Myers as the cat.

804 Alice's Dinah

In the classic children's book *Alice in Wonderland,* Dinah is the adored pet of Alice, and Alice is playing with the cat when she sees a white rabbit duck down a hole, thus beginning many strange adventures. Several of the weird Wonderland inhabitants—such as the Dormouse—get very upset when Alice speaks fondly of her dear cat Dinah.

805 Alice's grinning Friend

"Grinning like a Cheshire cat" (see 600) did not originate with *Alice in Wonderland,* but certainly the book has helped keep the phrase alive. The cat in *Alice* is quite large and has a big, toothy grin. In a memorable passage in the book, the cat disappears little by little, beginning at the tale and continuing until only the grin remains. The cat's head appears at the croquet game of the Queen of Hearts, who is infuriated because she wants to behead the cat but can't because the cat's head doesn't have a body! The famous illustrations of these scenes were done by artist John Tenniel.

806 Playing and slaying

It's true: cats like to play with their prey before they finally kill it. That truism made its way into the earliest American book, *The New England Primer.* Written and published by Puritans, the *Primer* sought to teach Christian beliefs and morals, as shown in its poem on the alphabet, where the entry for *A* is "In Adam's fall / We sinned all" and for *B,* "Thy life to mend, / This Book [the Bible, that is] attend." But the *Primer* was less explicitly religious for the letter *C*: "The cat doth play / And after slay." The charming woodcut illustration for this entry shows a cat romping over three terrified mice. Thus, the cat holds the distinction of being the first animal depicted in an American book.

807 Mr. Eliot and Old Possum

The poet T. S. Eliot was born in America but settled in England, where he wrote *very* serious poetry and won the Nobel Prize for Literature in 1948. But occasionally he felt playful, enough so that he created the poems in *Old Possum's Book of Practical Cats,* published in 1939. ("Old Possum" was Eliot's nickname.) The poems show that Eliot loved cats and was familiar with the "personality types" among them. Jenny Annydots, the "Gumby Cat," is the stereotypical "lap cat," adored and adorable, while the Rum Tum Tugger is the irritating tomcat who always makes trouble. Grizzabella is an alley cat whose face and body have seen better days. The poems would have been long forgotten had they not been used as the basis of the popular musical *Cats* (see 827).

808 Orlando and family

Some of the most delightful cats in children's literature were the products of the fertile imagination of the American author Kathleen Hale, who created the orange cat Orlando, his brown wife Grace and the kittens Pansy, Blanche and Tinkle. Orlando was basically just a human character in cat form. He did all sorts of human things, including visiting the moon in 1968—a year before humans landed there. Hale told Orlando's many adventures in a series of eighteen books.

809 Gingham and calico

The American author Eugene Field (1850–1895) was known as the "poet of childhood," and he did pen some delightful poems that appeal to children (of all ages). One that used to be read by practically every child in America was "The Duel," which begins "The gingham dog and the calico cat, / Side by side on the table sat." The two stuffed animals fight like real cats and dogs until they actually devour each other.

810 Mr. Lear's famous pair

The English humorist Edward Lear (1812–1888) wrote hundreds of delightful poems, many of them illustrated with his own distinctive drawings. Probably none of his poems is more famous than "The Owl and the Pussycat," who "went to sea in a beautiful pea-green boat." Lear had a favorite tabby cat, Foss, who was supposedly the model for the cat in the poem's illustrations. Lear was so fond of Foss that when the cat died at age seventeen, the author not only buried him reverently but set up a tombstone on the grave.

811 Generation gap cat

Can a pet help bridge the generation gap between father and son? That question is at the center of the award-winning novel *It's Like This, Cat* by Emily Neville. Written for older children, the 1964 book centers around eleven-year-old Dave, whose father wants him to get a dog—instead Dave gets an abandoned yellow tomcat, giving it the clever name Cat. He and Cat have various adventures in New York City, and by the end of the book, Dave's dad has (naturally) decided he rather likes cats in general, and Cat in particular.

Art and Artists

812 Theophile Steinlen

The Swiss-born artist Theophile Alexandre Steinlen (1859–1923) lived in Paris as the proverbial starving artist for many years, though his talent and persistence finally paid off. Steinlen adored cats so much that his home became known as Cat's Corner. The artist loved to sketch the many street cats of Paris, as well as the pets of friends. Unlike his contemporary Renoir (see 825), Steinlen didn't limit himself to depicting only placidly sleeping cats but also depicted them playing and hunting.

813 Poor mad Louis Wain

The English artist Louis Wain (1860–1939) began drawing cats as a way to cheer up his ailing wife, Emily, who nudged him into submitting the sketches to magazines. He did and became England's top cat artist. In his artistic world "Catland," cats (usually clothed) are shown boating, riding bicycles and engaging in all sorts of human activities. Alas, the successful artist became more and more eccentric and finally had to be committed to a mental hospital. He continued to draw and paint cats, and as his mental health continued to decline, his cat images became less cute and sentimental and more and more bizarre, a sad record of his inner state.

814 The Peaceable Kingdom

Christian artists have taken great pleasure in painting illustrations of the "peaceable kingdom" Bible passage (Isaiah 11:6–9) which prophesies a time when "the wolf shall dwell with the lamb, and the leopard shall lie down with the kid, and the calf and the lion together." That is, a heaven when creatures who are mortal enemies on Earth will instead coexist harmoniously. Artists love this theme because it gives them an opportunity to depict all sorts of animals, and, along with the big cats such as leopards and lions, they inevitably put in a domestic cat or two, lying down in blissful repose with some contented mice. A lovely image—*heavenly*—but far removed from real cats and real rodents.

815 Currier and Ives

Nathaniel Currier and James Ives went into business together in 1857, producing for fifty years lithographs that were a virtual history of American life. Among the hundreds of prints they produced (still highly valued by collectors) there were, inevitably, some delightful images of cats, such as *Little White Kitties into Mischief,* showing two shorthaired white kittens eagerly lapping up milk from an overturned cup.

816 Der Katzen Raphael

You probably know that Raphael (1483–1520) was one of the great painters of the Renaissance, but you may not have heard of Gottfried Mind (1768–1814), a Hungarian-born artist who specialized in pictures of cats. Living in Switzerland, Mind painted so many fine cat pictures that he became known as *Der Katzen Raphael.* Naturally, he had a houseful of cats of his own to use as models, and he was especially fond of Minette, who was near him when he worked.

817 Fifteen minutes of cat fame

The artist Andy Warhol (1928–1987) was either a creative genius or a cynical hack, depending on your point of view. Warhol was at the front of the movement called Pop Art, producing paintings of soup cans and celebrity photographs and operating from a studio called The Factory. Artists are rarely quotable, but Warhol is remembered for his statement that in the future "everyone will be famous for fifteen minutes." Warhol was fond of cats, as most artists are, and his affection is shown in his many delightful drawings of Sam and other cats.

818 Adam and Eve and perfect peace

"The Fall" is the name theologians give to the disobedience of Adam and Eve in the Garden of Eden. Before the Fall, the two lived in paradise, with no strife or hard labor, and this perfect peace extended to the animal kingdom as well, with all the beasts living in harmony. Thus the German artist Albrecht Dürer (1471–1528) was able to include in his famous engraving of Adam and Eve a cat and a mouse, with the cat totally ignoring the mouse. The cat wasn't being lazy, but instead Dürer was reflecting the traditional Christian belief that the world was a better place before man disobeyed God.

819 Jesus with a kitten

As noted elsewhere (see 508), cats are not mentioned in the Bible, but that didn't stop artists from painting cats into their pictures of the Bible. The master artist Leonard da Vinci (1451–1519) did so in his *Madonna and Child with a Cat,* which is a picture of the Virgin Mary and the baby Jesus, who is holding a kitten (though it's unlikely that the real Jesus ever did so). Leonardo, like all artists, appreciated beauty, whether in the human body or in nature, and he was intrigued by the shape of cats. He stated that "the smallest feline is a masterpiece." He sketched cats in numerous poses.

820 Madonna and cat

According to Christian folklore, at the moment the Virgin Mary gave birth to Jesus, in the same stable a mother cat gave birth to a litter of kittens—an interesting (and harmless) idea, and one that artists found appealing. The next time you are in an art museum, browse the medieval and Renaissance paintings of the Nativity and see if perhaps, tucked away in a corner of the painting, there isn't a mother cat with some newborn kittens.

821 Demon cats

Saint Anthony, an early Christian hermit, lived to the ripe old age of 105, dying in the year 356. Anthony claimed that in his many years in the Egyptian wilderness he was frequently tormented by tempting demons. Because Anthony was a popular saint, he was often depicted in art, and painters delighted in showing the skinny saint surrounded by all sorts of gruesome, demonic beasties. Many were in the form of monstrous cats, as in *The Temptation of St. Anthony* by the Flemish painter Hieronymous Bosch. He and other painters were probably aware of the long connection of cats with Egypt.

822 The ultimate: oriental rugs and cats

Take one of the most beautiful things made by man (an oriental rug) and one of the most beautiful things made by God (a cat), and you have the makings for a fine picture. This was the reasoning of the English artist Lesley Anne Ivory, whose many paintings of cats show the creatures on such exquisite settings as oriental rugs. Perhaps including the rugs was inevitable, given that she had studied textile design. Ivory owns several cats, naturally, and they serve as models for her paintings. Prints of her paintings are popular, as are her books *Cats Know Best, Cats in the Sun* and *Glorious Cats,* among others.

823 Picasso's wild cats

Most artists have chosen to depict cats in placid, adorable poses. Not so Pablo Picasso (1881–1973), the noted Spanish painter who was an unstoppable force in twentieth-century art. Picasso was intrigued with the very unadorable alley cats he knew, and he immortalized one in *Cat Eating a Bird.* (Nothing sweet or cuddly about *that* cat!) Picasso claimed he had painted a "real" cat, something wild and fiendish, quite unlike the stereotypical lap cat.

824 Frontier cat

The American artist George Caleb Bingham (1811–1879) was one of the Frontier Painters, known for their scenes of the American West. One of his best-known works is *Fur Traders on the Missouri River,* now housed at New York's Metropolitan Museum of Art. Rather surprisingly, on the fur traders' boat is a black cat, tied to a leash but seemingly at ease even though it is only inches from the water.

825 M. Renoir

The French Impressionist painter Pierre Auguste Renoir (1841–1919) was drawn to prettiness and serenity, as seen in his many paintings of women, children and gardens. Naturally a man attracted to serenity had to be attracted to cats, and so he included them in several of his paintings. The Renoir cats are inevitably asleep in the laps of his models (always girls and women), probably because Renoir liked the look of a sleeping cat, but, more importantly, because a sleeping cat is itself the perfect model.

826 Will and Fatso

"Fatso" is the nickname for Madame Butterfly, the plump cat belonging to the artist Will Barnet. She has appeared in many of his paintings of people with cats. (Happily, there are some modern artists like Barnet who paint objects people can actually recognize.) Madame Butterfly is a calico cat, though Barnet has been willing to alter her color to suit the other colors in the painting.

The Music Scene

827 In a word, Cats

Years after the poet T. S. Eliot's death, along came the pop opera composer Andrew Lloyd Webber, of *Jesus Christ Superstar* and *Evita* fame. Collaborating with the stage producer Trevor Nunn, he wove Eliot's poems fom *Old Possum's Book of Practical Cats* into a plotless but fascinating stage production, with some very athletic young singers and dancers romping about in cat makeup and costumes. *Cats* premiered onstage in London in 1980 and on Broadway in 1982, where it proved to be a durable crowd-pleaser, becoming Broadway's longest-running musical. Set to the bouncy music of Andrew Lloyd Webber, the poems have reached more people than has any of Eliot's serious verse.

828 Witty Mr. Gilbert, and partner

The team of the writer William S. Gilbert and the composer Arthur S. Sullivan gave the world such comical stage classics as *The Mikado, H.M.S. Pinafore, The Yeomen of the Guard* and other staples of musical theater. Scattered throughout Gilbert's wickedly funny lyrics are references to cats, mostly famously in a scene from *The Pirates of Penzance,* in which the goofy pirates stage a burglary and enter a home while singing the song "With catlike tread upon our prey we steal" at the top of their lungs, according to Gilbert's stage directions. Audiences still laugh out loud at the bungling pirates who clearly do not know how to be catlike. Gilbert's lyrics sometimes quoted popular proverbs about cats, as in the line from *H.M.S Pinafore*: "Once a cat was killed by care."

829 The Colette collaboration

The French composer Maurice Ravel (1875–1937) was a good friend of the author Colette (see 696), and they shared a love of cats. When Ravel and Colette collaborated on an opera, it was inevitable that there would be cat characters in it. Colette wrote the libretto and Ravel wrote the music for the 1925 opera *L'Enfant et Les Sortileges*—"the child and the magic spells," and this very unusual work includes a love duet sung by a tomcat and his lady love.

830 Bunyan's cats

The English composer Benjamin Britten wrote a curious opera, *Paul Bunyan,* that debuted in 1941. The hero, who is never seen, is the legendary giant lumberjack of the American woodlands. Two of the offbeat roles in this very offbeat opera are the cats Moppet and Poppet—both parts sung by women and in very "catty" voices. The opera's libretto was written by the poet W. H. Auden, himself a noted cat lover.

831 Miauliques

You might remember the *Three Stooges* episode where the three buffoons, working as pest controllers, bring a sack full of cats into a wealthy family's home, eventually hiding the cats in the piano. When someone attempts to play the piano, the cats let loose a very unmusical version of *The Blue Danube.* Believe it or not, in times past some impresarios actually would try to sell tickets to musical cat shows, known to the French as *miauliques.* Anyone who ever heard tomcats meowing in an alley can guess how unsuccessful these shows were.

832 Ragtime cat

Without a doubt you've heard the ragtime piano song "Kitten on the Keys." It was written by the composer Zez Confrey (1895–1971), who claimed the song was inspired by a visit to his grandmother's house. In the middle of the night he was awakened by her cat, who was treading on the piano keyboard. Thus was born one of the bounciest of ragtime tunes. Confrey insisted that at certain points in the song the pianist had to pound the keyboard with his fists in order to duplicate (more or less) the randomness of the "kitten on the keys."

833 Rydell's tomcat song

Bobby Rydell had a pop hit with "The Alley Cat Song" in 1963. The song isn't about a real cat but, rather, a man who is not exactly monogamous. "He goes on the prowl each night / Like an alley cat." The words to the song were written by Jack Harlen and set to the music of a Danish composer, Frank Bjorn. (The music originally had the title "Around the Piano" and had no connection at all with cats or philandering men.) The song—played often in a bouncy instrumental version on the piano—is just one other example of how the public connects alley cats to the concept of promiscuity.

834 The Barber guy, and cats

The Italian composer Giacchino Rossini (1792–1868) gave the world such opera classics as *The Barber of Seville* and *William Tell*. He was fascinated by cats, as seen in his *Duetto Buffo dei due*

Gatti—"comic duet of two cats." In this composition the two "cats" are actually two sopranos, "meowing" to each other in a truly delightful piece of music.

835 Peter and the cat

The Russian composer Serge Prokofiev's symphonic poem *Peter and the Wolf* premiered in 1936 and has remained popular. The piece is a "musical fable," using a narrator and different instruments to portray the boy, Peter, his grandfather, a pet duck and a wolf. A cat (portrayed by a clarinet) almost catches a bird (a flute), but Peter warns the bird just in time. Cat lovers still argue about whether the character—or voice—of the cat is properly conveyed by the sound of a clarinet.

836 Tchaikovsky's fantasy ballet

The Russian composer Pyotr Ilich Tchaikovsky's beautiful ballet *Sleeping Beauty* premiered in 1890, and its third act included the wedding of Princess Aurora, in which various fairy tale characters join the celebration. Among these were the famous Puss in Boots, who danced divinely (how else would a cat dance?) with his lady love, the White Cat.

837 The Gautier cat tribe

The French author Théophile Gautier (1811–1872) was noted for his fondness for cats, including one whom he named Madame Théophile. He also owned his adored Eponine, who dined at the table with him.

Gautier wrote at length about cats, including this astute observation: "If you are worthy of his affection, a cat will be your friend but never your slave." Gautier collaborated with the composer Frederic Massenet in writing the opera *Le Preneur de Rats,* "The Ratcatcher."

838 Year of the Cat

The Scottish pop singer Al Stewart had a hit in 1976 with his album *Year of the Cat*. The album and its popular title song had nothing to do with real cats, since the "cat" in the song was simply a very seductive woman. However, cat lovers were intrigued with the art on the album cover, showing a woman (wearing a cat mask and paws) at a vanity table with Cat's Whisker perfume, Kitty chocolates, Chat cigarettes and even coins and paper money graced with the figures of cats. At the very bottom of the image is the tail of one real cat, a gray tabby. A classic of 1970s pop music, and a classic album cover.

839 Stray Cats

The singer-guitarist Brian Setzer formed the rockabilly group the Stray Cats in 1979, and the group was popular in the 1980s, with "Stray Cat Strut" as their signature song. As in other songs about alley cats (see 833), the "cat" in the song is a thoroughly human "cat," one who observes, "I don't bother chasin' mice around"—not when there are so many "lady cats" to be had.

13

Silver Screen and Small Screen

Film Felines

840 The Harry Potter cats

J. K. Rowling's phenomenally popular Harry Potter books have become phenomenally popular movies, and since the stories deal with a school of witchcraft, naturally there are cat characters. Professor McGonagall (a human) can transform herself into a cat at times, but the most important cat in the stories is Mrs. Norris, the pet of Filch, the grumpy but protective porter at the Hogwarts School. Mrs. Norris and Filch have a kind of psychic bond as they keep a watchful eye on the school. In the movie versions, Mrs. Norris has been portrayed by three different Maine Coon cats.

841 Stuart Little's nemesis

Stuart Little, a mouse, is the title character in a beloved children's book by E. B. White. Published in 1945, the book was updated considerably for the 1999 film, but retained the familiar story of the mouse adopted by a human family. Stuart's nemesis is Snowbell, the family cat, who is extremely jealous and plots with his neighborhood cat cronies to do the mouse in. By the story's end, cat and mouse are good friends, of course. The movie Stuart was a mix of puppetry and computer images, but the cats were real, with Stuart's chief enemy (and later friend) played by a gorgeous silver Persian.

842 King cat horror

Cat's Eye, released in 1985, told three connecting horror stories by Stephen King, linked by the spunky stray cat involved in each tale. The third story, the most frightening, involved the cat being taken in by a nice family, with an adorable daughter (Drew Barrymore) who names the cat Charlie. The house is inhabited by an evil little demon who literally tries to suck the breath from the sleeping child, but the brave Charlie kills the demon. The story is, of course, based on the old myth about cats sucking the breath of children (see 521).

843 Blofeld's puss

In several of the popular James Bond movies, Agent 007 faces a sinister villain named Blofeld, the head of an international conspiracy called SPECTRE. Though evil, Blofeld is very refined, as evidenced by the attention he pays to his white Persian cat, whom he was always stroking. Blofeld was spoofed as Dr. Evil in the Austin Powers movies (see 844).

844 "When Mr. Bigglesworth gets upset . . ."

The hilarious (and sometimes tasteless) *Austin Powers* movies are, of course, a spoof of the James Bond films, so naturally the villain has, like the villain Blofeld in the Bond flicks, an adored pet cat. While Blofeld has a fluffy white Persian, Austin Power's nemesis Dr. Evil has a Sphynx, a breed pretty close to being hairless. The now famous cat is named Mr. Bigglesworth, and as Dr. Evil tells Austin Powers, "When Mr. Bigglesworth gets upset, people die!" The movies have had the effect of making the Sphynx breed more popular (see 179).

845 All the way from Japan

The delightful 1989 movie *The Adventures of Milo and Otis* was made in Japan—but since no humans appear in the movie, dubbing was no problem. The title characters—Milo the cat and Otis the dog—live on a farm until various adventures begin after the poor cat is swept down a rushing river. It's a delight watching a cat and a dog so devoted to each other. The comic actor Dudley Moore provided the narration in the English-language version of the film.

846 Missing an important balloon flight

Near the end of the beloved 1939 movie *The Wizard of Oz,* Dorothy and her dog Toto are about to fly back home to Kansas in a hot-air balloon along with the wizard. But Toto spies a cat in the arms of a woman and takes out after it. When Dorothy pursues him, the wizard's balloon comes untied and takes off without Dorothy and the dog. (Of course, we all know Dorothy did eventually get home, thanks to the magical ruby slippers.)

847 Cat wife vs. dog husband

The 1989 movie *The War of the Roses* takes a comical look at the bitter divorce battle of a wealthy couple. In the midst of some violent feuding, the husband accidentally runs over the wife's cat with his car, and naturally the wife assumes he did it on purpose. She gets even with him by cooking a fancy meal, then, after he has eaten his fill, makes him think she has served up his beloved dog. (The audience knows the dog is alive, but the husband doesn't.) The attorney who handles the divorce offers the audience some advice: maybe cat people shouldn't marry dog people.

848 Lucky cat!

A favorite "cat moment" is the ending of the 1961 movie *Breakfast at Tiffany's*. The sophisticated playgirl Holly Golightly (played by Audrey Hepburn) sees her life falling apart, and impulsively she turns out her beloved cat (named "Cat") onto the rainy streets of New York, then immediately regrets doing so. A cat owner is hard pressed to remain dry eyed while watching poor Audrey search the alleyways, yelling, "Cat!" All ends happily, with the orange tabby finding a dry spot in-between the embrace of Holly and the handsome man who loves her.

849 Cosuicide

The wacky 1986 movie *Crimes of the Heart* concerns three daffy Southern sisters, who, we learn, come from a—you guessed it—daffy family. Several times in the movie they refer to their mother's suicide—and to the fact that just before she took her own life, she killed her beloved cat as well. The sisters decide she did it because "she didn't want to die alone."

850 Poor Uncle Elizabeth

If you want to watch a heartwarming movie, you can't do better than *I Remember Mama,* the 1948 movie about a Norwegian family living in San Francisco. The family owns a cat named "Uncle Elizabeth"—so called because someone named the cat Elizabeth before realizing he was male. The cat, who has been in one too many alley battles, is ailing badly, and Mama reluctantly has to put him to sleep using chloroform. To the relief of the family, and the audience, the deep sleep under the chloroform is just what Uncle Elizabeth needed, and he recovers his health. The scene where the supposedly dead Elizabeth begins slowly twitching his tail is bound to tug on the heartstrings of anyone who loves cats.

851 Tough guys with cats

Audiences expect tough movie heroes to like dogs, so it is kind of a pleasant surprise to see a macho man doting on a cat. (Think of the tough Clint Eastwood character, stroking a kitten in *The Good, the Bad, and the Ugly*.) Perhaps the best example is tough guy John Wayne in the 1969 movie *True Grit*. His character, the hard-drinking, one-eyed marshal Rooster Cogburn, has only one real love in his life, a plump cat named General Sterling Price (named, by the way, for a Confederate general).

852 Pyewacket

In witch lore, Pyewacket is a common name for a cat. It is the name of the pet of the Kim Novak character in the 1958 movie *Bell, Book, and Candle*. Novak plays a modern-day witch who decides to use her powers to help her catch the right man.

853 A Feline E.T.

Jake is the unlikely name of the cat hero of *The Cat from Outer Space*, a 1978 live-action Disney film. Jake, from another planet, crashes on Earth and, of course, leads various humans through some wild escapades involving foreign spies and military secrets.

854 D. C., the First version

That Darn Cat was a popular 1965 Disney comedy about a Siamese cat who helps an FBI agent thwart kidnappers. He is referred to as "D. C."—for "Darn Cat." The movie was based on the book *Undercover Cat.* The human stars of the movie were Hayley Mills and Dean Jones.

855 D. C., the second version

That Darn Cat was remade by Disney in 1996, with a little less warmth and a little more hipness. As before, the scrappy cat leads his owner and the FBI on the trail of some bungling kidnappers. Dean Jones, who played the (human) lead in the 1965 version, also appears in this one.

856 Cat heaven

Cat lovers, prepare to cry your way through *The Three Lives of Thomasina,* a 1963 live-action Disney fantasy. Thomasina, a cat, has to be put to sleep, and we see some amazing scenes of kitty heaven. A mysterious healer appears from the woods and is able to restore the cat to life, to the joy of her owner, a little Scottish girl. The movie was based on a book by Paul Gallico (see 757).

857 Resuscitation by cats

In the 1992 movie *Batman Returns,* a secretary, Selena Kyle, is pushed out a skyscraper window by her nasty boss. She falls several stories and is presumed dead—but is mysteriously resuscitated, literally licked back to life by dozens of alley cats.

Revived and vengeful, the formerly meek Selena becomes the villainous Catwoman, the foe of Batman and of men in general. Later in the movie she experiences another fall from a tall building—but lands, unhurt, in a truckload of kitty litter.

858 Nothing to do with the Poe story

The Black Cat, a very silly 1934 horror movie with Boris Karloff and Bela Lugosi, has nothing to do with the classic Edgar Allan Poe story with the same title (see 768), but it is amusing anyway. Karloff is a Satan worshipper who possesses (naturally) a black cat. Lugosi, Karloff's archenemy, has a cat phobia and kills the creature with a knife.

859 Easier to work with than Jackie Gleason

The beloved comic actor Art Carney had a wonderful costar in the 1974 movie *Harry and Tonto*: a cat. Carney played an elderly New York widower who is evicted from his apartment and then heads across the country with his cat, Tonto. It's a thoroughly enjoyable movie, and Carney won an Oscar for his performance.

860 Two comic geniuses together

Combining Art Carney with a cat worked so well in *Harry and Tonto* that Hollywood tried the same match again, this time in the 1977 movie *The Late Show*. Carney plays a private detective who enjoys his solitude until a flaky woman (Lily Tomlin) with a missing cat works to become his sidekick and partner. Naturally they do find the cat, and they learn to like each other along the way.

861 The Incredible Journey

Walt Disney definitely had a knack for packing people into the theatres. He found the perfect story in a book by Sheila Burnford, describing the adventures of a cat and two dogs who are separated from their owners but who journey more than two hundred miles through the Canadian wilderness to find them. The live-action 1963 movie had audiences weeping over such calamities as the poor Siamese cat falling into a rushing stream, one of the dogs encountering a porcupine and all three pets facing off with a bear.

862 Incredible, again

The Incredible Journey was such a wonderful story that Disney could not resist remaking it, so in 1993 the studio released *Homeward Bound: The Incredible Journey*. In this version, the cat is a snooty longhair named Sassy—and she has a voice, as do the two dogs. Apparently the Disney people didn't think an audience could sit through an hour and a half of animal adventures unless those animals also had something clever to say. The cat's voice was provided by the actress Sally Field.

863 Incredible, yet once more

Disney had some success with its 1993 remake of *The Incredible Journey,* so naturally it got the two dogs and one cat together for another adventure, the 1996 movie *Homeward Bound 2: Lost in San Francisco*. This time Sassy the cat and her two companions find themselves in the toughest areas of San Francisco but, of course, all ends happily and they are reunited with their owners.

864 Rich Rhubarb

A perfectly silly idea, but it made for a good movie: an eccentric millionaire leaves his fortune, including a baseball team, to a stray cat. The title cat in Rhubarb, released in 1951, is fun to watch. The tabby cat who played the title character was the winner of a PATSY award (see 866) and later played the adored Cat, the pet of Audrey Hepburn in *Breakfast at Tiffany's* (see 848).

865 Electrocuted clue

The James M. Cain novel *The Postman Always Rings Twice* has been made into a movie twice (in 1946 and 1981). In both versions, a drifter falls in love with a young wife and helps her murder her husband. And in both versions the clue that tips off the police to the foul play is that a cat is found electrocuted at the bottom of a suspiciously placed ladder. Gruesome to see, although in the 1946 there is some humor when one of the cops keeps repeating, "That poor cat—dead as a doornail."

866 Animal Oscars

Human actors can win Oscars for their performance in movies and Emmys for their work on television shows, but did you know there are awards for animal actors, too? The award is the Picture Animal Top Star of the Year award, or PATSY. The American Humane Society of Los Angeles (where else?) began the awards in 1951, and the recipients have included not only cats but dogs, lions, tigers, chimpanzees, seals and dolphins. The cat Orangey, a red tabby who appeared in many movies, won in 1952 for his role in Rhubarb (see 864) and in 1962 for *Breakfast at Tiffany's* (see 848). Other feline winners were the cats who appeared in *That Darn Cat, Mannix, Harry and Tonto, The Cat from Outer Space* and *Bell, Book, and Candle*. We like to think that PATSY winners, unlike Oscar winners, do not develop oversized egos because of this acclaim.

867 Mack's cat

Mack Sennett was one of the great producer-directors of silent film comedies, best remembered for the frantic antics of the Keystone Cops. The story goes that during the filming of a Sennett comedy, a gray cat entered the set through a hole in the floor, and Sennett included the cat in the scene. The cat was christened

Pepper, and she was given roles in several Sennett films. Pepper formed an unlikely friendship with Teddy, a Great Dane who was also part of the Sennett family.

868 Shakespeare, cat style

Shakespeare's *Romeo and Juliet* has been made into several movies, none more unusual than the 1990 version starring cats instead of human actors. Juliet was played by a white angora, Romeo by a gray. Naturally real cats cannot be taught to recite Shakespeare, so the voices for the cats were provided by several stars of the British theatre, including Vanessa Redgrave, Maggie Smith and Ben Kingsley.

869 X-rated cat?

In 1972 animator Ralph Bakshi released the movie *Fritz the Cat,* which had the distinction of being the world's first X-rated cartoon film. Fritz was created by the cartoonist R. Crumb, and the naughty cat appeared in numerous "underground" comics in the 1960s. Not every cat owner is attracted to this sex-crazed character, but he does have a cult following.

And on the Tube

870 Spoofing the MGM lion

For decades, movies released by Metro-Goldwyn-Mayer (MGM, that is) opened with Leo the lion roaring. When the actress Mary Tyler Moore started her own TV production company, she realized her initials were darn close to MGM. So the MTM logo became an adorable orange kitten, uttering a soft "meow" at the close of every MTM show. The kitten, named Mimsey, was taken from an animal shelter and lived at the home of an MTM staffer. Mimsey lived from 1968 to 1988 and is still very much alive in the many reruns of *Newhart, Hill Street Blues* and the various other MTM productions.

871 Cocktail cats

From 1952 through 1954, CBS broadcast a comedy-mystery, *Mr. and Mrs. North,* in which the title couple worked to solve crimes. The amateur sleuths owned three cats named Gin, Sherry and Martini.

872 Alien diets

A brown cat named Lucky really was lucky, for he survived several seasons on the NBC sitcom *ALF*. You may know that ALF was a furry alien from the planet Melmac, a world where cats were considered desirable snacks. Both ALF and Lucky lived with the Tanners, and somehow, from 1986 to 1990, Lucky managed to avoid being eaten by the alien guest.

873 Minerva

The popular sitcom *Our Miss Brooks* (CBS, 1952–1956) starred Eve Arden as a wisecracking high school English teacher. Her landlady, Maggie Davis, owned an orange cat named Minerva, who, like many cats seen in movies and TV, had been rescued from an animal shelter.

874 Lonesome Sally's cats

On *The Dick Van Dyke Show* (CBS, 1961–1966), one of Dick's friends and coworkers was the unmarried Sally Rogers. Sally, always hoping to meet the right man to marry, confided in her two cats, Mr. Henderson and Mr. Diefenthaler.

875 Otto vs. Bob

In one of Bob Newhart's many TV sitcoms (*Bob,* CBS, 1992–1993), he shared his home with a cat named Otto. Bob, a greeting card artist, always found Otto to be in the way, so much so that he once threatened to microwave him.

876 What a witchy name

Since 1996, a black cat named Salem has been featured on the sitcom *Sabrina the Teenage Witch,* played not by a real cat but by a pretty lifelike robot. Salem and Sabrina were originally characters in the *Archie* comic books, and both appeared in the various Saturday morning cartoon versions of *Archie,* where Salem was often working his magic to the annoyance of Jughead's pet Hot Dog. The animated Salem could work his magic with an arrogant flip of his tail. Salem's name, of course, is meant to recall the infamous witch trials in Salem, Massachusetts.

877 Cartoonist's cat

There are lots of comic strip cats, so it's appropriate that the main character in *Caroline in the City,* a cartoonist, would own a cat. Caroline's cat was a beige Himalayan named Salty. The pampered (and declawed) cat wore a rhinestone collar, lounged on top of Caroline's drawing table and slept in her bed.

878 Even androids have cats . . .

On the sci-fi series *Star Trek: The Next Generation* (1987–1994), one of the main characters was the pale-skinned android, Lt. Commander Data. "Spot" was the clever name the brainy Data bestowed on his orange tabby cat. In an attempt to find just the perfect food for Spot, Data created seventy-four different kinds of food.

879 Driving the Clarkes

A recurring skit on *Saturday Night Live* during the late 1980s and early 1990s involved a Texas couple named Lyle and Brenda Clarke (played by Dana Carvey and Victoria Jackson) whose cat, Toonces, could drive a car. This always led to trouble, with the cat (wearing sunglasses and a leather jacket) driving himself and his owners off a cliff each time. Even so, the Clarkes liked to show home movies of Toonces driving the car into Niagara Falls, the Grand Canyon and other landmarks. Toonces was played by a gray tabby named Carocats Tyrone Fletcher.

880 Trailer puss

In the popular detective series *The Rockford Files* (NBC, 1974–1980), a stray cat named Valentino was the ownerless communal pet of the Paradise Cove Trailer Colony and was often seen at the home of detective Jim Rockford, played by James Garner.

881 AFHV

The long-running TV series *America's Funniest Home Videos* has gotten a lot of mileage out of the silly videotapes sent in by viewers. Among the most enjoyable (particularly for cat lovers) are the videos of cats, often lumped together in a segment called "Kitten Kaboodle." Part of the appeal of these, as with all pet videos, is that the audience knows they aren't "staged," as so many of the human videos appear to be. The cats aren't acting for the camera—they are just being themselves, as they fall off tables, fall into aquariums, claw oversized dogs, groom their groins in the middle of a church wedding and otherwise behave in the ways all cat lovers appreciate.

Cartoon Cats

Comic Strip Cats

882 Garfield: Fat, lazy and lucrative

On June 19, 1978, a droopy-eyed, fat, cynical, lasagna-eating cat named Garfield was launched on the world, appearing in forty newspapers. Within a decade, he would appear in 2,000 papers. No other comic strips have matched that feat except *Blondie* and *Peanuts*. The daily *Garfield* strips have been recycled in books that stay on best-seller lists for months. Plus there are primetime TV specials, a Saturday morning series, statues, clothing . . . in short, a regular industry centered on a totally selfish orange tabby cat, his dorky owner, Jon Arbuckle, and the dumb dog, Odie. Apparently people are drawn to a cat who wants nothing more than sleep and food, plus smashing an occasional spider.

883 Garfield's creator

Given the amazing success of Garfield, we can justify including more than one entry on the fat cat. Consider his creator: cartoonist Jim Davis borrowed the name Garfield from his own grandfather. Davis grew up on a farm, dropped out of Ball State University in Indiana and—big surprise!—does not own a cat because his wife is allergic to them. Davis has stated that Garfield isn't really a cat—like many comic strip animals, he is an obnoxious human in animal clothing. Traits that we find unattractive in human beings—laziness, gluttony, irresponsibility, malice—can be very amusing in a comic strip cat.

884 The "love a cat" guy

In 1975 a book of cartoons was published with the simple title *Cat,* and the artist was listed as "B. Kliban." Kliban (whose first name is Bernard) and his pen-and-ink sketches of plump tabbies in funny situations were the foundation of a veritable Kliban industry, as the cat images were reproduced on posters, calendars, stationery, T-shirts, sheets and a thousand other things. Perhaps the most memorable image from the Kliban line is a plump cat with a big red lip-print on his face and the caption "Love a cat." The name of Kliban's first cat, Noko Marie, often crops up in the cartoons. Kliban dedicated the original Cat book to her and his other cats.

885 Attila the cat

Mike Peters' comic strip *Mother Goose and Grimm* debuted in 1984 and is still popular. Grimm, as you may know, is Mother Goose's pet dog—yellow, ugly and thoroughly obnoxious. He has even been seen eating from the litter box of the other family pet, Attila, a purple cat with a big nose and a raccoon-like striped tail. Attila is the friend but, more often, the victim of Grimm. The strip also features occasional appearances by Sumo, an incredibly fat tomcat who silences Grimm by falling on him.

886 Pot-bellied Siamese

Comic strip cats are often obnoxious, none more so than Bucky, a pot-bellied Siamese who is the pet of single guy Rob Wilco in the strip *Get Fuzzy*. Rob's other pet is the sweet but dumb dog Satchel, who is the frequent target of Bucky's snide remarks. Owner and pets are all notorious couch potatoes. The strip is drawn by Darby Conley, who reports that he lives in a no-pets-allowed apartment building.

887 Pixel-ated cat

Cats have gone digital, as you can see in the comic strip *PC and Pixel*. PC Odata is a middle-aged computer nerd (with a ponytail, naturally) working out of his home, and Pixel is his computer-savvy cat, smarter (of course) than his owner. Pixel's buddy is Digit, a mouse (rodent, that is, not a computer mouse) who is also very computer savvy. The strip is drawn by the cartoonist Tak Bui, born in Vietnam but living in Canada.

888 Richer than Bill Gates

The cartoonist Charlie Podrebarac had a brainstorm: a comic strip about filthy rich business tycoons, only instead of humans have them be, literally, fat cats. So in 1998 he launched *Fat Cats,* centered around the brothers Bob and Leo, aided in their business dealings by the snobbish and savvy (and martini-sipping) Momcat. Their main servant is James, a dog, of course, who is not exactly happy working for this bevy of snooty, overfed cats.

889 No relation to Mötley Crüe

Motley's title character is a fluffy pet who is in most ways a typical house cat. He is finicky about food, claws the furniture and is alternately obnoxious and adorable. In a typical *Motley* cartoon strip, the cat's owner tells him that if he refrains from clawing the newly bought chair, he will get a reward in his food dish. Naturally Motley proceeds to shred the chair, assuring the reader, "Cats can't be bought." Motley is drawn by Larry Wright, who also draws *Kit 'n' Carlyle* (see 890).

890 Cat versus boyfriends

In the one-panel daily comic *Kit 'n' Carlyle,* Kit is a single working woman who shares her home with Carlyle, a lovable but mischievous black cat with a pencil-thin neck. The pair made their debut in 1980, and Carlyle still does his best to annoy Kit's various boyfriends. He does agree with the suitors that Kit is a terrible cook. He also observes that Kit isn't the best caregiver in the world: one time she bought him some "6 Lives" cat food at a discount store. Cartoonist Larry Wright, who also draws *Motley* (see 889), claims, "I just draw whatever my real cat does at home."

891 Typical retirees?

Brian Crane's comic strip *Pickles* debuted in 1990 and is centered on the retired couple Earl and Opal. The loving but bickering twosome share a home with Roscoe, a dumb dog, and Muffin, an aloof and furniture-shredding cat. Typically, Muffin is doted on more by Opal than by Earl.

892 One of many -berts

You probably know that the comic strip *Dilbert,* drawn by Scott Adams, centers around the unhappy white-collar employees of an engineering firm, who spend their days amidst cubicles and mindless company rules. The firm's human resources director is the malicious Catbert, a cute but sadistic cat who loves to vex, underpay and occasionally fire the employees. Catbert has to share the strip with the less malicious Ratbert and Dogbert.

893 Pre-Garfield fat cat

Five years before *Garfield* was launched, the cartoonist George Gately gave the world *Heathcliff,* a large, troublemaking cat who managed to vex his owners and the local dog. Where Garfield was lazy, Heathcliff was hyperactive, romancing his Persian cat girlfriend Sonja, harassing his owners, the Nutmeg family, and irking the bullying bulldog Spike. The strip premiered in 1973, and the animated *Heathcliff and Dingbat* show begin airing on Saturday morning TV in 1980. *Heathcliff: The Movie* hit theatres in 1986. George Gately died in 2001 but left the strip in the hands of his nephew. Despite the fact that Garfield is more popular, Heathcliff still has a loyal following.

894 Snoopy versus the cats

Charlie Brown's dog, Snoopy, was the only regular nonhuman character in *Peanuts,* but on occasion Snoopy did face cat adversaries. "The stupid cat who lives next door" was an ongoing opponent. Snoopy would taunt him over the fence, then the cat's large paw—claws out—would be seen knocking Snoopy senseless. Another cat was Faron, the pet of Frieda, the girl who boasted of her "naturally curly hair." She carried the nearly comatose cat around in her arms, limp as a wet noodle. The *Peanuts* creator Charles Schulz got rid of Faron pretty quickly, for he realized that a cat in the strip made Snoopy too much like "a real dog."

895 Bloom County Bill

The wacky comic strip *Bloom County,* drawn by Berke Breathed, ran from 1980 to 1987 and featured all manner of odd human and animal characters, notably the big-nosed penguin, Opus. The strip also introduced the most unattractive cartoon cat ever, Bill the Cat, a mangy, bedraggled creature who never spoke but seemed always to be throwing up, as indicated by the words "Oop! Ack!"

896 Only Dennis would do this . . .

There are lots of inappropriate names for cats, but "Hot Dog" has to be one of the worst. It happens that this is the name that the comic strip brat Dennis the Menace bestowed on his family cat. Hot Dog made his debut in the comic strip in 1975, while the real dog, named Ruff, had been with the family since 1951. Ruff and Hot Dog have always gotten along just fine.

897 The Far Side of cats

The cartoonist Gary Larson entertained millions of readers with the off-the-wall humor of his syndicated cartoon *The Far Side.* Pets were a common feature of the cartoons, and Larson seemed to delight in drawing comical cats. In one cat cartoon, typical of *The Far Side* style of humor, an elderly couple is gazing out their living room window. The wife laments that their cat is playing with a mouse before killing it. What we see in the front yard is the cat tossing a ball to the mouse. In another cartoon a woman standing next to a tub that holds an enormous shark warns her tiny cat, "Remember, I don't want to catch you bothering the fish!"

898 The First comic strip cat

Long before *Garfield,* there was *Krazy Kat,* among the earliest of the newspaper comic strips. In 1910 the cartoonist George Herriman introduced the world to *The Dingbat Family* and the characters Krazy Kat, Ignatz Mouse and Offissa Bull Pup. A year later the strip was renamed simply *Krazy Kat,* and readers followed the weird adventures of the odd cat who adored mice platonically and not as food. The mouse was constantly hurling bricks at Krazy and finding himself in jail for the offense. The strip was set in a kind of surreal desert, and thanks to being syndicated by the Hearst newspapers, was widely read.

899 Rose's Peekaboo

The cartoonist Pat Brady (male) has drawn the popular strip *Rose Is Rose* since 1983, introducing the world to the Gumbo family, which includes the longhaired cat Peekaboo, who is adorable but (typical of comic strip cats) provides many "catty" observations on the family's life. Peekaboo is the companion of the family tot, Pasquale.

900 Japan's atomic cat

The bright blue bizarre-looking cat Doraemon was created by Japanese artist Hiroshi Fujimoto (1934–1996) and debuted in 1969. Doraemon is a robot cat from the twenty-second century, sent from the future to be the aide and friend of a human named Nobita Nobi. Though he is atomic powered, Doraemon is afraid of mice. And he is earless because rats ate off his ears. This peculiar but endearing creature has made a splash in millions of comic books, mostly in Japan, though he has his fans around the world.

901 Cat in the moon

Cosmo was a comic book cat in the late 1940s. He resided on the moon and took "cosmic catnip capsules." He kept watch on Earth, located people needing his aid and flew by rocket to Earth, where he was super fast and super powerful. Naturally he wore a cape (as all superheroes do) with a big letter *C* in the middle of his chest. It's odd that the brave, dynamic Cosmo never made it into animated cartoons.

The Animated Cartoon

902 Felix the First

A newfangled thing called television got a test run in 1928 when the RCA Company sent an image from New York to Kansas. That image—seen by very few people—was of a papier-mâché statue of the cartoon cat Felix. You might say that a cat was the first TV star. Felix had been around since 1919, the creation of the animator Otto Messmer. The black cat, with his enormous oval eyes and habit of walking with his "arms" behind him, appeared in numerous cartoons—all black-and-white and silent, of course—until he was "retired" in 1929. He continued in comic books until 1959, when he entered a new life in made-for-TV cartoons (still black-and-white but now with sound). The new Felix had a magic "bag of tricks" that aided him in his various adventures. Most of the cartoons ended with the squeaky-voiced Felix enjoying a hearty belly laugh at the expense of his foes.

903 Operatic cat and mouse

Animated cartoon characters singing opera instead of speaking dialogue? That's exactly what the old *Mighty Mouse* cartoons were about. In 1945 the Terrytoons animators found the classic formula: pit the small but beefy mouse hero against a villainous cat named Oil Can Harry, who was always trying to do in Mighty Mouse's sweetie, Pearl Pureheart. It was all very melodramatic, and in the tradition of opera, the bad guy was a bass and the hero a tenor. Among the many cat villains of cartoons, Oil Can Harry was the nastiest—and the one with the best singing voice.

904 Four-footed demon

In Jewish and Muslim folklore, Azrael is the name of the angel of death. In the legends he is hideously ugly, the very embodiment of evil. If you're familiar with the Smurfs, the blue-skinned elflike beings created by the Belgian cartoonist Pierre "Peyo" Culliford, you know that he chose Azrael as the name of the malicious cat belonging to Gargamel, the sorcerer who is the Smurfs' archenemy. Azrael the cat isn't quite as fearsome as Azrael the angel of death, of course, and like most cat villains in cartoons, he is always on the losing side.

905 The Pink Panther

In the original movie *The Pink Panther,* released in 1964, the "panther" was actually a gem, not a cat. But audiences delighted in the animated cartoon panther seen over the credits, accompanied by the now-familiar Pink Panther theme music by Henry Mancini. There were several sequels, all with more of the slim and slinky animated panther over the opening credits. Inevitably DePatie-Freleng, the studio that produced the animated cat, cashed in on his popularity with a Saturday morning cartoon series in the 1970s. The Pink Panther is still seen today in ads for the fiberglass insulation produced by the Owens-Corning Company. (The insulation is *pink,* of course.)

906 Early Walt

Long before he headed his own movie studio, the cartoonist Walt Disney worked on a series of animated cartoons featuring a live girl named Alice having various adventures with animated creatures. One of Alice's companions was a black cat named Julius, who could remove his tail and use it as a club. Julius bore an uncanny resemblance to another cartoon cat of that period, Felix.

907 Pursuing a French-Canadian rodent

If you remember the Saturday morning cartoon show *Tennessee Tuxedo* that ran from 1963 to 1966, you might remember Klondike Kat, a bungling Canadian Mountie, stationed at Fort Frazzle in the frozen north. His criminal nemesis was a French-accented rodent named Savoir Faire (with his catchphrase "Savoir Faire eez everywhere!"). As always in cartoons, rodents are much smarter than their feline pursuers.

908 Why not "Catman"?

Bob Kane, the cartoonist who created the character Batman for DC Comics, spoofed his own creation in the syndicated TV cartoon *Courgaeous Cat*. Making his debut in 1961, Courageous Cat lived in the Cat Cave and fought colorful criminals with the aid of his sidekick, Minute Mouse. Like Batman, Courageous Cat wore a caped costume and had lots of gadgets to help him battle evildoers. He and Minute Mouse rode in the Catmobile and were spurred to action by the Cat Signal.

909 Black Snowball

On a show like *The Simpsons,* you have to figure that a cat named Snowball would be black, not white. The original Snowball (who was female, by the way) got run over by a car but was soon replaced by another black cat and given the name Snowball II.

910 Crimefighting cats

The same man who created *ALF* (see 872) for TV also created *Spacecats* (NBC, 1991–1992), a kids' series mixing animation and puppetry. The Spacecats were three extraterrestrials named Tom, Scratch and Sniff. The comic actor Charles Nelson Reilly played a bodiless head named DORC—"Disembodied Omnipotent Ruler of Cats."

911 Poor dumb Katnip

The MGM movie studios had a big hit with the Tom and Jerry cartoons, so Paramount studios created their own cat-and-mouse team. Herman (a mouse in a bow tie and pants) and Katnip first appeared together in the 1947 cartoon *Naughty But Mice.* Most of the cartoons followed a standard formula:

some mice were having fun, Katnip showed up to spoil things and Herman had to come to the rescue, which wasn't hard, considering how dumb Katnip was. (Unlike Tom and Jerry, who were mute, Herman and Katnip did have voices.) As if Herman weren't enough trouble, Katnip also had to face the mischievous crow Buzzy in several cartoons.

912 Pushing the envelope of taste . . .

Nickelodeon, the cable network that caters to kids, launched *The Ren and Stimpy Show* in 1991, and it definitely got people's attention. Centered around Ren Höek (a Chihuahua with, oddly, a German accent) and Stimpson J. Cat, the show was violent and featured numerous jokes about bodily functions, almost slipping into obscenity. But kids and their parents both responded favorably, raising questions about standards for modern TV.

913 Purple and able

"It never hurts to help!" is the motto of Eek! the Cat, an enormous purple puss whose good intentions always get him into trouble. Eek! made his debut on the Fox network in 1992, appearing with his fat girlfriend Annabelle, Elmo the Elk and the vicious Shark Dog, who lives next door.

Warner Bros.' Looney Tune Cats

914 Sylvester the slobberer

Probably the most famous animated cat in the world is the slobbering, bird-chasing creation of the Warner Bros. studios, the infamous Sylvester. Black with a white belly, muzzle, "hands" and feet, Sylvester made his debut (unnamed) in the 1945 cartoon *Life with Feathers,* in which he chases a depressed lovebird. It wasn't until 1947 that he appeared as the pursuer of the yellow bird Tweetie, in *Tweetie Pie.* (The cat was named Thomas at this point and didn't become Sylvester until later.) Big and not too bright, Sylvester was inevitably thwarted in his efforts to devour the tiny but clever Tweetie, whose famous line was "I tawt I taw a putty tat!" Naturally Sylvester and Tweetie both appeared in the 2003 *Looney Tunes* movie.

915 Confused mouser

Sylvester was a mouser as well as a bird chaser, and he never quite caught on to the fact that the character Hippety Hopper was a baby kangaroo, not a giant mouse. Cat and kangaroo first appeared together in the 1952 cartoon *Hoppy Go Lucky*. Poor Sylvester was as unsuccessful in capturing the bouncing Hippety as he was in catching the bird Tweetie. Adding to his humiliation was the fact that his son was a witness to his failure in capturing the "giant mouse." He had no more luck with a real mouse, the infamous "fastest mouse in all Mexico," Speedy Gonazales.

916 Silent Sylvester

In a few cartoons, the usually vocal Sylvester was mute—but extremely funny. In the 1948 cartoon *Scaredy Cat,* he was the pet of Porky Pig, who buys an old home, which, Sylvester learns to his horror, is inhabited by murderous mice. The formula was repeated in the 1954 *Claws for Alarm,* where, again, Porky remains blissfully unaware that his life is in danger from homicidal mice in an old hotel. In the 1955 *Jumpin' Jupiter,* Porky and the cat are abducted by birdlike aliens, though only Sylvester knows it.

917 Poor Elmer

Sylvester wasn't always chasing Tweetie Bird. In one cartoon, he did something alley cats are famous for: creating a racket at night and keeping people awake. In the 1948 cartoon *Back Alley Oproar,* the obnoxious cat not only meows but sings opera, plays musical instruments and does everything else possible to keep poor Elmer Fudd from falling to sleep. At the end of the cartoon, Elmer succeeds in killing the cat—only to realize that all nine of Sylvester's lives are still around to harass him with their caterwauling.

918 Neurotic Claude

Sylvester was the most famous cat creation of Warner Bros., but the studio also produced cartoons with a pampered, high-strung yellow house cat named Claude. Poor, nervous Claude appeared in several cartoons in the 1940s and 1950s, facing such antagonists as the mice Hubie and Bertie and, even worse, the obnoxious Frisky Pup, who had the habit of sneaking up behind Claude and barking furiously. A running gag in the Claude cartoons is that the nervous cat would literally jump to the ceiling, hang by his claws, then fall straight down—flipping himself upright just before landing.

919 Finally, a sweetiecat

Most cartoon cats are obnoxious, but in 1952 Warner Bros. debuted the most adorable cat ever, a tiny black-and-white kitten named Pussyfoot. The kitten is adopted by a huge bulldog, Mark Antony, and the dog goes out of his way to protect the tiny puss. A running gag in the cartoons is watching Pussyfoot dig his claws into the dog's back until finally, to the dog's great relief, he settles into the dog's fur for a nap.

920 Before Garfield, Dodsworth

Long before Garfield, the Warner Bros. animators had already created a fat lazy cat, named Dodsworth. In the 1952 cartoon *Kiddin' the Kitten,* the fat slob's owner threatens to throw him out unless he starts catching mice. The cat solves the problem by opening an academy for mouse catching, using a dumb little kitten to do his mousing for him. The kitten gets his revenge by releasing the captured mice, recatching them, then taking Dodsworth's place. In another Dodsworth cartoon, the fat puss is more active, pursuing a woodpecker for his lunch and (as happens to cats in all cartoons) becoming victim instead of predator.

921 Scented cat-chaser

Skunks don't live in France and don't mate with cats, but anything is possible in a cartoon. Beginning with the 1951 cartoon *Scent-imental Romeo,* Warner Bros. used the formula of having a lovesick French skunk, Pepe Le Pew, pursue a "female skunk"—actually a cat who had a stripe of white paint spilled on her back. Mouthing romantic phrases in both bad English and bad French, Pepe hopped gaily after the disgusted cat. Part of the fun in these cartoons is that real skunks are not graceful but real cats are, and the Pepe cartoons reverse this, with the frantic cat tripping over herself to flee the skunk.

922 Hey, Babbit!

The comedy team of Abbott and Costello were spoofed in several Warner Bros. Cartoons in the form of two mice, Babbit and Castello. The two debuted in the 1942 *A Tale of Two Kitties*. In all the

Babbit and Castello cartoons, the chubby Castello was used as a stooge by the wily Babbit in his schemes to outwit an extremely vicious (and toothy) house cat.

923 Speedy versus the cats

Speedy Gonzales, "the fastest mouse in all Mexico," faced several foes, including Warner Bros.' favorite cartoon cat, Sylvester. But in one of the funniest cartoons ever made, Speedy faces a chubby cat named Jose and a skinny cat named Manuel. *Mexicali Schmoes* (1959) shows the two hungry cats being constantly outwitted and outrun by Speedy. At the end, Jose catches the slowest mouse in all Mexico, Slowpoke Rodriquez—who, unfortunately for the cat, also packs a gun.

The Hanna-Barbera Factory

924 The cat-and-mouse cartoon game

The MGM movie studios employed two talented animators, Bill Hanna and Joe Barbera, who in time would become two of the greatest names in TV cartoons. In 1940 they directed the MGM cartoon *Puss Gets the Boot,* which introduced the world to Tom the cat and Jerry the mouse. Tom would pursue the clever Jerry through more than 150 cartoons. The two characters hardly ever spoke, so the cartoons relied on nonstop action. Six of the cartoons won Academy Awards. MGM ended the series in 1957, but later Hanna and Barbera created new Tom and Jerry adventures for TV.

925 The granddaddies of TV cartoons

Bill Hanna and Joe Barbera were animators for MGM film studios, where they produced the many Tom and Jerry cartoons (see 924). In 1957 the two men formed their own company and began concentrating on fast production of animated cartoons for TV. Over the years the Hanna-Barbera team managed to produce some of the most famous cartoons cats in the world, including Top Cat, Snagglepuss and others described elsewhere in this section.

926 A TV First

The first animated cartoon show made for TV was *Ruff and Reddy,* produced by the Hanna-Barbera team. The show debuted on NBC in 1957 (in black-and-white, of course) and featured a live host, Jimmy Blaine. The show centered on the adventures of a smart cat, Ruff, and a dumb dog, Reddy. Aided by Professor Gismo, they faced such villains as Killer and Diller, the Chickasaurus and the Goon of Glocca Morra. While it wasn't a major hit, *Ruff and Reddy* proved that low-cost, fast-produced animated cartoons could keep kids entertained.

927 Just the facts, cat

The Hanna-Barbera animation team produced the famous Tom and Jerry duo, but they also produced cartoons featuring a cat and mouse working as a team. These were Snooper and Blabber, two trench coat–wearing detectives that were part of the *Quick Draw McGraw* cartoon show that debuted in 1959. Super Snooper (the cat) and Blabber Mouse often seemed to be a parody of the popular Dragnet series. Like other Hanna-Barbera shows, this one spun off comic books, lunchboxes, toys and other items.

928 Snickering Sebastian

Josie and the Pussycats were created by the Hanna-Barbera studios and ran on Saturday mornings for many years. The Pussycats were an all-girl rock group, its members dressing in cat costumes (including tails). The group was accompanied by a snickering, mischievous black-and-white cat named Sebastian, who could pick locks with his claws and do other things to help foil the bad guys who inevitably turned up on each show.

929 Not quite country

In 1969, ABC and Hanna-Barbera planned to launch an animated Saturday morning cartoon show called *Nashville Cats,* but at almost the last minute the show was renamed *Cattanooga Cats*. The cats were a country-rock band (dressed in hillbilly garb, of course) who had various adventures and tried to avoid the annoying Chessie, the autograph hound. The show also included the *Autocat and Motormouse* cartoons, a sort of race-car version of the familiar cat-chases-mouse routine.

930 "T. C." to his Friends

Those of us over age forty fondly remember *Top Cat,* an animated cartoon show that ran in prime time in 1961. The half-hour show, produced by the Hanna-Barbera animators, centered around a yellow alley cat, Top Cat ("T. C." for short) and his urban gang: Spook, ChooChoo (who was pink), Brain (who was dumb), Fancy-Fancy and Benny. The gang loved nothing more than vexing the dopey policeman, Officer Dibble. The show ran only one season but was rerun constantly and spawned numerous comic books.

931 Pink and civilized

"Exit, stage left!" and "Heavens to Murgatroyd!" were the trademark phrases of Snagglepuss, a pink lion wearing a formal tie and cufflinks. Snag, who debuted on the Hanna-Barbera cartoon show *Quick Draw McGraw* in 1959, was perfectly harmless, but he was often pursued by the big-game hunter Major Minor, who somehow got the impression that Snagglepuss was ferocious. The cat's distinctive voice reminded everyone of the character actor Bert Lahr, who played the lion in *The Wizard of Oz.*

932 Meeses to pieces

Mr. Jinks, the frustrated cat of the *Pixie and Dixie* cartoons, never did learn that *mice* is the plural form of *mouse,* so in every cartoon he uttered his tagline, "I hate those meeses to pieces." The two mice and their cat adversary debuted in 1958 as part of the *Huckleberry Hound* show produced by the Hanna-Barbera studio. Through four seasons, poor Jinks was always outdone by the bow tie–wearing Pixie and the Southern-accented Dixie.

Full-length Feline Features

933 Cinderella's mice pals

In the 1950 Disney animated movie *Cinderella,* the heroine's best friends are the household mice. And while Cinderella must cope with her wicked stepmother and snooty stepsisters, the mice must cope with the menacing cat, Lucifer. (Lucifer is another name for Satan, but you knew that already.) Lucifer is a nasty character but also very funny as we watch him writhing in agony while Cinderella's ugly stepsisters sing and play music badly off-key.

934 "No cats in America!"

Lots of European immigrants who arrived in America in the late 1800s imagined that America was a heaven on Earth. This idea was spoofed in the 1986 animated movie *An American Tail,* about the adventures of a band of Russian mice who settle in New York. They had been told that America is wonderful—in fact, no cats there! They soon learn the truth, of course, though they manage to vanquish their cat foe with a clever motorized mouse.

935 Oh so French

The Aristocats, released in 1970, is a delightful Disney animated film about a pampered French cat, Duchess, and her three kittens. Their mistress dies and leaves her estate to the cats, but naturally a greedy human (the butler) wants to get the cats out of the way. The cats have various adventures in the French countryside, aided by a very un-French alley cat named O'Malley. Eva Gabor provided the voice of the cat mama.

936 Of course cats dance

The 1997 animated movie *Cats Don't Dance* centered on the cat Danny, a dancer in 1930s Hollywood who couldn't figure out why he could never get *human* parts in movies. A silly but generally enjoyable movie.

937 Miss Garland, unseen

One of Judy Garland's last projects was *Gay Purr-ee,* a 1962 animated movie about cats finding love in Paris. Judy provided one of the cat voices (and got to sing, of course); ditto for Robert Goulet. Judy's character was Mewsette, a farm cat who set out for Paris with her tomcat beau, Robespierre.

938 What the Dickens?

Oliver Twist, the classic Dickens novel about an orphan boy falling in with lowlifes, was resurrected in the 1988 Disney animated movie *Oliver and Company*. This time Oliver is a kitten in New York, taken in by a gang of thieving dogs.

939 Finally, the cat has a tongue

In the numerous Tom and Jerry cartoons (see 924), neither the cat nor the mouse spoke, but that isn't so in *Tom and Jerry: The Movie,* released in 1993. In fact, although the two characters looked the same as ever, the old formula of frantic-cat-chases-frantic-mouse was discarded completely, as the two talked, sang and danced their way through a harmless movie for kids.

940 Siamese, if you plee-eez

Disney's wonderful 1955 animated movie *Lady and the Tramp* is basically about dogs, but two of its most memorable characters are Si and Am, a pair of Siamese cats who make serious mischief in Lady's household. The troublemaking twosome sing "We are Siamese if you plee-eez" while raising a ruckus. Oddly, their squeaky voices were provided by husky-voiced singer Peggy Lee.

941 Street cats and "can openers"

Here's an odd item: released in Germany in 1994, an animated movie about cats with ample sex and violence—about as far removed from Walt Disney and Looney Tunes as you can imagine. The movie is *Felidae,* released in a dubbed English version in 1998. (Felidae, you may recall, is the scientific name for the cat family.) In the movie, the cat Francis and his streetwise buddy Bluebeard investigate several cat murders and uncover a plot for a "master race" of cats. One quirk of the movie: cats refer to their human owners as "can openers," apparently thinking of them merely as suppliers of food.

942 Puppets and cats

The wonderful 1940 Walt Disney movie *Pinocchio* featured two animated cats in prominent roles. One was the adorable Figaro, the pampered pet of old Gepetto, who created the Pinocchio puppet. Figaro is with Gepetto when he is swallowed by the whale Monstro. The other cat, quite different, is Gideon, the dopey companion of the fox J. Worthington Foulfellow; these two form a pair devoted to Pinocchio's moral downfall.

Cats as Marketing Tools

943 Morris, the ultimate cat snob

Think of "spoiled cat" and you probably think of Morris, the spokes-cat for the 9-Lives brand of cat food. Morris was found at an animal shelter in a Chicago suburb, and the Leo Burnett ad agency turned the big orange tabby into a superstar. He debuted in ads in 1969 but died in 1975 and was quickly replaced by a Morris lookalike. The "real" Morris the cat was John Irwin, the man who provided the bored, haughty voice of the oh-so-finicky cat.

944 The Hello Kitty phenomenon

One of the merchandising marvels of the last twenty years has been Hello Kitty, the brainchild of the Sanrio Company of Japan. Buyers consider the countless Hello Kitty products—toys, watches, clothing, figurines and other collectibles—to be *adorable* with a capital A. The main character is Kitty White, who is (big surprise) a white kitten, always sweet and considerate, always with a red bow on one ear. She lives with her family in London and loves to give tea parties and bake cookies. The cast includes her adorable parents and grandparents, her adorable twin sister (who wears a yellow bow) and her adorable animal friends—monkeys, moles, raccoons, even dogs and mice. One thing all the characters have in common, besides being adorable: they have no mouths. It is a "cult of the cute," but what cat lover would complain?

945 The grand-daddy of all cat logos

Most of the cat advertising images mentioned in this section are long gone, but one lingers on, and that is the Cat's Paw cat, the black mascot of Cat-Tex shoe soles and rubber heels. Cat's Paw began in the early 1900s when the Massachusetts Chemical Company began using the name for its rubber shoes and then later for soles and heels. Knowing that people were aware of how surefooted cats are, the company employed slogans like "I never slip" and "The heel with nine lives." The most familiar image, still seen on Cat's Paw products, shows the head, shoulders and (of course) extended paw of a black, red-eyed cat. Many a U.S. shoe repair shop had (and has) a Cat's Paw clock prominently displayed.

946 The cat decade

What was there about the 1970s that made it the Decade of the Cat? The popular comic strip cat *Heathcliff* debuted in 1975, B. Kliban's best-selling illustrated

Cats appeared in 1975 and *Garfield* hit the world in 1978. Kliban's cats and Garfield became veritable industries, with posters, toys and a zillion other products. Culture watchers are still scratching their heads over it all, but long-time cat lovers understand it perfectly: in the 1970s, society as a whole was catching on to the fact that cats are wonderful. Manufacturers and advertisers were not slow to make the most of it.

947 Ah, slumbering Chessie

The Chesapeake and Ohio Railroad still exists, but you can no longer sleep on a C & O car, since the line no longer has passenger cars. But in days past the railroad advertised you could "sleep like a kitten" on C & O trains, and the railroad's logo was an adorable tabby kitten, Chessie, snuggled under a sheet with its head and one paw showing. Chessie was taken from a picture made by the artist Guido Gruenwald that was purchased by a C & O executive. C & O ran its first ad with Chessie in 1934, and the company was flooded with requests for copies of the image. The railroad knew a good thing when they saw it and started marketing the Chessie image on clothing, bags, playing cards and other consumables. The tiny kitten was, at that time, the best-known cat in America.

948 Thread cats

You might be familiar with the Coats and Clark Company, a maker of thread. Back before Coats and

Clark merged, Clark's Thread hit upon a rather obvious advertising ploy: show an adorable kitten playing with the thread. (After all, everyone knows that cats and kittens like to chase strings and threads.) The idea caught on, and other thread companies used cats in their ads. The Corticelli Company, for example, showed two adorable white kittens frolicking with spools of thread of all colors, with the slogan "Too strong to break." In their day—the first decade of the twentieth century—the Corticelli kittens were among the most famous ad cats in the world.

949 Before Socks, stockings

Black cats with white paws were being named Socks well before the Clinton presidency, and perhaps that suggested the brand name Black Cat to the Cooper brothers of Kenosha, Wisconsin, who founded the Black Cat Hosiery Company in the 1890s. All the socks and hose produced by the company bore the image (on the toe) of a grinning black cat with a ribbon around his neck. (It was actually "grinnier" than the Cheshire cat of *Alice in Wonderland*.) In time the *a* in *black* and *cat* morphed into the front legs of the black cat image.

950 . . . And nearby, his white brother

One of the Cooper brothers who founded the Black Cat Hosiery Company started a firm (just across the street) to manufacture underwear. In a remarkable leap of creativity, the company chose to use a grinning cat with a ribbon around his neck as its logo, and the company was called White Cat. Many years later, this company morphed into Jockey, now a well-known maker of underwear.

951 The Coke cat

The Coca-Cola Company has been around for a long time, and has, naturally, produced some memorable ads to promote its products. One ad from the 1920s showed a stylishly dressed woman of the period drinking Coke, while her equally stylish white cat drank milk from a blue bowl.

952 The Kellogg's cats

Producing various cereals over so many decades, the Kellogg's Company has inevitably featured cats in some of its ads (even though cats have zero interest in eating cereal themselves). An ad for Kellogg's Toasted Corn Flakes from the early twentieth century depicted a child holding a gray cat, with the tag line "For Kiddies, Not Kitties." A couple of decades later, the kiddies could order, from the back of a Kellogg's cereal box, a huggable doll, Crinkle the Cat.

953 Tiddledywinks, Feline style

The old children's game of tiddledywinks seems pretty quaint compared to today's video games, but it is still available, and basically unchanged. It was ridiculously simple: coinlike disks were used to flip smaller disks into a cup to score points. In the 1930s the English firm of J. W. Spear and Son produced its Little Kittens version of the game, in which the cups were mouths and paws of some gaping kitten figurines.

954 Dueling tomcats

Parker Brothers, the famous board-game company that gave the world Monopoly, Sorry, Risk and other classics, is an old firm, dating back to the 1800s. One of its early products was the Amusing Game of Kilkenny Cats, obviously a takeoff on the old expression "fighting like Kilkenny cats" (see 597). The game box depicted two cats (presumably toms) in waistcoats, aiming their dueling pistols at each other while their cat friends stood nearby awaiting the outcome.

955 Psychic cats

Parker Brothers later produced another cat parlor game, the Black Cat Fortune Telling Game, which debuted in 1897. The game involved cards of the four standard suits, each with a cat image on the back. Matching the words on the cards' backs could (supposedly) tell the players' fortunes. No doubt Parker Brothers was counting on buyers to connect cats (black ones especially) with the occult and witchcraft.

956 Rodent-killing competition

Inevitably some of the products sold to kill rats and mice would have to use cats as part of their marketing strategy. In the 1870s, the businessman Ephraim Wells developed a product he called Rough on Rats (field-tested in his own rat-infested home). Some of the ads for Rough on Rats showed a bevy of disappointed and alarmed cats, lamenting that they had been replaced by the amazing product.

957 Tsuda's costumed cats

"Cats can't be taught tricks." Well, some can, as proven by Satoru Tsuda of Japan. He came up with the idea of using trained cats in TV ads in unconventional ways. He took in four strays and taught them not only to pose for the camera but to wear costumes of various types, including street thugs, punk rockers, policemen and soldiers. The costumed cats were seen on TV, billboards, print ads and naturally made their way via merchandising into calendars, posters and jewelry. Not bad for a band of homeless cats and a very patient (and later very wealthy) trainer.

958 Cats and cigar logos

Cigars were (and, mostly, still are) a "guy thing," so perhaps it is surprising that cigar companies in the 1800s so often used cats in their names and logos. In those days it was generally assumed that "real men" (the kind who smoked cigars, that is) were more fond of dogs than cats. Nonetheless, cigar boxes and wrappers from the nineteenth century testify to the many cat names and images used by cigar companies: Two Toms, Old Tom, Mr. Thomas, Cats, Tabby, Me-Ow, Our Kitties, White Cat and, yes, even Pussy. Some showed cats smoking cigars (fat chance!), and the Me-Ow logo showed two black tomcats in the claws-out, backs-up fighting stance.

959 Cats and stoves

The days of the black stove that burned wood or coal are long gone, but in the old days keeping the stove's iron finish free of rust was essential, so various companies marketed "stove polish." One brand was Black Cat, manufactured by the J. S. Prescott Company. Naturally the label pictured a black cat (with a red ribbon on his neck). While there is no connection between cats and stoves, the sleek coat of a black cat surely would have reminded buyers of how their stoves *ought* to look.

960 Cat compacts

Back in 1930s America (there was that Depression, remember?) store customers were always happy to get something for free. One "freebie" was the paper compact, a cardboard-encased compact mirror given free to women, always (of course) bearing inside it an ad for some store or service. Some of these compacts bore the face of a cat on the inside, perhaps because most women find cats appealing and perhaps because cats (like mirrors) are associated with grooming.

961 Cat-and-dog product

If you had to guess, what would you think a product called Honest Scrap would be? The answer: chewing tobacco. Honest Scrap was a brand of chewin' backy produced by the Lorillard company, and one of its advertising images was a black cat facing off with an only slightly larger white dog. The image bore the title "An everyday scrap."

962 The catnip toy guy

Catnip-filled balls and catnip-filled mice toys have been around a long time—in fact, since 1907, when a veterinary supplier, A. C. Daniels, patented his Catnip Ball, a small wooden ball, hollowed out for holding catnip and serving as a great toy for felines. Later he patented the first catnip-filled toy mouse. Naturally Mr. Daniels also marketed his own catnip, under the brand name Summit.

963 Babies and tires

The Michelin tire company has been using its adorable baby image for several years now, accompanied by the slogan "There's a lot riding on your tires." Back in the 1920s, the Fisk Tire Company of Massachusetts was already using a protective parent image, but not a human one: one of the company's ads showed a fierce-looking mother cat frightening a dog away from her basket of wide-eyed kittens. Interestingly, on the wall behind the kitten basket is a pre-Michelin image of a tot holding a tire, with the slogan "Time to Re-tire—get a Fisk." We can assume that tire buyers were expected to connect new tires with the parental protectiveness of the mother cat.

964 Preferring cream (gasoline) to milk

With the exception of the Exxon tiger, cats haven't been used much in gasoline ads, but back in 1929 there was a wave of advertising for Ethyl, the new antiknock compound developed by the General Motors Corporation. An Ethyl Gasoline Corporation was established to promote the new product, and its ads featured a longhaired white cat, with the slogan "To make your engine purr . . . use Ethyl." The ad also noted that "the aristocratic Angora and the proletarian puss have at least one thing in common: that is, both prefer cream to milk." The "cream" was the new Ethyl additive.

965 The pre-tire Goodrich

Most folks know how much most cats dislike water, so inevitably some companies would employ "cat hates water" images in their ads. One such company was B. F. Goodrich, the rubber company famous today for its tires. In its pre-tire days the company manufactured boots and galoshes, and some of the Goodrich ads from the early 1900s depicted smiling cats walking through the rain while wearing Goodrich galoshes.

966 The Umbstaetters' cat 'zine

It's hard to imagine now, but decades ago there were literally hundreds of monthly magazines featuring short stories. In the era before movies, TV and radio, fiction magazines were a prime source of entertainment. One of the most popular ones was *The Black Cat,* begun in 1895 by Herman Umbstaetter and illustrated by his wife, Nelly. The covers featured Nelly's illustrations of a black cat in various human poses—painting, playing a flute, sailing a ship and so on. The cat's face also appeared in the initial letter of each short story. Many of the ads in the magazine also used a black cat image. By the time the Boston-based magazine ceased publication in 1923, it had featured some noted writers, including Jack London. The covers were and still are considered collector's items.

967 Inky cats

What does ink have to do with cats? Not a thing, but that hasn't stopped a couple of ink companies from using cats in their ads. In the early 1900s, the

Thomas Company of Chicago used a rather stern-looking black cat in its ads, along with a slogan advising buyers to ask for "the ink with the cat on the bottle." Beginning in 1941, the Carter's Ink Company used a mother cat with kittens on some of its ink bottles, and its full-color ads depicted a white mother cat hanging out her nine kittens—each a different color—to dry on a clothesline. The nine Carter ink colors fit perfectly with the slogan "Carter's Ink has 9 dyes."

968 From cats to newly hatched chicks

Bon Ami scouring powder has been around awhile, along with its familiar baby chick logo and the slogan "Hasn't scratched yet." Bon Ami was launched on the world in 1886 by the soap manufacturer John Robertson, who used the mineral feldspar as the "magic ingredient" in Bon Ami. In the early days, long before the baby chick logo, Bon Ami ads sometimes showed a fierce cat, claws out, on the verge of scratching two dogs, with the slogan "Cats can, but Bon Ami cannot scratch, for it lacks grit."

969 Soapy cats

In the public's mind, cats hate water, and thus they hate bathing . . . so using a cat image in soap advertising doesn't seem to make sense, except that people also know that cats are fanatically clean. Thus more than a few soap companies have used cats in ads for soap, including the famously pure Ivory Soap, which has been around since 1879. One Ivory Soap ad from more than a century ago showed a snow-white cat surrounded by twelve malicious-looking dirty gray cats. The ad had a one-word caption: “Envy.”

970 The Sunkist cat

You no doubt associate the name Sunkist with citrus fruit, oranges in particular. Back in the 1930s, some of the fruit sold under the Sunkist label also bore another label: Tom Cat, as seen in the image of a blue-and-white cat on boxes of citrus.

971 Before the Energizer bunny . . .

Decades ago, a company called National Carbon began producing batteries with the brand name Eveready, a brand that is still around today. In the 1930s, many Eveready ads featured cats, such as one of a curious tot shining her flashlight on a contented mother cat with a litter of kittens. Another Eveready ad showed a couple in pajamas, who have apparently been awakened by the sound of a beribboned kitten walking on the piano keys. The image of the kitten on the keys, looking both surprised and amused at the flashlight shining on it, is priceless.

972 The Fancy Feast dandy

Any commercial for Fancy Feast Gourmet Cat Food had to star a very sophisticated and beautiful cat. The original one was SH III, the pet of Scot Hart (which should enable you to figure out who the cat was named for). SH III was a gorgeous Chinchilla Persian who also appeared in such movies as *The Jerk, Scrooged* and *National Lampoon's Christmas Vacation.*

973 Tiger into cat, Olympic style

You might remember the 1988 Olympics, held in Seoul, South Korea. The mascot of the games was Hodori, a tiger, though he was presented as a frisky (meaning "very athletic") house cat. Hodori the tiger gained worldwide recognition through all the Olympic souvenir paraphernalia. But of course Koreans had been aware of him for centuries, since he was a key figure in numerous folk tales and legends.

And a Few Bits of Potpourri

974 -Philes and -phobes

You are probably aware that an *ailurophile* is a person who likes cats, while an *ailurophobe* is someone who hates or fears cats. Both words are rooted in the Greek word *ailuros,* meaning (surprise!) "cat." (The Greek word *philia* means "love" and the word *phobos* means, of course, "fear.") It is the author's assumption that most of the people reading this book are ailurophiles—or will be by the time they finish perusing this book.

975 Is it curable?

Cat lovers have a hard time comprehending ailurophobia, the fear or hatred of cats. But for some people it is very real, in many cases rooted in a childhood experience of being scratched or bitten by a cat. Some people have fainted at the sight of a cat, while others experience panic or anxiety attacks. Considering how seldom cats attack people, is this fear "all in the head"? More importantly, is it curable? The good news is that, yes, any phobia is curable, and some ailurophobes have become avid ailurophiles. The bad news is that some people do not fear cats but actively *hate* them, and such people are unlikely to seek out a cure.

976 Name trends

There are trendiness patterns in human names, with some names popular at one time and then unpopular at others. (For example, in the author's school days, there were lots of Cathys, Rickys, Lindas, Gregs, Marks and Tims—names rarely bestowed in our present flood of Brittanys, Jacobs, Ambers and Matthews.) According to a recent issue of *Cat Fancy* magazine, the most popular names for female cats are: Muffin, Misty, Fluffy, Patches, Samantha, Tigger, Tabitha, Missy and Pumpkin. And for the toms: Tiger, Max, Charlie, Rocky, Toby, Sam, Smokey and (oddly) Mickey. We'll check back with the magazine in about ten years to see if a new wave of cat names has come into vogue.

977 Cat stamps

This won't surprise you: there were official U.S. stamps featuring dogs before there were any honoring cats. Cat fans complained, and the Postal Service responded in 1988 with a set of four cat stamps, each featuring two breeds of cats, including (of course) an American shorthair and a Maine coon. The stamps were given their public premiere at an appropriate place: New York's Winter Garden Theatre, which at the time housed the long-running musical *Cats*. The stamps sold for twenty-two cents, by the way.

978 The spay stamp

If you're a stamp collector, you probably have seen the thirty-seven-cent U.S. stamp with the message "Spay or Neuter" and an image of either a puppy or a kitten. Some people jokingly refer to it as the "Bob Barker stamp," because of the TV game show host's longtime advocacy for spaying and neutering pets (see 713).

979 Mouser Towser

Scotland's landscape is dotted with the many distilleries that produce world-famous Scotch whiskey. Where there is whiskey, there is grain, and where there is grain, there are rodents, so cats have long been an essential part of the distillery scene. One of the rodent killers at the Glenturret distillery, a cat named Towser, died in 1987, having killed approximately 29,000 mice in his lifetime.

980 Pack rat

Detestable as rats are, they are actually intelligent creatures, much more capable of social organization than cats are. The black rat (*Rattus rattus*) is one of the most intelligent species, and it also happens to grow up to eighteen inches in length. Couple that size with the fact that black rats learn to fight in packs, and you can see that cats over the centuries have had their work cut out for them. Fighting large, intelligent and organized rats requires speed and courage on the part of cats.

981 Catgut (the real thing)

While the so-called catgut used in violin strings is (thankfully) *not* made from cat intestines (see 673), real catgut has in fact been used in other musical instruments. In Japan, a plucked stringed instrument called the *samisen,* somewhat like a banjo, has strings made from actual catgut—and with a cat skin stretched across its soundboard.

982 Beauregard of Richmond

Artists like cats, and so museums and galleries often have their resident cat (or cats). Appropriately, in the 1990s the resident cat at the Virginia Museum of Fine Arts in Richmond had a good Confederate name, Beauregard. The plump gray-brown tabby often wandered around the museum's classrooms and sometimes became an unpaid model, situating himself near the seated (and usually naked) human model.

983 Cat people, as proven by their names

Know anyone named Katz, Gatti, Duchat, Lechat or Gatteschi? All these surnames are some variation on the word *cat* in one European language or another. How did any family come to have a "catty" name?

One theory is that a family decided to include a cat in its coat of arms—no doubt out of affection for cats, but also because of admiration for some quality of cats, such as stealth, swiftness or beauty.

984 "Two mice-cats per ship"

Cats don't like water, but, oddly, they travel well by sea, since they don't get motion sickness. It was discovered long ago that they will serve as rodent exterminators on ships as well as on land, and ships are never without rodents. Back in the 1600s the value of cats at sea was realized by Jean Baptiste Colbert, the head of France's treasury under King Louis XIV. Hoping to keep rodents—and thus disease—at a minimum on French ships, Colbert mandated that all ships leaving French ports should have a minimum of "two mice-cats" on each ship.

985 Feline Fest

In Belgium, the city of Ieper (that's a capital *I* as in "Irving") hosts a cat festival every three years, partly in the spirit of fun and partly to atone for the cruel treatment of cats in the Middle Ages, when Ieper and other cities applauded as droves of cats were slaughtered. The Ieper parade features people in cat costumes, an enormous "queen cat" float, the Norse goddess Freyja in her cat-drawn chariot (see 545), "witch cats" frolicking in mobile cemeteries and other feline floats, balloons and vehicles. Even in the years when there isn't a cat festival, the city bears the nickname *kattenstad,* "city of cats."

986 Cat or horse?

Horses were and still are symbols of social prestige. In times past, a man who owned horses was clearly higher on the social scale than the mere commoner who had to (horrors!) walk from one place to another. This was true in China as in every other place, but the Chinese had a proverb that put things into perspective: "A lame cat is better than a swift horse when rats infest the palace." Put another way, the symbols of power don't always amount to much. Horses might impress the population at large, but the palace is as subject to ruin by rodents as the poor man's hut is.

987 The artsy hotel cat

You can safely assume that any place where artsy and literary people gather might be open to having a cat around. That is certainly true of the famous Algonquin Hotel in New York City. Located in the city's theatre district, the hotel has long been a gathering (and drinking) place for the artsy set. Rumor has it that the first "Algonquin cat" was Rusty, who was taken in in the 1930s after he played in a Broadway show. The hotel cat is generally given the run of the place and, needless to say, never goes hungry.

988 Pursuing cats trivially

The game Trivial Pursuit became all the rage in the 1980s, but it wasn't until the 1990s that a cat version became available. This was Cat-a-Muse, distributed by GAMES 2000. The object of the game is to be the last surviving cat. Players answer questions from various cat-egories and face numerous catastrophes before the game concludes. The game is a pleasant way to learn facts about cats. (Then again, you could just continue reading this book.)

989 The Key West cathouse

A business at 411 Green Street in Key West, Florida, sells all sorts of cat merchandise—figurines, pictures, posters, T-shirts. It is called the Cat House, and its Key West location is appropriate, given the city's connections with Ernest Hemingway (see 680). The story goes that the building was, in an earlier time, the more traditional type of cathouse—that is, a house of prostitution.

990 No, not what you think

In the town of Sebring in southern Florida you can visit "Florida's Only Legal Cathouse," not a whorehouse but a restaurant, which of course is decorated with thousands of cat paintings, photos and figurines. The Cathouse's restrooms are referred to as the "Sandbox," and a private dining room is the

Persian room. The many decorations are actually the gifts of restaurant patrons.

991 Stuffed cat

When we think of taxidermists, we think of people who stuff and preserve *wild* animals, but one person who specialized in stuffing pets, cats in particular, was the Englishman Walter Potter, who not only practiced his art on the bodies of cats, but liked to pose and dress the cats in human settings, such as weddings. The Victorians, who had a kind of "cuteness cult," were quite fond of Potter's preserved-cat art.

992 The cathouse cats

The story goes that the houses of prostitution in seaports—there is a long and obvious connection between sailors and prostitutes—had a "catty" way of signaling to potential customers. Ceramic cats were set in the windows: when the cats were facing outward, the establishment was open for business; when the cats faced inward, the place was closed. (Do those places ever close? Hmm.) The "in-between" signal was that the ceramic cat might have two red marbles at its feet, meaning that the human "cats" inside were all busy at the moment, so please try again later.

993 Artifacts (or "catifacts"?)

There are a number of cat museums scattered across the globe, including the Katzen Museum in Riehen,

Switzerland. Like most of the others, this one features a broad collection of cat figurines and images, plus artifacts—or "catifacts," as the cat museum people like to call them—from ancient times. In Ainville in northwestern France you can visit the Musee du Chat ("museum of the cat," that is). Appropriately, considering cats' long history as mousers, the museum is housed in a former barn. It houses more than two thousand objects related to cats—paintings, sculpture, engravings, jewelry, porcelain, etc.

994 The British naval cat rule

Until 1975, the British navy required all its vessels to have a cat on board. As noted elsewhere in this book, cats were "working pets" on ships, their main purpose being to keep down the rodent population. But humans are human, and naturally they got attached to their four-legged friends. Many sailors believed that cats were the guardian spirits of their ships, and that as long as a cat was on board, the ship was safe. If the cat happened to fall overboard and drown, the ship (so the superstition went) was doomed.

995 Fiddle Inn

There are numerous theories about the source of the nursery rhyme about the cat and the fiddle (see 459). Whatever the source, we do know that as far back as the year 1085 there was an English inn named the Cat and the Fiddle. Keep in mind that in the Middle Ages most people were illiterate, so if you ran an inn or a tavern you had to make it identifiable by a visual clue, such as a picture of a cat with a fiddle. Apparently there were Cat and Fiddle Inns scattered across England (not part of a *chain*), perhaps because people simply expected (for whatever reason) an inn to be called Cat and Fiddle.

996 Cheetahs and their small cousins

The Greek playwright Sophocles wrote numerous plays, such as the famous *Oedipus Rex*. The majority of his plays have been lost, existing only in a few scattered fragments. In one of these fragments one of the characters asks, "Is it likely the cat grows up into a leopard?" The obvious answer is "No," but the "leopard" referred to here might actually have been the cheetah, the "hunting leopard" that the Greeks had semi-tamed to go after game. Cheetahs could be walked on leashes and more or less became pets (for the wealthy, at least). Cheetah cubs are about the size of adult house cats, and it is possible that in some Greek households the cats and cheetah cubs played together.

997 Lucky Fourteen

The prestigious Savoy Hotel in London had an amusing tradition: believing that thirteen is an unlucky number, especially for the number of guests at a dinner party, the hotel staff ensured that there will always be a fourteenth "guest" at the party, specifically, a black cat statue named Kaspar. He would be placed in a chair, a napkin tied around his neck, and his place settings changed through the various courses of the meal. Silly, of course, but innocent enough, and in time it was less a matter of superstition and more a matter of a whimsical tradition of the hotel.

998 The dual executions

The Catholic Church sent many witches (or *alleged* witches) to their deaths and, as noted elsewhere in this book, it was commonly assumed that the witches had a cat nearby (see 505). In the year 1484, Pope Innocent VIII decided it made sense to eliminate both the human witch and her satanic pet as well, so he decreed that when a witch was burned at the stake, her cat would die with her, too.

999 The Maneki Neko Figure

The Japanese are fond of the Maneki Neko figure, the "beckoning cat," a cat sitting on hind legs with one paw raised in a kind of salute. The figures are often seen in Japanese stores, restaurants and hotels. Though made in various colors, they usually are white with red and black markings, and they may be made of metal, porcelain, pottery or wood. Aside from the fact that they are simply cute, and that the Japanese are just generally fond of cats, they symbolize good luck and good health. The

Maneki Neko is assumed to be of the Japanese Bobtail breed (see 188).

1,000 Cat and kittens in pewter

In merry olde England, Cat and Fiddle was a common name for an inn or pub (see 995), and so was Cat and Kittens. In some of these establishments, the "cat and kittens" were, in fact, the slang names given to large and small pewter tankards used for serving beer. Naturally the pubs' signs depicted an actual cat with kittens.

1,001 Lion-taming, on a modest scale

Every circus and variety show used to have a trained dog act, but it was widely assumed that cats are untrainable, because they are so individualistic and independent. This is largely true, but in fact there have been a few "cat acts" in history. In Italy in the 1800s, Pietro Capelli began training the street cats he had befriended. To his great surprise and delight, he found cats could learn to juggle with their hind legs, walk on tightwires, play toy musical instruments and do other feats that dazzled audiences, even the jaded rich. Amazing what time and love and patience will do.

INDEX

Numbers here refer to the 1,001 entry numbers, not to page numbers.